POLITICS IN THE RC

The politics of the Roman Republic has in recent decades been the subject of intense debate, covering issues such as the degree of democracy and popular influence, 'parties' and ideology, politics as public ritual, and the character of Rome's political culture. This engaging book examines all these issues afresh, and presents an original synthesis of Rome's political institutions and practices. It begins by explaining the development of the Roman constitution over time before turning to the practical functioning of the Republic, focusing particularly on the role of the *populus Romanus* and the way its powers were expressed in the popular assemblies. Henrik Mouritsen concludes by exploring continuity and change in Roman politics as well as the process by which the republican system was eventually replaced by monarchy. This original and readable book will be important for all students and scholars of Roman history and of politics in general.

HENRIK MOURITSEN is Professor of Roman History at King's College London. He has published widely on aspects of Roman history from local and republican politics to slavery, manumission and epigraphy. His books include *Elections, Magistrates and Municipal Elite* (1988), *Italian Unification* (1998), *Plebs and Politics in the Late Roman Republic* (Cambridge, 2001), and *The Freedman in the Roman World* (Cambridge, 2011).

KEY THEMES IN ANCIENT HISTORY

EDITORS

P. A. Cartledge
Clare College, Cambridge
P. D. A. Garnsey
Jesus College, Cambridge

Key Themes in Ancient History aims to provide readable, informed and original studies of various basic topics, designed in the first instance for students and teachers of Classics and Ancient History, but also for those engaged in related disciplines. Each volume is devoted to a general theme in Greek, Roman, or where appropriate, Graeco-Roman history, or to some salient aspect or aspects of it. Besides indicating the state of current research in the relevant area, authors seek to show how the theme is significant for our own as well as ancient culture and society. It is hoped that these original, thematic volumes will encourage and stimulate promising new developments in teaching and research in ancient history.

Other books in the series

Death-Ritual and Social Structure in Classical Antiquity, by Ian Morris
978 0 521 37465 1 (hardback) 978 0 521 37611 2 (paperback)
Literacy and Orality in Ancient Greece, by Rosalind Thomas
978 0 521 37346 3 (hardback) 978 0 521 37742 3 (paperback)
Slavery and Society at Rome, by Keith Bradley
978 0 521 37287 9 (hardback) 978 0 521 37887 1 (paperback)
Law, Violence, and Community in Classical Athens, by David Cohen
978 0 521 38167 3 (hardback) 978 0 521 38837 5 (paperback)
Public Order in Ancient Rome, by Wilfried Nippel
978 0 521 38327 1 (hardback) 978 0 521 38749 1 (paperback)
Friendship in the Classical World, by David Konstan
978 0 521 45402 5 (hardback) 978 0 521 45998 3 (paperback)
Sport and Society in Ancient Greece, by Mark Golden
978 0 521 49698 8 (hardback) 978 0 521 49790 9 (paperback)
Food and Society in Classical Antiquity, by Peter Garnsey
978 0 521 64182 1 (hardback) 978 0 521 64588 1 (paperback)
Banking and Business in the Roman World, by Jean Andreau
978 0 521 38031 7 (hardback) 978 0 521 38932 7 (paperback)
Roman Law in Context, by David Johnston
978 0 521 63046 7 (hardback) 978 0 521 63961 3 (paperback)

POLITICS IN THE ROMAN REPUBLIC

HENRIK MOURITSEN

King's College London

CAMBRIDGE
UNIVERSITY PRESS

CAMBRIDGE
UNIVERSITY PRESS

University Printing House, Cambridge CB2 8BS, United Kingdom

One Liberty Plaza, 20th Floor, New York, NY 10006, USA

477 Williamstown Road, Port Melbourne, VIC 3207, Australia

4843/24, 2nd Floor, Ansari Road, Daryaganj, Delhi – 110002, India

79 Anson Road, #06–04/06, Singapore 079906

Cambridge University Press is part of the University of Cambridge.

It furthers the University's mission by disseminating knowledge in the pursuit of
education, learning, and research at the highest international levels of excellence.

www.cambridge.org
Information on this title: www.cambridge.org/9781107031883
DOI: 10.1017/9781139410861

First published 2017

Printed in the United States of America by Sheridan Books, Inc.

A catalogue record for this publication is available from the British Library.

Library of Congress Cataloging-in-Publication Data
Names: Mouritsen, Henrik, author.
Title: Politics in the Roman Republic / Henrik Mouritsen, King's College, London.
Description: New York : Cambridge University Press, 2017.
Identifiers: LCCN 2016047823 | ISBN 9781107031883 | ISBN 9781107651333 (pbk.)
Subjects: LCSH: Rome – Politics and government – 510–30 B.C.
Classification: LCC JC88 .M68 2017 | DDC 320.93709/014–dc23
LC record available at https://lccn.loc.gov/2016047823

ISBN 978-1-107-03188-3 Hardback
ISBN 978-1-107-65133-3 Paperback

Contents

vii

Acknowledgements

During the long gestation period of this book. I have received the help and advice of numerous colleagues and friends. I have had the opportunity to present chapters at the ICS in London and at the universities of Manchester, Princeton, Columbia, Dresden, Chemnitz, and Kyoto. I would like to thank my hosts at these institutions as well as the audiences for their constructive feedback. Maggie Robb, Sophie Lunn-Rockliffe, Yasutaka Uchida, and William Fitzgerald kindly read and commented on the manuscript, which has also benefitted from discussions with Martin Jehne, Bernhard Linke, John North, Walter Scheidel, and Dominic Rathbone. My doctoral student Steven Cosnett accepted the onerous task of compiling the index and checking the references, for which I owe him many thanks. I am grateful to the editors of the Key Themes in Ancient History series, Paul Cartledge and Peter Garnsey, and to Michael Sharp at Cambridge University Press for their patience and understanding; I am particularly indebted to Peter for his unfailing encouragement and sound advice throughout the process. Finally, I would like to thank my family and friends for their support and interest in my work.

Abbreviations (Authors and Works)

App. *BC*	Appian, *Bella civilia*
App. *Pun.*	Appian, *Punica*
Arist. *Pol.*	Aristotle, *Politics*
Asc. *Corn.*	Asconius, Comm. on Cicero, *Pro Cornelio*
Asc. *Mil.*	Asconius, Comm. on Cicero, *Pro Milone*
Auct. de vir ill.	*Auctor de viris illustribus*
Caes. *Civ.*	Caesar, *Bellum civile*
Cic. *Ac.*	Cicero, *Academic Questions*
Cic. *Agr.*	Cicero, *De lege agraria* (*In Rullum*)
Cic. *Amic.*	Cicero, *De amicitia*
Cic. *Att.*	Cicero, *Epistulae ad Atticum*
Cic. *Brut.*	Cicero, *Brutus*
Cic. *Caec.*	Cicero, *Pro Caecina*
Cic. *Cael.*	Cicero, *Pro Caelio*
Cic. *Cat.*	Cicero, *In Catilinam*
Cic. *Corn.*	Cicero, *Pro Cornelio de maiestate*
Cic. *Clu.*	Cicero, *Pro Cluentio*
Cic. *De orat.*	Cicero, *De oratore*
Cic. *Div.*	Cicero, *De divinatione*
Cic. *Div. Caec.*	Cicero, *Divinatio in Caecilium*
Cic. *Dom.*	Cicero, *De domo sua*
Cic. *Leg.*	Cicero, *De legibus*
Cic. *Fam.*	Cicero, *Epistulae ad familiares*
Cic. *Fin.*	Cicero, *De finibus*
Cic. *Flac.*	Cicero, *Pro Flacco*
Cic. *Har.*	Cicero, *De haruspicum responso*
Cic. *Man.*	Cicero, *Pro lege Manilia* (*De imperio Cn. Pompeii*)
Cic. *Mil.*	Cicero, *Pro Milone*

Cic. *Mur.*	Cicero, *Pro Murena*
Cic. *Off.*	Cicero, *De officiis*
Cic. *Parad.*	Cicero, *Paradoxa stoicorum*
Cic. *Part.*	Cicero, *Partitiones oratoriae*
Cic. *Phil.*	Cicero, *Philippics*
Cic. *Planc.*	Cicero, *Pro Plancio*
Cic. *Prov.*	Cicero, *De provinciis consularibus*
Cic. *Q.fr.*	Cicero, *Epistulae ad Quintum fratrem*
Cic. *Rab. perd.*	Cicero, *Pro Rabirio perduellionis reo*
Cic. *Red. pop.*	Cicero, *Post reditum ad populum*
Cic. *Red. sen.*	Cicero, *Post reditum in senatu*
Cic. *Rep.*	Cicero, *De re publica*
Cic. *Rosc. Am.*	Cicero, *Pro Sexto Roscio Amerino*
Cic. *Sest.*	Cicero, *Pro Sestio*
Cic. *Sul.*	Cicero, *Pro Sulla*
Cic. *Tusc.*	Cicero, *Tusculan Disputations*
Cic. *Vat.*	Cicero, *In Vatinium*
Cic. *Ver.*	Cicero, *In Verrem*
Comm. pet.	*Commentariolum petitionis* (Q. Cicero)
Diod. Sic.	Diodorus Siculus
Dion. Hal. *Ant.Rom.*	Dionysius of Halicarnassus, *Antiquitates Romanae*
Fest.	Festus, *Gloss. Lat.*
Gaius, *Inst.*	Gaius, *Institutes*
Gel. *NA*	Aulus Gellius, *Noctes Atticae*
Gran. Lic.	Granius Licinianus
Hdt.	Herodotus
Liv. *per.*	Livy, *Periochae*
Macr.	Macrobius (*Saturnalia*)
Ov. *Fast.*	Ovid, *Fasti*
Plut. *Ant.*	Plutarch, *Life of Antony*
Plut. *Caes.*	Plutarch, *Life of Caesar*
Plut. *Cat. Mi.*	Plutarch, *Life of Cato the Younger*
Plut. *CG*	Plutarch, *Life of Gaius Gracchus*
Plut. *Crass.*	Plutarch, *Life of Crassus*
Plut. *Fab. Max.*	Plutarch, *Life of Fabius Maximus*
Plut. *Flam.*	Plutarch, *Life of Flaminius*
Plut. *Luc.*	Plutarch, *Life of Lucullus*
Plut. *Mar.*	Plutarch, *Life of Marius*
Plut. *Marc.*	Plutarch, *Life of Marcellus*
Plut. *Mor.*	Plutarch, *Moralia*

Plut. *Pomp.*	Plutarch, *Life of Pompey*
Plut. *Sull.*	Plutarch, *Life of Sulla*
Plut. *TG*	Plutarch, *Life of Tiberius Gracchus*
Pind. *Pyth.*	Pindar, *Pythian Odes*
Plin. *Nat.*	Pliny (The Elder), *Natural History*
Polyb.	Polybius
Rhet. Her.	*Rhetorica ad Herennium*
Sall. *Cat.*	Sallust, *Bellum Catilinae*
Sall. *Iug.*	Sallust, *Bellum Iugurthinum*
Sall. *Hist.*	Sallust, *Histories*
Schol. Bob.	*Scholia Bobiensia*
Serv. *A.*	Servius, Commentary on the Aeneid
Suet. *Iul.*	Suetonius, *Divus Iulius*
Thuc.	Thucydides
Val. Max.	Valerius Maximus
Var. *L.*	Varro, *De lingua Latina*
Var. *R.*	Varro, *De re rustica*
Vell.	Velleius Paterculus
Zonar.	Zonaras

Introduction

As Caesar crossed the Rubicon and quickly took control over Italy, he was faced with an urgent problem – how to legitimise his position as de facto ruler of Rome. Both consuls had followed Pompey to Greece, which seriously limited Caesar's options, since only they could preside over a consular election or appoint a dictator. To overcome this obstacle Caesar had the senate and augurs issue a decree that was then ratified by the assembly, exceptionally allowing a praetor to nominate a dictator. Caesar's ally, the praetor M. Lepidus, could therefore appoint him to his first dictatorship and in turn enable him to preside over his own election to the consulship of 48.[1] It was transparently a fudge that deceived no one in Rome; Cicero calls it illegal and compares it to the way Sulla had gained his dictatorship in 82. Still, the fact that Caesar went to this length to achieve a veneer of legitimacy is telling.

A similar preoccupation with procedure is noticeable among Caesar's opponents, the 'government in exile'. According to Dio, at the height of the civil war in 48 there were two sets of magistrates representing the two sides in the conflict, but only those appointed by the Caesarians in Rome were 'normal' officials elected according to established rules. Those of the senatorial side, which had fled to Thessaly, merely had their tenure extended as proconsuls, propraetors, proquaestors etc. The reasons for this arrangement are intriguing; for as Dio further explains, although they had 'appropriated a small piece of land for the taking of auguries, in order that these might seem to take place under some form of law, so that they regarded the people and the whole city as present'; 'they had not appointed new magistrates for the reason that the consuls had not proposed the *lex curiata*'.[2] The latter was in political terms a formality, a ritual performed by thirty lictors in Rome, which granted (or enabled) the

---

[1] Cic. *Att.* 9.9.3 (SB 176); 9.15.2 (SB 183); Caes. *Civ.* 2.21.5. Vervaet 2004: 80–3.
[2] Cass. Dio 41.43.1–3 (Loeb), cf. Stasse 2005: 398–400; Fiori 2014: 104–6, with lit.

imperium of senior officials.[3] Still, it mattered sufficiently to stay the hand of the rulers of the empire during one of the most dramatic confrontations the republic had yet experienced. As Dio observed, the senators in Thessaly were 'very careful about precedents' and 'anxious that the acts rendered necessary by the exigencies of the situation should not all be in violation of the strict requirements of the ordinances' (41.43.4 Loeb).

Five years later the dictator was gone and Rome was again engulfed in civil war. At that point Cicero unleashed a fierce campaign against Antony, which caused such a stir in the senate that hostile rumours suggested that he was preparing to seize the *fasces* and make himself dictator. In his final Philippic oration, Cicero strongly denies the accusation, declaring that he is no Catiline but on the contrary the staunchest defender of the *res publica*. But he then changes tactic and points out the formal obstacles such an adventure would face, asking his audience: 'Under what auspices should I, an augur, receive these *fasces*? How long should I possess them? To whom should I hand them over?'[4] In other words, a serious allegation of planning a coup is publicly rebutted by reference to the procedural difficulties involved in an attempt of this nature.

Examples such as these illustrate how even in times of extreme political turmoil when any semblance of normality had disappeared formal procedure was still painstakingly observed. As such they reveal an almost obsessive concern about due process, which seems detached from any underlying political principle. Thus, Vervaet noted that although Sulla had gained power by 'unrestrained atrocities, brutal force and sheer terror', the terms of the *lex Valeria* which formalised his position 'still responded to legalistic scruples and the need of public legitimacy'.[5] Similarly, Caesar carefully notes in the *De bello civili* (3.1) that his second consulship – achieved through civil war – met the statutory interval between offices required by the *leges annales*.

This attention to proper form and procedure, even in the midst of complete social and political breakdown, reminds us that when studying Roman politics we enter a world where power was not just negotiated but also conceptualised in ways quite different from those with which we are now familiar. Therefore, to understand their political institutions and processes on their own terms requires a conscious leap of the imagination.

---

[3] On the nature of the *comitia curiata* and its resolutions, see Nicholls 1967; Develin 1977b; Hermon 1982; Stasse 2005; Humm 2012; Fiori 2014: 102–14.

[4] *Phil.* 14.14: 'Quibus auspiciis istos fascis augur acciperem, quatenus haberem, cui traderem?'

[5] Vervaet 2004: 75, who also observed that Marius refused to enter Rome in 87 until the *comitia* had formally undone the law that had driven him into exile, App. *BC* 1.70; Plu. *Mar.* 43.2.

Political systems, in antiquity as well as today, develop conventions and practices which may appear paradoxical and illogical to outsiders, but are taken for granted and regarded as natural by those who view it from within. The Athenians famously would not have recognised modern representative systems as 'democratic', while their use of the lot to fill public offices nowadays strikes most people as eccentric, as does the Spartan practice of 'voting by shouting'. Even in the modern world, where universally embraced democratic ideals have led to a high degree of 'homogenisation' of political systems, otherwise comparable countries still display features which cause bafflement among foreign observers.[6]

As frameworks for day-to-day government and administration, political systems are rarely questioned by those who operate within them, certainly not with regard to their basic principles. A government's legitimacy is generally accepted as long as it conforms to the rules and procedures which are themselves justified by tradition and custom. Rome was no different in this respect. The overriding concern among Roman politicians was the observance of correct procedure, a feature that is often seen as an expression of a distinctive Roman type of formalism, apparent also in their religious practices. It could also be argued that the emphasis placed on 'formalities' is characteristic of societies with poorly developed 'Staatlichkeit'. The Romans had no 'state' in the modern sense and only a limited set of public institutions. In their place we find the *res publica*, the shared public interests, which were to a great extent upheld through a dense web of rules and procedures scrupulously observed even when they seemed to serve no 'rational' purpose. The mass of accumulated rules and conventions served to regulate who could claim legitimacy, which is key to any political system. By defining who could wield power, how they could do it and for how long, they safeguarded the common interest against the 'law of the jungle'. The more complex and detailed the rules, the less the risk of uncontrolled power; in the same way as the gods were 'tied' through ritual and procedures, so were those who governed in the temporal sphere.

This study will explore aspects of Roman notions of legitimacy and the often paradoxical expressions they found in the world of 'real' politics. They created striking incongruities between political practices and

---

[6] For example, although coalition governments have long been the norm in most European countries since the war, the 2010–15 coalition government in the UK was greeted as an anomaly and potential threat to basic principles of accountability. Conversely, the fact that British majority governments regularly take office with only a minority of the vote behind them (unthinkable in most other European states) rarely causes much debate or affects the perceived legitimacy of a government and its legislation.

constitutional principles, which often stood in glaring contrast to each other. Thus, part of the inspiration comes from my previous work on political participation in the late republic, which suggested a discrepancy between the constitutional role of the *populus* and the small crowds which in practice represented it.[7] To capture the logic behind these apparent contradictions we need to question our preconceptions about what a political system should look like and how it functions. Any attempt to 'defamiliarise' Roman politics and recover a more genuinely Roman understanding of their system of government faces basic obstacles, however. The process of 'normalisation' began already in antiquity under the influence of Greek experiences and theorising. It is therefore natural to start our survey with Polybius who laid the foundations for this approach with his 'interpretatio graeca', and then turn to Cicero, who embraced the Greek models while at the same time modifying them in important ways.

Moving on from that discussion, we will then look at the political institutions and their articulations, which seem to reflect a uniquely Roman conceptualisation of power and legitimacy. Most importantly, the *populus* occupies a central but also highly complex role in this system. Its role in the political process was highly formalised, reduced almost to abstraction. As noted, the aim is to get closer to the Romans' own understanding of their political system and the logic that informed it. The problem is that when we analyse it in conventional terms and try to identify the location(s) of power, we are confronted with a basic indeterminacy that seems to be integral to the Roman 'constitution' itself. As part of this survey we will then consider the historical evolution of the institutions during and after the so-called Struggle of the Orders, in many respects the formative period of the republic. Special attention is given to a little-known reform of the assembly that introduced an element of lottery in elections which illustrates the particular rationale that shaped these procedures.

While the first section looks at institutions and their underlying principles, the second turns to actual practice – what happened in Roman politics on a day-to-day basis? The central question is again the location of power and the long-debated issue of the influence of the people. In line with recent scholarship it will be argued that the assemblies functioned as civic 'rituals' rather than decision-making bodies. However, following the 'communicative turn' attention has now shifted from the assemblies to the public meetings, *contiones*, which are now seen as the main fora for popular

---

[7] Mouritsen 2001; 2015a.

influence. After a critical assessment of the tenets of this theory, it will be suggested that Roman politics, like most other historical polities, was controlled by the elite, albeit an elite that extended well beyond the narrow confines of the senate. The office-holding class was, moreover, in many ways distinct from that of other aristocratic societies, displaying 'merito-cratic' features that may have helped to consolidate Roman society during what has become known as the 'middle republic'. In this context the question of 'political culture' also becomes significant, suggesting as it does that the 'secret' of Rome's success may be sought outside the political sphere, in social, economic, and not least military structures.

Finally, no study of Roman politics can avoid dealing with the 'fall of the republic', and one of the themes explored in the third section will be the impact of the political system itself on the catastrophic series of events that led to the advent of monarchy. It will be argued that intrinsic weaknesses in the political structure contributed to the growing instability of the later period. In this context the notion of 'political instability' will have to be considered as well as the question of 'periodisation', which has a direct impact on the conceptualisation of the process leading up to the 'fall'. Was there a 'late republic', and if so, what did it look like? The question involves a discussion of the nature of political conflict in the last century, including the modern 'two-party'-model of 'optimates' and 'populares' which will be examined in some detail since it lies at the heart of the conventional 'crisis narrative' of the late republic.

Needless to say, this study makes no claim to presenting a full picture of 'Roman politics' (however one defines that) covering all relevant topics. It is by necessity selective, and issues are chosen primarily for their exemp-lary qualities and ability to illustrate aspects of Roman public life and governance that have perhaps not previously been viewed from this parti-cular perspective. It is therefore essentially an attempt to draw attention to elements that question our preconceptions about political structures and processes, and thereby contribute to a discussion about how one studies a polity like the Roman republic.

CHAPTER I

Senatus Populusque Romanus
Institutions and Practices

In its essential features the Roman republic may seem deceptively familiar, broadly conforming to the 'standard' city-state structure found across the ancient Mediterranean. In most polities a tripartite structure can be reconstructed, composed of popular assembly(ies), council(s) and a variety of magistracies. Within this simple scheme the interrelations between the institutions and their internal structures and procedures may vary, creating different balances of power between rulers and ruled, elite and populace. The Roman version of these institutions, the *comitia*, the senate and the magistrates, thus fits into a known pattern, even if there were additional complications in the form of specifically plebeian institutions, which have no parallel in the ancient world. Despite its apparent familiarity the Roman system nevertheless presents questions as regards the distribution and exercise of power, especially in relation to the role of the people; for, while the popular assemblies had the final say in all matters of legislation and public appointments, they were at the same time subject to the authority of powerful magistrates. Similarly, the senate, although formally an advisory body, clearly wielded decisive influence over public policy and administration.

Until recently scholars resolved these contradictions by assuming that the elite effectively neutralised the powers of the assembly through clientelistic networks which acted as instruments of social control. This theory has since been challenged, and will be returned to later.[1] Others have therefore proposed that in the absence of comprehensive patronage and bonds of obligation, the people did indeed act as a free and active political agent, exercising their constitutional powers in ways that almost made Rome comparable to classical Greek democracies.[2] While most scholars have not

---

[1] See below pp. 94–5.
[2] Millar 1984; 1986; 1989; 1995; 1998; followed by e.g. Lintott 1987; Wiseman 1999. More sceptical, Gabba 1990; North 1990; Harris 1990; Eder 1991; Jehne 1995a; Hölkeskamp 2000; 2010; Mouritsen 2001; Ward 2004. Overview of debate Marcone 2005; Hurlet 2012.

gone that far, they still tend to identify the assemblies as a popular power base, which might be neutralised by external factors or – in their absence – function more or less as intended.

It is at this point that the conceptual models which we – consciously or not – employ to make sense of Roman institutions become important. Traditionally, historians have followed a systematic constitutional approach and analysed the formal distribution of powers in the Roman state. The legal approach reached its pinnacle in Mommsen's *Römisches Staatsrecht*, but in recent years this line of inquiry has come under increasing criticism for its formalism and lack of consideration of extra-legal factors influencing the institutions.[3] But to understand the roots of this conceptual model we have to go further back, to the earliest surviving attempt to analyse the Roman system which was produced by Polybius.

Polybius and the Roman Political System

No study of Roman politics can ignore Polybius (*c.* 200–120 BCE), not just because of his status as a contemporary source, but also because of the lasting impact his approach has had on subsequent – ancient and modern – analyses of the Roman constitution. A Greek statesman from Megalopolis, Polybius was exiled to Rome in 167, where he spent the following seventeen years, developing close ties with the leading men of the time. During his exile he began work on a monumental history of Rome that would trace her conquest of the Mediterranean world in forty books, the first five of which survive intact, the rest only in fragments of varying length. The work is remarkable for its 'factual' style of reporting, which makes it a prime example of pragmatic, 'didactic' historiography.[4] The approach is analytical rather than rhetorical, always looking for general causes behind historical occurrences. Polybius' discussion of the political system, presented in the fragmentary book six, offers the first, indeed only, original attempt to subject Roman institutions to theoretical analysis. Polybius' impact can hardly be overestimated and his legacy arguably lives on to the present day; many scholars still regard Polybius' model as the best guide to understanding the Roman constitution.[5]

The central tenets of Polybius' analysis are well known and need only be broadly outlined. Essentially, the Roman political system is presented as

---

[3] Mommsen 1887; cf. the papers collected in Nippel and Seidenstecker eds. 2005.
[4] See e.g. Walbank 1972: 66–96; Champion 2004.
[5] Millar 1984: 2; Lintott 1999: 8, 16–26, 214–19; Welwei 2002; Rogers 2002; Polverini 2005. See also Nicolet 1973; 1983.

the embodiment of the 'mixed constitution', blending elements of monarchy, oligarchy, and democracy into a single, well-balanced entity.[6] The internal stability ensured by the mixed system allowed Rome to direct her energy outwards towards military expansion, thereby explaining her remarkable drive and success. According to Polybius, the purpose of his work was to explain Rome's conquest of the civilised world to a Greek audience – although he may also have hoped to impress his Roman hosts. In antiquity constitutions were generally assumed to hold the key to the success or failure of states since they determined their degree of stability and upheaval, freedom and tyranny, and it was this linkage that provided the rationale for Polybius' constitutional digression. Moreover, given the traditional Greek ideal of the golden mean, a 'mixed' constitution that blended different types of government and balanced opposing interests against each other was – in analogy to the doctrine of the bodily humours – naturally deemed the best, and the only guarantee of long-term stability.[7] Therefore, since Rome's military superiority was indisputable, it followed logically that it must have a matching superior constitution, which from a Greek perspective meant a mixed constitution.

This premise lends Polybius' analysis a certain aprioric aspect but, as importantly, the particular version of the 'mixed constitution' he presents is in many respects unusual, not just in its application of Greek theory to Roman institutions but also in the way he uses his theoretical models. Polybius' basic framework was provided by the traditional tripartite division of constitutions into monarchy, democracy, and oligarchy that can be found already in Herodotus' constitutional debate, and even earlier in Pindar.[8] Later it became a standard fixture of Greek political thinking and theorists further refined the model by dividing each of them into good and bad forms. The terminology and categories varied, but in Polybius' work the positive forms appear as monarchy, aristocracy, and democracy, and their negative versions as tyranny, oligarchy, and ochlocracy (mob rule). The constitutional archetypes were considered to be in a permanent state of flux, invariably degenerating into their negative forms and causing upheavals that would lead to their eventual replacement by another type of government. In Polybius' model the different types succeeded each other in a fixed cyclical movement, the *anakyklosis*, which represented a variant of the Platonic idea.

---

[6] On the theory of the 'mixed constitution' see e.g. von Fritz 1954; Nippel 1980; Lintott 1997; Blösel 1998.

[7] Hahm 1995: 9 suggested Polybius drew on a mix of different Greek philosophical traditions.

[8] Hdt. 3.80–2; Pind. *Pyth.* 2.86–8.

Faced with the problem of endemic political instability Greek theorists came up with a number of solutions. In Plato's ideal constitution the state was ruled by an enlightened guardian, whose benevolent reign would overcome the conflict between rich and poor. Later he moved towards a mixed system which combined elements of the different constitutions. Aristotle, on the other hand, while in principle accepting Plato's elevation of kingship, also developed a less utopian ideal, the so-called *Politeia*, which blended oligarchic and democratic features. Although presented as the perfect form of democracy, Aristotle's 'polity' was in practice closer to a moderate oligarchy. This constitution was intended to bring an end to political upheaval and class conflict by offering a measured compromise between the interests of the elite and the populace. In Aristotle's analysis the polis was naturally torn between the well-to-do (*euporoi*) and the indigent (*aporoi*). By focusing on the structural causes of political instability and stressing the significance of economic inequality, Aristotle's solution thus remained firmly rooted in the social reality of contemporary Greek poleis. The conflict between rich and poor was to Aristotle the root cause of instability, and his solution involved a broad compromise between the two groups and the application of balanced, bipartisan policies that respected the concerns of both sides.

Polybius' 'mixed constitution' is a very different creature from Aristotle's 'Polity'. To Polybius the *anakyklosis* did not reflect the instability caused by the competing interests of different social groups but was entirely ethical in nature. It was brought about by the moral corruption of the rulers which inevitably followed within 'pure' systems, leading to their overthrow and replacement. Thus, as Nippel observed, with Polybius Greek constitutional theory lost its sociological dimension, and it was this analytical shift which enabled Polybius to combine all three 'positive' archetypes, kingship as well as aristocracy and democracy.[9] The inclusion of monarchy altered the character of his model, for while monarchy evidently existed as a constitutional type, it did not reflect the rule of any particular group in society in the same way that democracy and oligarchy did. Monarchy is in a sense the primitive default option that emerges when an open, participatory political process has broken down and power is left in the hands of a single individual. To Aristotle monarchy was therefore essentially tyranny, although he accepted that the enlightened rule of one man, defined as kingship, in theory represented an ideal and possibly supreme form of government. While elite and masses were

[9] Nippel 1980: 145.

the given constituents of any ancient society, whose – self-interested – rule was conceptualised as oligarchy and democracy, respectively, there could in the nature of things be no specific constituency behind a monarchy. Polybius' notion that an effective 'mixed constitution' required a monarchical element is therefore based on a mechanistic construction of the problem. Kingship was included in order to create a correspondence between the perceived problem – the constitutional cycle – and the solution – the 'mixed constitution', which combined all the 'pure' forms and neutralised their individual weaknesses. Or, in other words, since monarchy was part of the problem – the *anakyklosis* – it must also be part of the solution, i.e. the ideal constitution. This schematic logic, however, remains divorced from socio-economic considerations of the causes of political instability.

In this context the example of Sparta, the classic Greek paradigm of a 'mixed' constitution to which Polybius explicitly – and favourably – compared Rome, becomes significant. Sparta's unique combination of monarchy, democracy, and oligarchy meant that in order to carry that comparison through a monarchical element had to be found also in Rome. That was obviously difficult in a system founded on the explicit disavowal of all things regal, and Polybius' attempt at identifying kingship in the role of the Roman consuls remains weak. It ignores a number of features: that there was more than one consul, that they held equal powers, were elected by the assembly for one year only, held no legislative powers, answered to the senate which could issue instructions, and might be held responsible for their actions after their time in office. Some Romans, as we shall see, may have interpreted the consuls as the inheritors of the king's *imperium*, but that did not make their role monarchical, especially since they also saw the office as deliberately conceived in opposition to the ousted kings.

Polybius' 'monarchical' consuls highlight the mechanical nature of his approach, which shows little direct engagement with the nuts and bolts of the Roman institutions and their practical functioning. Each element of the constitution is identified as the embodiment of one of the conventional Greek archetypes. Thus, while the consuls are made to represent kingship, the assembly is labelled the democratic element and the senate the oligarchic. That approach differs radically from that found in Aristotle, for whom the basic distinction in any society was that between the wealthy who had sufficient means to take active part in government and those without. Oligarchy was therefore defined as the rule of the well-to-do, while democracy existed when poorer people held power despite their lack of resources. Crucially, Aristotle did not operate with an either/or distinction, since each type represented a continuum of constitutional forms;

Aristotle envisaged no fewer than four degrees of oligarchy.[10] The character of a constitution depended on a number of variables, of which the most important were property assessments (*timema*) for citizenship and office holding, the level at which the thresholds were set, the provision of payment for officials and the degree of access to the assembly. In addition, Aristotle's distinction between oligarchy and democracy took into account the general distribution of wealth in society, the rule of law, and the extent of inherited powers.

None of these factors are considered by Polybius, who simply attaches to each institution a constitutional label that sums up its political 'value' and defines it as the incarnation of a particular constitutional principle. According to Polybius their political character was so unequivocal that when each element was viewed in isolation, the constitution appeared either to be fully democratic, monarchic or aristocratic. Polybius therefore does not allow for the possibility that they might contain internal contradictions or compromises, thus ignoring what Nippel called 'Intraorgankontrolle', the internal control mechanisms that play such a prominent role in the models of Plato and Aristotle.[11] There is no hint that assemblies, magistracies, and councils might themselves cover the full range from democratic to aristocratic. Thus, we search in vain for a discussion of the property qualifications which determined the structure of the assemblies, access to public office and membership of the senate. Polybius seems unaware of the fact that councils, assemblies and magistracies had no definite political character but could fall at any point within a broad continuum of popular and aristocratic politics.

We might therefore ask whether Polybius' Roman constitution was not a 'composite' constitution rather than a 'mixed' one, combining elements of different political systems which remain essentially separate. However, this is precisely where Polybius makes his original contribution to ancient political theory. Since each element was 'pure', the stabilising 'mixture' lay entirely in the interrelation between individual institutions, whose powers were moderated through a system of 'checks and balances'. The interdependency of the Roman institutions represents the central tenet of Polybius' analysis, which argued that none of them could act independently but had to rely on the co-operation of the others, a co-operation that was forced upon each element and essentially was motivated by self-interest tempered by fear.[12]

---

[10] Arist. *Pol.* 4.5, 1293a12–34. Cf. Ostwald 2000: 71.   [11] Cf. Nippel 1980.
[12] Lintott 1997: 79; Asmis 2005: 380.

Demonstrating this interdependency in practice is not without difficulty, however, and many scholars have noted the problems Polybius faced when trying to apply his thesis to the specifics of the Roman political system. It is, for example, hard to accept the consuls as counter-balancing the senate, since consuls and senators all belonged to the same socioeconomic class; indeed the consuls were themselves members of the senate and would remain so after their tenure. Some of the interdependencies claimed by Polybius also seem forced, not least the people's reliance on the senate, which exaggerates the importance of public contracts and the proportion of citizens sharing in them (6.17).

Examples such as these cast doubt on the assumption that the analysis grew out of Polybius' own personal observations of Roman politics and his close acquaintance with leading protagonists. Polybius' constitutional digression should in this respect be treated as distinct from his 'pragmatic' historical reporting. It is perhaps better understood as an intellectual 'tour-de-force' which served to divert and impress his readership – and rival historians – with a dazzling display of political theorisation. Polybius embraces the challenge of making Roman institutions comprehensible to a foreign audience that would often have found them baffling, and he does so by fitting them into a conventional Greek theoretical framework. As a result the unfamiliar becomes familiar – to the Greeks as well as to us; Rome emerges as the perfect embodiment of the long-standing Greek ideal of the mixed constitution, able to take its rightful place alongside Sparta.

The question is where this leaves the study of the Roman political system. Polybius' analysis is too schematic to be of much help in understanding the location of power in republican Rome, and despite recent attempts to 'rehabilitate' his model, most scholars have recognised its basic shortcomings.[13] There is, however, a much wider legacy of Polybius' work, and to grasp that we may shift our focus from the specifics of his analysis to his overall approach; for what was truly innovative in Polybius' constitutional digression was his application of Greek concepts to Roman institutions. This example of 'interpretatio Graeca' has raised few eyebrows, probably because most modern scholars consider these analytical tools to be universally applicable. But as Ostwald noted, the classification of constitutions as the rule of one, few and many, is now so conventional, 'that we tend to forget how uniquely Greek it is'.[14] The concepts employed by

---

[13] Following Walbank 1972: 155–6 and Cornell 1991: 61–2, Seager 2013 dismisses Polybius' model as inadequate and simplistic.

[14] Ostwald 2000 13; cf. Marcone 2005: 91–2; Zecchini 2006: 403–4; Hurlet 2012: 33.

Polybius – and indeed his entire analytical framework – were developed in a Greek context and shaped by experiences specific to the Greek *polis*. Given their cultural contingency, we may consider the possibility that they in fact impose an alien perspective that obscures what was uniquely Roman.

Polybius' approach was basically a functional one that perceived Roman politics as a logical system, in which each element fulfilled a specific role in maintaining the all-important stability. As components of political machinery they were endowed with rational purpose as a means of negotiating power within the state, balancing the interests of different groups and upholding social peace. Polybius' identification of a distinct political 'value' in each Roman institution has wide implications, for in the end it is this approach that has defined the *comitia* as essentially 'democratic' in their rationale.

Cicero's *Res Publica*

Polybius' analysis of the Roman state was that of an outsider, which raises the question how a Roman writer would apply the Greek models. This is where Cicero's contribution becomes important, for in the *De re publica* and *De legibus* he offers a glimpse of a different conceptualisation of Roman institutions.[15] Unlike Polybius, Cicero was not a detached foreign spectator, but a Roman aristocrat with long experience in dealing with the institutions he describes. Although he builds on the same Greek theoretical foundations as Polybius, whom he acknowledges as an authority (*Rep.* 1.34), and uses identical models and categories, there are slight but significant shifts in emphasis and the addition of crucial new accents.[16]

The *De re publica*, written between 54 and 51 during Cicero's self-imposed withdrawal from the political scene, belongs to a period of upheaval and instability in Rome. The text has a clear remedial function, exploring possible solutions to the disunity and instability that currently threatened the republic. It therefore presents a positive and uplifting vision of the *res publica*, with particular stress on the importance of consensus, co-operation and unity of purpose as the original impulses that had first led to its creation.[17]

---

[15] For an overview, see e.g. Atkins 2000.

[16] Ferrary 1984a: 90 suggested Cicero's *De re publica* remained independent of Polybius.

[17] *Rep.* 1.1, 39, 42, 49, as emphasised in his famous definition of a political community as 'coetus multitudinis iuris consensu et utilitatis communione sociatus', 1.39; cf. Asmis 2005: 380.

Cicero's description of the constitutional types and the advantages derived from a balanced mixture does not depart significantly from his Greek sources, but the overall conception of the constitution is nevertheless quite different. He abandons the idea of opposing constitutional elements locked in perpetual competition over power and resources and kept in equilibrium only through mutual fear. Strikingly, he uses a Platonic image of dissimilar sounds creating musical harmonies to illustrate the distinctly Roman consensus he envisages. Importantly, this is a harmony between social classes held together by common accord, not distinct constitutional forces or principles.[18] The resulting *concordia* is therefore very different in nature from Polybius' checks and balances.

In line with conventional Roman thought and political practice, Cicero readily accepts the people's right to *libertas* and stresses its overall centrality to the *res publica*, but it was also self-evident to him that the elite would provide leadership. He therefore introduces a concept absent from his Greek models, namely senatorial *auctoritas*, the pervasive influence that went far beyond what was formally enshrined in law (*Rep.* 2.57). Essentially therefore, Cicero's constitution is both aristocratic and bipartite, with the *populus* holding the power but exercising it on the advice of experienced councillors and delegating executive functions to appointed magistrates.[19]

Thus, in contrast to Polybius the central virtue of the mixed system was to Cicero its ability to satisfy the people's desire for *libertas* without compromising the power of the elite or the strong magistracy. But because the basic principle of the people's *libertas* was beyond contention, its precise articulation became much more crucial. A key concept was *aequabilitas* – equity, equality or fairness – which represents the particular kind of equality that is proportional to merit and thus responds to the fundamental aristocratic objection against the egalitarian principle which is its failure to take into account naturally occurring differences in status or ability.[20]

Cicero's other constitutional treatise, the *De legibus*, goes into greater detail with regard to the practicalities of politics and here the discrepancies between his and Polybius' approach become even more apparent.

---

[18] Like music 'so also is a state made harmonious by agreement among dissimilar elements, brought about by a fair and reasonable blending together of the upper, middle, and lower classes, just as if they were musical tones', *Rep.* 2.69 ('sic ex summis et infimis et mediis interiectis ordinibus ut sonis moderata ratione civitas consensu'). Cf. Asmis 2005: 405.

[19] Ferrary 1984a: 91–3; Asmis 2005: 403–14. Schofield 1995: 77 noted that the *De re publica* 'marries a fundamental recognition of popular sovereignty with an unshakeable and deep-seated commitment to aristocracy as the best practicable system of government'.

[20] *Rep.* 1.53, 69, cf. 2.39–40; cf. Fantham 1973, who highlights variations in Cicero's use of the concept.

The popular tribunate is presented as a means of pacifying the people, a necessary concession which ensures that the common people make no desperate attempt to assert their rights (*Leg.* 3.24–5). Cicero further outlines a procedure designed to give voting procedures the 'appearance of liberty', 'libertatis species', a point echoed in his praise for the republican hero Publicola, who by granting the people a moderate amount of liberty had entrenched the power of the elite.[21] Thus, the popular institutions and their prerogatives emerge as institutionalised guarantors and symbolic representations of the people's liberty, serving to integrate the people into an aristocratic regime – without conveying any real power.[22] In Cicero's version of the 'mixed constitution', institutions could exist to create a semblance of representation, being gestures of inclusion and shared citizenship rather than vehicles of actual popular influence.

Cicero's model remains a negotiation between, on the one hand, the Greek conceptual framework he had adopted and, on the other hand, his personal vision and experience of the Roman state. As such it hints at a more complex and subtle understanding of institutions than Polybius' model of formalised checks and balances. In particular, the suggestion that institutions could have symbolic functions may give us a clue as to how to resolve the paradoxes inherent in the Roman political system. Polybius' functional approach has, as noted, encouraged a 'normalisation' of Roman institutions, but a better understanding of the Roman political system and the particular logic which governed it may be gained by focusing on those elements that do not fit easily into his model. In that context the ambiguous role of the *populus* attracts particular attention.

'The Power of the People': The *Comitia* in the Roman Republic

The Roman People was, as most textbooks explain, 'sovereign'; only the *populus* could make laws, declare war and make peace, appoint leaders of the Roman state and condemn a citizen to death. The 'sovereignty' of the *populus Romanus* was implied already in the fifth-century law code, the Twelve Tables, which according to Livy stated that: 'whatsoever the people decreed last should have the binding force of law'.[23] The role of the people as the source of public legitimacy was undisputed; as Giovannini noted,

---

[21] *Leg.* 3.39; *Rep.* 2.55: 'qui modica libertate populo data facilius tenuit auctoritatem principum'.
[22] Cf. Nippel 1980: 155.
[23] Liv. 7.17.12: '. . . quodcumque postremum populus iussisset, id ius ratumque esset'. Badian 1996: 211 notes that the passage is not a general statement of 'sovereignty' but deals with conflicts in law.

the supremacy of the *populus* was, judging from our sources, never called into question.[24] Certainly, in historical times the principle of the people's 'sovereignty' was for all Romans the self-evident foundation of political life. The concept of popular 'sovereignty' is, of course, an anachronism in a Roman context, invented as it was in the early modern period.[25] But Roman notions of the 'power of the people' may not only have differed from anything we would today recognise as 'sovereignty'; it was probably also quite unlike the 'democratic' principles debated by ancient Greek theorists. In fact, the people's 'sovereignty' may have been rooted in a very different construction of the Roman state. In order to investigate that issue we will look first at the ways in which the 'will of the people' was expressed and articulated in the popular institutions.

The classic Roman republic had a bewildering variety of popular assemblies, the *comitia curiata, centuriata, tributa,* and the *concilium plebis*, in addition to the non-decision taking meetings known as *contiones*. They were created at different moments in Rome's history, and for different purposes. They did, however, share the same formal structure and procedures, particularly concerning the relationship between the assembly and the presiding magistrate. Political gatherings, needless to say, always require some form of organisation and leadership. In Rome, however, the role of the organiser went far beyond the strictly practical. The presiding official was in full control of every aspect of the proceedings. Unlike classical Athens, Rome had no statutory assembly days, allowing the people to come together on a regular basis to deliberate current issues. The various assemblies and meetings convened only when called by an authorised official. An assembly thus came into being through the actions of an official, who could dismiss it again at any time, thereby preventing it from reaching any decision.

The fact that it was the magistrate who constituted the people politically also determined the workings of the *comitia*. Again the contrast with Athens is striking, since there was no possibility of popular initiatives or proposals emerging from the meetings themselves, which were not even allowed an open debate. Discussions were formally separated from the decision-taking meetings (*comitia*), and relegated to so-called *contiones*, which were defined as formal public gatherings where no vote was taken. *Contiones* were called by an official, who

---

[24] Giovannini 1990: 406–8 on the so-called 'Struggle of the Orders'.
[25] Cf. Badian 1990b: 469; cf. Jehne 2005: 134–42 with lit. For the modern concept of sovereignty, see Grimm 2009.

held the required authorisation, the so-called *potestas contionandi*, and they might be held on their own or precede a *comitia*. But even these occasions did not offer the opportunity for a free or open debate. The proceedings were strictly regulated and remained under the direct control of the presiding official. It was he who decided not only the time and place, but also the issue(s) to be debated and crucially who were permitted to speak – usually arranged in advance.[26] The *contio* was therefore more an address to the people than a consultation of it.[27] There was no formal interaction between speakers and *populus*, just a one-way communication, which was fully controlled by the magistrate who convened the meeting, selected the speakers and could dismiss the crowd at any point. It follows that the Roman people had no legitimate ways of convening or expressing its views without formalised leadership. When this was not forthcoming the people could not voice any opinion; in other words, the *populus* did not exist as a political body independently of its leaders.

The essentially passive role of the *populus* is also reflected in the legislative procedure. The presiding magistrate would present proposals to the assembly, whose response was limited to yes or no without any opportunity to modify or change what was put before it. The lack of active input into policy-making means that a legislative *comitia* can be defined as an *ad hoc* meeting convened by a magistrate for the purpose of ratifying a specific proposal (rejections, as we shall see, hardly ever happened). The limitations imposed on the Roman *comitia* may not strike modern observers as that exceptional, perhaps because of the similarities between the Roman procedure and that of a modern-day referendum, where politicians put a simple proposition before the electorate for its approval or rejection – a process which is commonly perceived as a fair and democratic solution to the practical problem of consulting large numbers of people. The parallel is misleading, however; for the modern equivalent to a Roman legislative assembly is not a referendum but a meeting of parliament. The basic principle in contemporary political systems is that of representation, referendums usually being the rare exception. The modern popular assembly is therefore a parliament, and to appreciate fully the constraints imposed on the Roman *comitia* we must envisage a parliament with no regular meetings, no debates, and no ability to formulate or modify policies; in short, a parliament completely controlled by the executive.

---

[26] On the *contio*, see Pina Polo 1995; 1996.
[27] *Contio* could therefore also refer to a speech delivered at the meeting, cf. Mouritsen 2013.

The relationship between magistrate and assembly in Rome also differed fundamentally not just from that found in current political systems, but also in, for example, classical Athens. Unlike Athenian office holders, the magistrates were not simply officials in charge of specific public functions and accountable to the *ekklesia*. They were, as Meyer noted, superior to the *populus*, as indeed underlined by the etymology of their title *magistratus*, derived from *magis* – greater.[28] The power of the people was expressed via – and only via – the actions of its elected officials. The unique position of the Roman magistrate was also underlined symbolically. Thus, his powers were embodied and directly expressed in the symbol of the *fasces*, which had no parallel in the Greek world.[29] Moreover, the relationship between magistrate and *populus* manifested itself spatially in the fact that the magistrate presided over the assembly from an elevated tribunal, physically standing above the *populus* which gathered before him.

Given the extensive powers of the magistrates, the method used to appoint them becomes significant. The process is conventionally described as popular election, but the formal procedure is revealing as to the underlying logic of the occasion. Again we find the *populus* playing a peculiarly passive role. As Badian has demonstrated, the people were neither 'sovereign' nor active in the elective assemblies.[30] They were convened by a magistrate, who formally guided the *comitia*, and the technical language used for the appointment of magistrates indicates that it happened through the joint action of the presiding magistrate and the *populus*.[31] Without the guidance of a magistrate the *populus* could not appoint new leaders. In this context it is significant too that the new appointment formally was made only when the leader announced it. This feature gave the process an element of internalised succession, where the new magistrate was 'created', '*creatus*' by the incumbent rather than by the popular vote.[32] It was the magistrate not the people who was responsible to gods and humans for the succession and its consequences.[33] When the chain between them was broken, an *interrex* had to be appointed to carry out the ritual handing over of power to the successor. In formal terms the occasion was therefore one

---

[28] Cf. Meyer 1961: 80, who describes the extraordinary position of the magistrates in Rome that made them 'sovereign' and superior to the people.

[29] Cf. Marshall 1984.   [30] Badian 1990b: 471.

[31] As the phrase found in e.g. Cic. *Rep.* 2.31: ' . . . Tullum Hostilium populus regem interrege rogante comitiis curiatis creavit . . . ' illustrates, 'a validly elected magistrate can issue solely from the question plus the answer', Badian ibid.

[32] Meyer 1961: 66 described it as a 'persönlichen Schöpfungsakt', 'a personal act of creation'. The phrase is recorded in Cic. *Leg.* 3.9; Liv. 4.7.10; 25.2.4; 32.27.5; 40 35.1; 45.44.1.

[33] Meyer 1961: 67–8.

where the outgoing magistrate presented his successor to the assembly, asking it to grant its approval.[34]

The procedure is commonly assumed to go back to regal times and originate in the traditional acclamation of the new king by the *comitia curiata*, which the ancient tradition identified as the oldest Roman assembly, predating the republic.[35] Supposedly, the kings had received their powers through a *lex curiata de imperio*, which in effect was an oath of allegiance sworn to the new ruler, expressing the people's consent.[36] That interpretation is supported by the terminology used. Thus, it has been suggested that etymologically *suffragium* may refer to the sound made by an assembled crowd banging their weapons as a sign of approval. That would indicate a primitive act of acclamation by a crowd collectively responding to a request, rather than an elective process where votes were cast and counted.[37] The political language of the Romans points in the same direction, since Latin had no word expressing the exercise of an active political choice by the citizens. The word for voting, vote, and voter – *suffragor, suffragium* and *suffragator* – are all positive terms of approval and support, not of choice. The vocabulary thus reflected a system where the *populus* could either express its approval or withhold it.

Later real elections offering a choice of several candidates were introduced, but there is no evidence that the assembly was then free to vote for whomever it wanted. As Badian concluded: 'The comitia had no right of initiative'.[38] The magistrate was still formally and in actual fact in charge, and he could refuse to accept a vote by the *populus*, as happened on several occasions.[39] Thus, in 215 the consul Q. Fabius Maximus threw out the result of the first century, the *centuria praerogativa*, and asked it to reconsider its decision, which it duly did.[40] In 184 the election of Q. Fulvius Flaccus as praetor was rejected, because he was already designated aedile.[41]

---

[34] Linke 1995: 147. Levick 1981, argued that no formal *professio* of a candidature to the presiding magistrate was required, which might reflect the tradition by which magistrates presented their successors for the assembly's approval.

[35] Cic. *Rep.* 2.25, 31, 33, 35, 38, cf. Gel. *NA* 13.15.4.

[36] Rüpke 1990: 48–51 noted the unanimity implied in the procedure of the *comitia curiata*, cf. Nicholls 1967; Rieger 2007: 606. Prugni 1987: 135 suggested that the *lex de imperio* was not a law but a declaration of loyalty. According to Humm 2012, the *lex curiata* did not confer *imperium* but the auspices which enabled magistrates to receive the *imperium*, essentially granted by Jupiter.

[37] Vaahtera 1993b; cf. Jehne 2001; 2013b: 130–2, with refs. n.10.   [38] Badian 1990b: 470–1 n.20.

[39] When presented with the results of a vote the presiding magistrate could refuse 'nomen accipere', cf. Rilinger 1976: 60–75. On recorded cases, see Eder 1990a and Badian 1990b: 466–75, who counted thirteen. As late as 67 the consul C. Piso had declared that if the assembly chose M. Palicanus as consul he would not return him, 'non renuntiabo', Val. Max. 3.8.3.

[40] Liv. 24.7.10–9.3. cf. below pp. 46–7.   [41] Liv. 39.39.

Later, at the consular elections of 148, the presiding magistrate refused to acknowledge the election of Scipio Aemilianus, who was formally a candidate for the aedileship.[42] When on some occasions the magistrate backed down and compromised, it was because the candidates in question forcefully invoked the principle of popular 'sovereignty', which always had the potential to create conflicts between different constitutional and legal conventions.[43]

The 'sovereignty' of the Roman people in important respects turns out to be restricted by and subject to the power of the magistrates. So how are we to understand the nature of this 'sovereignty'? The relationship between *populus* and *senatus* may give us an idea, suggesting as it does that the people were subjected to another much more fundamental authority. According to Roman tradition the senate was, as the name suggests, a council of elders which had been more or less informally constituted in order to advise the kings and – after their expulsion – the consuls. In accordance with its advisory role, its formal powers were strictly limited. Its position in relation to the assemblies is therefore intriguing, since our sources insist that any decision by the assembly required the formal approval of the senate, the so-called *auctoritas patrum*. As Cicero stated: ' . . . no act of the popular assembly should be valid unless ratified by the *auctoritas* of the Fathers'.[44] Little is known about the precise nature of this nebulous concept, and the clearest evidence comes from two laws which reformed its application. The *lex Publilia* of 339 prescribed that it must be given to new laws before the vote was taken in the *comitia centuriata*, while the *lex Maenia* (third century) required that *auctoritas patrum* be given before, not after, the elections.[45]

The practical significance of the *auctoritas patrum* is unclear: there are no reported instances where it was withheld, and many scholars have therefore suggested that it later became a formality.[46] But its existence is nevertheless important, not least because of the implicit claim that the will of the people was not the highest authority but subject to the approval of an aristocratic body of elders. Without senatorial consent

---

[42] App. *Pun.* 112; Val. Max. 8.15.4. See Develin 1978b.

[43] Cf. Liv. 27.6.7 and the dispute over M. Claudius Marcellus' third consulship in 152. As Badian 1990b: 473 observed, the magistrate did not 'persist in this course. He asked for support – or else his opponents did – and gave up if he saw himself to be isolated.' For such conflicts, see Lundgreen 2009b.

[44] *Rep.* 2.56: ' . . . populi comitia ne essent rata nisi ea patrum adprobavisset auctoritas'; Cf. 2.25; Serv. *A.* 9.190; Liv. 1.18.6–10.

[45] Liv. 8.12.15; Cic. *Brut.* 55; cf. Cic. *Planc.* 8; Sal. *Hist.* 3.48.15Maur; Liv. 1.17.9.

[46] Disputed by Graeber 2001.

the 'will of the people' was null and void, and interestingly this relationship was also reflected in the layout of the political venues. Thus, the Curia occupied an elevated position above the people's meeting place, the Comitium, which it dominated visually and symbolically. It might be tempting to see the senate's role as part of a 'Polybian' compromise which balanced the interests of the aristocracy against those of the masses. But the power of the senators was not, as one might have expected, founded on conventional aristocratic claims to leadership, such as superior wealth, responsibility, and capability. It was a claim of a very different nature.

'Religion' and 'Politics'

The approval of the senators was, as we saw, expressed as *auctoritas patrum*, and this concept is a key to understanding their power. *Auctoritas* carries strong religious associations, and it has been suggested that the ancient expression describing the senators' approval 'patres auctores fiunt', goes back to sacral law. Moreover, the senators who gave their *auctoritas* were historically the *patres*, i.e. the patrician senators.[47] The existence of this particular group played a central role in the development of Rome's political system. Two aspects are crucial. First, it was a hereditary status, and, second, its members held special privileges primarily of a religious nature. Although much remains obscure, it appears that at some early stage in Rome's history a group of families, *gentes*, established themselves as a separate class with particular religious rights and responsibilities. Above all they seem to have assumed the right to interpret the will of the gods through signs and rituals, and it was that role which underpinned their political ascendancy.[48]

In order to understand this connection we may briefly consider the religious construction of the Roman state as a whole. Our understanding of Roman religion has been vastly enhanced by recent scholarship which above all has stressed that modern notions of 'politics' and 'religion' as discrete and ideally separate spheres of life did not apply in Rome; in fact the conceptualisation of the two was alien to Roman mentality and indeed

---

[47] Cf. Fest. s.v. *adlecti* 6L: 'nam patres dicuntur qui sunt patricii generis'. Liv. 6.42.10; Sal. *Hist.* 3.48.15Maur; Cic. *Dom.* 38; Gaius *Inst.* 1.3.

[48] Giovannini 1985: 29–31 interpreted *patrum auctoritas* as religious approval and essentially identical to the *auctoritas* of the augurs and the *ius auspicii; contra* Graeber 2001: 13. Giovannini further argued that the *leges Publilia* and *Maenia* obliged magistrates and augurs to take the auspices before the vote in order to bring an end to political manipulation.

absent from their language.[49] As Scheid stated: ' . . . in the Roman world there was no difference between "secular" life and religious life. Every public act was religious and every religious act was public', and it therefore followed that 'a magistrate was invested . . . with a function that extended to two complementary fields of action, namely relations with the gods and relations with men'.[50] Both 'politics' and 'religion' were ultimately concerned with preserving the community.

The Roman *res publica* was founded on a partnership between the *populus Romanus* and its gods, and the continued support of the latter was considered vital to the well-being of the community. This 'peace with the gods' (*pax deorum*) was ensured through public ritual and sacrifice, and through the continuous consultation of the gods before any collective action was taken. Obtaining the gods' consent was essential for any public decision-making, and a complex system of divinatory rituals allowed the Romans to interpret the will of Jupiter. The Roman preoccupation with divination may seem obsessive to modern observers, but the continuous consultation of the gods gave the Romans the freedom and confidence to act without unduly worrying whether a particular action had the gods' approval or not.[51]

The practice of divination in Rome involved the gods far more directly in the political process than in almost any other known political system. It meant that the people did not decide autonomously, but in close cooperation with the gods. Every decision was taken in consultation with Jupiter, who responded to inquiries whether meetings should go ahead or be called off. The decision-making thus involved a crucial third party, since it was the augurs, the magistrates and the senate who managed the relationship between the people and the gods. It meant the people could never act on its own, but only in conjunction with the two other partners. Legislation passed or elections conducted without favourable auspices would be vitiated and could for the sake of the community not be upheld.

In the early republic priestly and magisterial functions were, according to the ancient tradition, monopolised by the patrician order, whose main characteristic was their inherited religious authority. Significantly, it appears that the right to consult the gods, the *auspicia*, formally lay in the hands of the patrician senators, though normally delegated to the holders of *imperium*, who later came to include also non-patricians. On the death of a king the *auspicia* had apparently passed to the *patres* during the

---

[49] Rüpke 1990; Beard, North, Price 1998; Scheid 2003.   [50] Scheid 2003: 130.
[51] I owe this observation to John North, pers. comm.

interregnum, 'auspicia ad patres rederunt', and after the end of monarchy the patricians still resumed control whenever the normal handover of power was interrupted.[52] In that situation a patrician senator would be appointed *interrex* in order to restore the magisterial succession. Since the auspices were essential to the exercise of power, to the passing of legislation and to military leadership, the patrician hold over the *auspicia* in effect meant a monopoly on executive power. But although the patricians may have monopolised the public priesthoods, the senate remained the highest religious authority, settling all disputes in that sphere. Cicero could thus with full justification describe 'auspicia et senatus' as the foundation of the *res publica*.[53]

The existence of the patriciate provides a clue to understanding central aspects of the republican constitution; the patrician privilege represented an autonomous source of authority – embedded in religious concepts and practices – and allowed them to claim formal ascendancy over the *populus*. The magistrate and his council therefore held an independent authority, distinct from the popular mandate granted by the assembly. Their religious power allowed them to intervene in any decision of the *populus*. The augural prerogative of the *patres* was always exercised indirectly by magistrates assisted by augurs, which was the reason why Roman magistrates could halt or annul popular decisions (Cic. *Leg.* 3.27). Simply by declaring: 'alio die' – on another day – they could bring comitial proceedings to an end – a right unheard of in democratic Athens. The presence of a hereditary class, controlling the mediation between gods and state, shaped Roman public life and institutions. It placed the focus of the 'constitution' firmly on the (patrician) magistrates, who in turn were 'greater' and endowed with authority to nominate their successor, who would hold similar personal authority. It also limited the pool from which the leaders could be drawn and ensured broad aristocratic homogeneity, setting the leaders formally apart from the *populus*.

The relationship between *populus* and magistrates, priests, and senate thus casts a revealing light on the nature of the 'sovereignty' of the Roman people. In terms of legislation it meant that every law had to be approved by the *populus*, but not that every wish of the people would become law. Likewise, in the case of appointments all magistrates required the approval of the people but not all those approved would necessarily become

---

[52] Badian 1990a: 84–5.
[53] *Rep.* 2.17: 'Romulus ... haec egregia duo firmamenta rei publicae peperisset, auspicia et senatum ... '.

magistrates. What emerges is therefore a very different notion of political institutions from that found in the writings of Greek theorists. To gain a clearer understanding of the people's 'sovereignty' we may briefly consider the Roman 'state'.

As Cornell observed, the Romans had no 'concept of the state in the modern abstract sense ... as an impersonal entity that stood apart from the individuals who composed it. Rather it was simply the Roman people, the collectivity of the citizens'.[54] The famously untranslatable concept *res publica*, often rendered as 'state', summed up all the affairs pertaining to the public, the *populus*, its antonym being *res privata*, the property/affairs of individual citizens. *Res publica* was, as Cicero stated tautologically, identical with *res populi*, and it has been argued that the *res publica* in a very literal sense belonged to the people.[55] The 'power' of the people was therefore not a question of popular 'sovereignty' as a distinct constitutional principle in the modern sense, simply because the people *were* the state. It followed axiomatically that in a free *res publica* the *populus* were the only source from which law and legitimacy could be derived. Accordingly, the authority of the senate and the patricians was never a power to legislate or to appoint leaders of state but one that entitled them to a mediating role – between the Roman people, its gods, and foreign powers. Decisions might have to be approved by gods and senate but they carried no legitimacy without the formal ratification of the *populus*. As far as we know, this fundamental understanding of state and *populus* was never disputed, and it shaped both political ideology and practice throughout the republican period. But the Roman notion of the free *res publica* and the central role which it accorded the *comitia* did not involve any recognition of basic 'democratic' principles or the people's right to self-government. It was essentially an acknowledgement that there could be no legitimacy without the people's consent.

This conclusion puts the spotlight on the nature of this consent, its significance and its practical expression. To what extent was this merely a formal requirement with little or no political content? An interesting answer was suggested by Scheid, who compared the consultation of the

---

[54] Cornell 1991: 63; cf. Kunkel 1973: 9; Brunt 1988: 299; Schofield 1995: 66. For a discussion of the concept of 'state' in a Roman context, see Eder 1990a: 17–21; Walter 1998; Hölkeskamp 2010: 67–71; Lundgreen 2014b.

[55] Schofield 1995: 79–81 interpreted the *res publica* as a concrete *res* belonging to the *populus*, but entrusted to and managed by their chosen leaders, a relationship defined through the key Roman values of *tutela* and *fides*; cf. Atkins 2013: 128–38.

gods with that of the people.[56] He noted that: 'Divination was a deliberate and precise human technique which consisted not so much in an empirical and direct consultation with the gods, but rather in the recitation of a kind of prayer that revealed the gods' agreement with whoever was consulting them. In a way, that consultation with the gods was comparable to the magistrate's consultations with the people'. The similarities between the two procedures are indeed striking, both carefully designed to produce affirmative outcomes; as we saw, the entire format of the assembly aimed at eliciting a positive response to the magistrate's request for approval. In both spheres the magistrate can be seen as the originator of the action, for which he seeks the consent of the two other bodies involved, the *populus* and its tutelary gods. This rationale lends the *comitia* a ritual aspect that is brought out even more clearly when we look at the ways in which the *populus* expressed its consent.

Voting and Assemblies

In antiquity political participation was, in the absence of the modern concept of representation, by definition direct; people could be politically active only by turning up in person and casting their vote in the assembly. In Rome, however, popular participation was structured in a unique way, which minimised the role of the individual citizen. Whenever a vote was to be taken the citizens were organised into groups, which voted together as blocks casting a single set of votes each. Different assemblies were based on different units, *curiae, centuriae* or *tribus*, but the fundamental principle remained the same.

The Roman system of block voting had no direct parallel in the ancient world,[57] and its origins remain obscure, although it has been linked to the structure of Roman society in pre-historic times. Thus, the oldest Roman assembly, the *comitia curiata*, divided people into *curiae*, and it has been suggested that these groups, 'co-viria', may have been the original units from which the Roman population had been formed. The traditional designation of the Roman citizens as *Quirites* goes back etymologically to the members of *curiae*, which Prugni argued were not artificial political constructs but autonomous units existing before the creation of the state.

---

[56] Scheid 2003: 112.
[57] Jehne 2001: 92 n.13 rightly questions the suggested Boiotian parallel. According to Stanton and Bicknell 1987, the Athenians voted in *trittyes*, tribal groups, but that was not comparable to Roman block voting, since the purpose merely was to facilitate the counting of votes.

Supposedly, all Roman citizens were members of a *curia*, which retained some religious functions under the leadership of a *curio*.[58]

In the late republic the *comitia curiata* had very limited functions, and its original responsibilities are largely a matter of speculation. However, the *curiae* were involved in granting *imperium*, executive powers, to the chief magistrates, as they had previously done to the kings in an act of formal acclamation. Perhaps the *curiae* had once met separately to acclaim the new king, and only at a later stage were turned into a single assembly in which each unit continued to deliver a separate vote of consent.[59] The hypothesis would provide a historical explanation for this unique invention. Still, whatever its origins the real significance of the block vote in the *comitia curiata* lies in the pattern it came to provide for all political participation in the Roman republic. As other types of assemblies were created they invariably adopted the ancient practice of the block vote, which persisted long after the archaic structures that first inspired it had vanished.

There are wide implications of the block vote, since it meant that it was no longer the mass of assembled citizens who collectively gave their backing to a proposal or a candidate, but the largely artificial units to which each of them had been assigned. Constitutionally the vote cast by individual citizens did not count, only the vote of their units. The block vote thus introduced an element of abstraction into the people's participation, which marked an important modification of the 'direct' principle that otherwise prevailed in the ancient world. Ultimately, it enabled the *populus* to convene and act constitutionally without large-scale participation. It separated the *populus* as a political concept from its physical reality by allowing the former to be formally present in all its constituent parts without the mass of Roman citizens actually being there.

The most startling illustration of this separation comes from the late republic when the *comitia curiata* had been reduced to pure ritual. At that time the highest state officials would still be granted their powers by a vote in the ancient assembly of the *curiae*. The traditional procedure would be followed as before, the magistrate would call the *curiae*, votes would be cast and counted, results declared, but with the important difference that each

---

[58] Prugni 1987: 102. The Fornacalia, whose last day was for those who did not know which *curia* they belonged to, suggests universal membership of *curiae*, Ov. *Fast.* 2.529–32.

[59] Cic. *Rep.* 2.31 states that the position of Tullus was 'officially ratified by each district in turn'. Botsford 1909: 157; Vaahtera 1990: 173–4; 1993b: 73–5; Linke 1995: 63; Jehne 2013b: 132; 2014b: 121. Palmer 1970: 202 suggested *curiae* represented different peoples incorporated into Rome, which met separately and conducted their own vote.

of the thirty *curiae* now was represented by a single *lictor*.[60] The procedure was, of course, a formality and the outcome never in doubt, but constitutionally it still carried validity and was in some way deemed necessary for the formal exercise of power. This requirement could have serious practical implications, not just, as we saw, during the civil war but also in 54, when the consul Ap. Claudius Pulcher apparently found himself unable to assume his duties as proconsul and take up the governorship of Cilicia because no curiate law had been passed. While he himself seems to have claimed that none was needed, he still took the radical step of procuring a false *lex curiata* through bribery and fraud. Thus, two of the consular candidates made a compact with the consuls promising that 'if they were themselves elected they would furnish three augurs who would state that they had been present at the passing of a *lex curiata* which had never been passed ... '.[61] Although the precise significance of the *lex curiata* is contested in this case, the incident shows that a vote by thirty lictors could have real political implications. It may be tempting to dismiss the late republican *comitia curiata* as a constitutional anomaly, an archaic relic from the distant past preserved because of the Romans' innate conservatism. But the important lesson to be drawn from this story lies in the fact that the people *did* act constitutionally and delivered a binding *votum* of real political significance – without actually being present. Because the vote was taken by abstract units, all that was required was the representation of these units.

The *comitia curiata* was, of course, unusual in its complete formalisation of political participation, but it was not entirely anomalous; it merely expressed in extreme form the underlying principle behind the people's participation in all Roman assemblies. The block vote, whether taken in *centuriae* or *tribus*, meant that the actual number of participants became irrelevant from a constitutional point of view. A vote was valid when passed by the units, not when a representative section of the population had given their approval. The implication was that statutory quorum, a common feature in Greek constitutions, and other measures to ensure numerical and social representativity were redundant in Rome.[62] In effect, any crowd convened according to the formal rules and divided into their respective units *was* the Roman people. The validity of a law or an appointment was not dependent on how many people had taken part, and logically no efforts

---

[60] Develin 1977b: 55 summarises the – mostly religious – functions of *curiae*. Cf. note 36 above.
[61] Cic. *Fam.* 1.9.25 (SB 20); *Q. fr.* 3.2.3; *Att.* 4.17.2 (SB 91). Cf. most recently Fiori 2014: 102–4 with lit.
[62] Gauthier 1990 on quorum in Greece, where we find inscriptions with exact, often substantial figures of votes cast in favour, suggesting a general ideal of unanimity. Most likely therefore the quorum was not primarily concerned with absenteeism.

were therefore made to ensure a representative turnout. In fact large-scale participation was rather discouraged, as indicated by a number of features: the venues were kept small; complex and time-consuming procedures were never effectively rationalised; no provisions were made to promote lower class participation by e.g. remuneration; and *comitia* were even banned on market days, thereby preventing visiting *rustici* from taking part.[63] The result was that by the late republic only a tiny proportion of the citizen population could participate, although that did not affect the perceived legitimacy of legislation or appointments; even highly contested bills or elections were never challenged on the grounds of poor or unrepresentative turnouts.

Political legitimacy was achieved through proper procedure, which meant a mandate given by the units into which the Roman people were divided. The formalisation of consent had paradoxical consequences, for while block voting made actual numbers irrelevant, it remained crucial that all units be represented. We happen to know through an aside of Cicero's that if no one had turned up from a *tribus* (itself an indication of the small numbers involved) a few voters would be transferred from other *tribus* to represent the empty one (*Sest.* 109). Just as striking as the creation of fictitious *tribules* was the requirement that all tribes should deliver their votes even when they no longer counted. Tribes voted successively in legislative assemblies but when a majority had been reached and the bill effectively was passed, all the remaining tribes still had to come forward and cast their votes.[64] Again the practice suggests that the popular vote had originally been unanimous, since there would be no point in obliging tribes to deliver a redundant vote if it expressed no agreement. The aim was for all units to state their consent, which was symbolically important not just in terms of its formal legitimacy, but perhaps also for the relationship between the law and the citizens, who in a sense became bound by the vote of their unit.

The same logic could also be applied to the direct opposite – but equally paradoxical – effect, namely to deny that a particular decision had been handed over to the *populus* when in fact it had. In 104 the *lex Domitia* transferred the election of the higher priesthoods to the *comitia*, presumably to make it less divisive and limit the opportunities for politicking and

---

[63] On the duration of *comitia*, see Mouritsen 2001; cf. Jehne 2001: 96.

[64] Fraccaro 1957: 249–50; Hall 1964: 285; Taylor 1966: 77–8; Staveley 1972: 181–2; cf. Jehne 2013a: 113 n.36, who doubted whether all tribes had to vote given the waste of time involved, but Roman assemblies were not rationally organised and numerous passages in Livy demonstrate that all the tribes would have to be called forward, cf. Fraccaro 1957 ibid.

intrigue which the previous co-optive process had offered – and Domitius personally experienced. However, for religious reasons this prerogative could officially never be taken away from those with privileged religious authority and an ingenious solution was therefore found which left the choice to just seventeen of the thirty-five *tribus*, to be selected by drawing lot.[65] Although the assembly now de facto elected the priests, the decision had not formally been taken by the *populus* since a majority of the *tribus* had not taken part in the proceedings.

Overall we are dealing with a system in which there was a *formal* requirement that laws, verdicts, and appointments be approved by the *populus* in order for them to hold any legitimacy. It is logical therefore that the *populus* which gave its approval was a highly formalised, even symbolic, version of the people, and one that was not expected to act but to respond affirmatively, i.e. give its *suffragium*. But there was one important exception to this pattern, which related to the judicial role of the *populus*. When the assembly convened as a court, the outcome was not given beforehand. Instead of simply ratifying a proposal put before it, the assembled citizens had to make a decision, and a hugely important one to the individuals concerned. The need to reach a verdict made participation in judicial *comitia* a very different issue, and it is here that we come across the only recorded Roman concern about assembly attendance.

Emilio Gabba drew attention to a passage in Varro, which preserves a rule from M'. Sergius *commentarium vetus anquisitionis* (third/second century) that provides detailed instructions on how to call judicial assemblies dealing with capital cases.[66] It gives elaborate prescriptions on the announcement of the meeting, which must be called from the Rostra, and on the closure of the *tabernae* of the *argentarii*. The presence of senators should also be ensured, and the text reveals how seriously trial attendance was regarded, not just in terms of numbers but also of the quality of the participants. The measures aimed at creating a well-attended assembly dominated by the well-to-do, and the importance of large-scale attendance in capital trials is documented already in our earliest legal source, the Twelve Tables, where a *maximus comitiatus* was required for such occasions.[67]

---

[65] Cic. *Agr.* 2.18. Brunt 1988: 523, suggested the curious voting method may have been intended to indicate divine approval of the tribes selected, highlighted by the use of the lot.

[66] Gabba 1988: 44–7; Var. *L.* 6.90–3.

[67] Cic. *Leg.* 3.11, and 3.44. Gabba 1987, showed that *comitiatus maximus* was not, as commonly assumed, a name for the *comitia centuriata*, supposedly the most important assembly which dealt with war and peace as well as capital cases. Rather than 'the great assembly' it probably refers to a particularly large assembly as specifically required for capital cases. Thus, we must distinguish between *comitiatus* and *comitia*, the former referring not to an actual assembly but to the people

The official concerns about participation at capital trials highlight the general absence of such considerations. The block vote gave the people's political role an abstract quality, which reduced the significance of the individual citizen as a political agent. This point is underlined also in the different Greek and Roman definitions of the state. Eder noted that while Aristotle defined the polis as a *koinonia ton politon*, and the citizen according to his functions in the polis, Cicero famously defined the *res publica* as *res populi*.[68] Thus, whereas the Greek definition mentions individual citizens, the Roman refers to a totality, the *populus*. *Res publica* was not a *koinonia* of citizens but, as Eder observed, an 'abstract entity', which might be subdivided into smaller units; Roman citizens could, in short, be politically active only as members of a group, as 'a small part of a part' – 'ein Teilschen eines Teiles'.[69]

These differences in definition are further reflected in the sharply contrasting citizenship policies pursued in Rome and the Greek world. Athens was extremely restrictive with its citizenship, largely because of a political system which allowed and expected extensive participation of the citizens who were defined in terms of their political activity.[70] Rome, on the other hand, was famously open with her citizenship, which was extended to foreign communities as well as freed slaves, feasible precisely because her citizenship was not conceived of in terms of political participation or direct personal influence.[71] It enabled the Roman state to develop along very different lines and to expand through the large-scale incorporation of outsiders into its citizen body.

Briefly returning to our opening question concerning the 'power of the people', the way forward may be to distinguish between formal powers and powers that were to be actively exercised. Thus, the people could in one sense do virtually everything and in another very little. Formally, the 'people' had unlimited powers but in practice hardly any means of exercising them. Because of the simple equation of the state with the *populus*, the

---

convened for the purpose of an assembly. Twelve Tables 9.1–2, 6, with comment *Roman Statutes* 699–700.

[68] The Greek *polis*: Arist. *Pol.* 1.1, 1252a1, 3.1, 1274b41, 3.4, 1279a21, 7.7, 1328a36; the Greek citizen: Arist. *Pol.* 3.1, 1275a22, 4.5, 1293a23–4, 5.7, 1308a5–7; Rome: Cic. *Rep.* 1.39. Eder 1990a: 18–19, esp. 19 n.11.

[69] Eder 1990a: 19 n. 11: ' . . . eine tendenziell abstrakte Gesamtheit, die – falls sie gegliedert wird – wiederum in Teile, nämlich ordines, tribus, centuriae und partes zerfällt, die jeweils grössere Mengen von Bürgern zu einer Einheit zusammenschliessen'.

[70] E.g. Thuc. 2.40. Cf. Meier 1997. See also Whitehead 1991: 144–5; Gauthier 1974; 1981; cf. Meyer 1961.

[71] Meier 1997: 55 noted that Roman citizens primarily were active in the military: 'Politisch war das Gros eher passiv'. The most important aspect of their citizenship was their 'Freiheit'.

people were by definition the only source of legitimacy in a free *res publica*. But in Rome the people was also defined as profoundly passive and reflective. Things happened for and through the *populus* but not by the *populus*. It might therefore be tempting to dismiss the people's consent as a mere formality, but that would be a mistake, for in Roman public life there were no 'mere formalities'. We are again reminded that observance of correct procedure was essential to the validity of any public action and the people's consent was as important as that of the gods. Both parties – gods and *populus* – could in principle withhold it, although that would defy the logic and rationale of the ritual.

The paradox of the Roman popular assemblies may ultimately be rooted in our own approach to political institutions, which remain deeply influenced by Greek conceptualisation and Polybius' constitutional labelling. His model did not envisage the possibility of formal, even symbolic, powers, and he therefore missed the peculiar nature of the Roman assemblies. To him each institution served a well-defined, rational function in spreading or concentrating power, and on that premise the contradictions of the Roman assemblies become inexplicable. Since it made little sense to Polybius that the Roman people had total power but no way of exercising it, he fitted the Roman situation into a model of balancing forces, which implied that the powers of each institution were complete and subject only to the limitations imposed by the powers of competing institutions. In that way the apparent lack of internal logic could be construed as a logic on a different level, one where the rationale of the system lay not in the articulation of the individual institutions but in the whole ensemble of institutions and above all in their interaction.

The 'Struggle of the Orders' and the Evolution of the Roman Political System

The basic principles of the Roman constitution outlined in the previous pages remained largely constant and were over time elevated to venerable ancestral custom. No constitution remains static, however, and also in Rome new institutions and offices were introduced and old ones modified, though rarely abolished. Since few strands of reliable information survive from the early republic and most of our knowledge has to be inferred from later institutions and practices, any attempt at tracing constitutional developments must in the nature of things have to remain tentative.

Our main, indeed only, contemporary evidence, the Twelve Tables (mid-fifth century), suggests a fairly 'primitive' rural society, which only very slowly developed centralised powers, laws and institutions.[72] Power appears to have been in the hands of great families whose position was based on land ownership. As noted, one group of families had early on established itself as a ruling class – the patricians, who claimed religious privileges and prerogatives that served to underpin their social and political ascendancy. Magistrates were appointed annually – how many and under what titles remains uncertain – and their powers were confirmed by popular acclamation. Alongside the magistrates a body of elders existed, drawn from the leading – mostly patrician – families who advised the magistrates and oversaw their actions. Collectively, the patrician senators claimed the right to annul any appointment or piece of legislation, presumably in order to check the magistrates rather than the assembly, which held no political initiative. Membership of the senate may not have been formalised until the late fourth century, but we should not overestimate the fluidity of the early Roman senate. It did after all hold substantial collective powers, and even an informally constituted senate represented the collective authority of the great families, whose senior members presumably could expect a seat on the magistrates' advisory council.

The aristocratic nature of early republican society is hardly open to doubt, and the political system appears to have been designed primarily to check the powers of individual members of the ruling class. This was achieved through short-term tenure of public office and the collegiality which also limited the scope for independent action. Paradoxically, it could be argued that the elevated position of the magistrates and the immense powers invested in them suggest a considerable degree of cohesion and internal discipline within the early Roman elite, given that aristocratic systems normally delegate such authority only when there is a reasonable expectation that office holders will act in their collective interest.

We have no reliable information about the selection of magistrates in the early period. Presumably, it happened consensually through more or less formalised negotiations among the patrician elders – who already had the power to block unsuitable appointments.[73] It would therefore appear that the early republic was ruled by a small hereditary class of families, which took turns to fill the magistracies and perform the largely military responsibilities that came with them. The *populus*, organised in its various

---

[72] Cf. Linke 1995.
[73] Rilinger 1976: 87–8 suggests a scenario where the patrician senate formally nominated the new magistrates similar to that by which *interreges* were selected.

subdivisions, was called upon to ratify proposals and declarations of war and approve their new leaders.

Changes to the system happened mostly as a result of the challenge presented by the so-called plebeians, which has become known as the 'Struggle of the Orders'. Reconstructing this conflict poses fundamental problems because of the almost complete lack of contemporary sources. It has come to us through the filter of later republican history, and whatever information was available to the writers of that period – and that was probably quite rudimentary – would inevitably have been coloured by more recent experiences of political conflict, casting fundamental doubts on most aspects of the traditional narrative. As Linderski noted, 'the only thing not in contention is that it did take place'.[74] And the most compelling evidence for its existence comes from the specifically plebeian institutions which grew out of the 'Struggle' and eventually became integral parts of the Roman constitution.

The plebeian institutions were created in opposition to the established political structures dominated by the patricians, and included plebeian officials, *tribuni plebis* and *aediles plebis*, and an assembly, the *concilium plebis*, which issued formal resolutions, known as *plebiscita*. The most striking aspect of these institutions is the fact that they represent a direct mirror image of the official institutions of the Roman state. Thus, the nature of the relationship between tribune and *concilium* appears to have been similar to that between magistrate and *comitia*. The *concilium* was called and controlled by the tribune and subject to limitations identical to those imposed on the *comitia*. We also find the same formalisation of popular attendance, using block votes rather than individual votes. In historical times the *concilium* was convened in *tribus* but there are indications that it may originally have been organised in *curiae*, further suggesting that the *concilium* was modelled directly on the *comitia curiata*.[75] The main difference between the two systems lay in the role of the tribunes and in the source of their powers. They had the right, perhaps even the obligation, to intervene on behalf of the plebeians and protect their interests against (patrician) magistrates, and their power to do so came from a *lex sacrata*, a formal oath taken by the plebeians to protect their tribunes, which conferred *sacrosanctitas* and made them inviolable.

---

[74] Linderski 1990: 34; *pace* Mitchell 1990, who questioned the very existence of a 'Struggle'.

[75] The title of the tribune may also have been derived from that of the chief magistrate, although that remains conjectural. Scholars have drawn attention to the curious fact that not just the tribunes but also the praetors presided over a tribunal and suggested that the early Roman magistrates formally might have been tribunes too.

The plebeian 'movement' has traditionally been seen as a genuinely popular reaction against patrician domination and exploitation. It is therefore often assumed that the 'Struggle' in the early stages was focused on the socio-economic issues concerning ordinary plebeians, and that only later, as a plebeian elite gradually emerged, did demands for full political equality and participation arise.[76] The plebeian institutions, however, are difficult to reconcile to this model, since they appear to have been no more 'democratic' in their structure than those of the supposedly oppressive patrician state, which they replicate in almost every respect. Like the *comitia* the *concilium plebis* was entirely controlled by their leaders and allowed no independent initiative.

This puzzling situation opens up two lines of explanation: either the plebeians were unable to conceive of any other form of political organisation and believed that only this structure would command sufficient authority to enforce their demands; or, alternatively and perhaps more plausibly, the plebeian institutions reflected a social structure which was as hierarchical and unequal as that of Roman society as a whole. In other words, they point to the formation of a plebeian elite already during the early stages of the 'Struggle', an elite which used the institutions as vehicles for their claim to authority and legitimacy equal to that of the patricians. That interpretation would help explain why the leadership structure of the 'popular' *concilium plebis* was not qualitatively different from that found in the existing assemblies, presumably so unresponsive to the needs of the *populus*. The plebeians appear to have entertained the same basic notions of the state, legitimacy and power as other Romans at the time. The implication is that a truly 'democratic' movement may never have existed in Rome, the plebeian 'state within the state' being closer to a paternalistic aristocracy which embraced the interests of the masses, in part perhaps to its own advantage.[77]

The plebeian resistance was, of course, rooted in discontent – with the rule of the patricians or perhaps just with specific social issues. In the early stages the sources suggest it was focused on alleviating particular problems: debt and bondage; access to public law, personal security, and land. But the late introduction of constitutional issues, including the demands for plebeian access to state offices, does not necessarily make it a popular

---

[76] For an outline of the 'Struggle', see Raaflaub 1993, who doubts the existence of a plebeian elite in the early stages and – against De Sanctis 1907: 1.224–5 and Cornell 1995: 252–6 – questions the 'closure of the patriciate' implied by the presence of plebeian names in the early *fasti*.

[77] Bleicken 1982: 93, questioned the notion of 'a state within the state' and suggested it was 'die Erklärung eines Teils zum Ganzen'.

movement 'from below'. Initially, the religious monopoly of the patricians may have seemed so fundamental an obstacle that any attempt to gain full equality appeared futile. Moreover, the major disadvantage suffered by leading plebeians – their inability to hold military commands – may have become a pressing concern only as Rome began her Italian expansion in the fourth century.

The 'Struggle of the Orders' has often been seen as uniquely Roman in its origins, character, and articulation, probably because of the special status of the patrician elite, but comparative studies of city-states in medieval Italy have revealed interesting parallels. There we find similar patterns of social conflict with oligarchic monopolies challenged by *il popolo*, whose council, the *consiglio del popolo*, appointed its own leaders and protectors, the *capitani del popolo*, separate from the governing institutions. They would typically gain official recognition over time and become established parts of the government. Moreover, despite their popular rhetoric these leaders were generally of relatively high economic standing, i.e. members of an excluded class of property owners who championed the cause of the people in order to gain access to the inner circle of the ruling class.[78] A similar scenario cannot be ruled out in early Rome.

In 367 a compromise appears to have been reached with the passing of the Licinio-Sextian laws, which formally granted plebeian access to the chief magistracy. However, the *fasti* suggest that it only took effect in 342 when the plebeians were finally guaranteed one of two annual consulships.[79] It may not have been until this moment that the dual consulship with equal powers came into existence, i.e. as an ingenious solution to the problem of accommodating the claims and interests of two distinct constituencies while at the same time keeping effective check on the plebeian office holders. According to the annalistic writers and the *fasti* the collegiate system went back to 509, the first year of the republic, but Livy's famous reference to a *praetor maximus* who would hammer a nail into the Capitoline temple each year casts doubt on this tradition (7.3.5). As many scholars have argued, the story implies that the early republic was headed by a single senior magistrate, perhaps assisted by two lower officials.[80]

After the settlement the auspices may formally have remained in the hands of the patricians, who also continued to control the *interregnum*

---

[78] Summary in Finer 1997: 950–85, esp. 954–6, 979–80.   [79] Cornell 1995: 337–400.
[80] For the double consulship as a creation of the reform of 367 see e.g. Eder 1990a: 28–9; Wiseman 1995: 106–7; 2004: 65–9; Welwei 2000: 49–50; Richardson 2008: 338. *Contra* Cornell 1995: 215–39; Forsythe 2005: 150–5.

throughout the republic. The plebeian magistrates, as Linderski suggested, would have been allowed to use the auspices, although they would never 'have' them.[81] Since the consulship primarily was a military office and the holders were away on campaigns most of the year, a third magistrate, known as the *praetor*, was appointed.[82] He was expected to stay in the city and be in charge of jurisdiction, while the consuls were in the field. The compromise also changed the role of the plebeian tribunate and the *concilium plebis*. The tribunes became state officials with the power to propose laws binding for the whole community – and to block all public proceedings. However, the tribunes' lack of *auspicia* meant that their resolutions had no divine approval, a problem that might have been solved by extending the *auctoritas patrum* to *plebiscita*.[83] It is probably in this context that the changes to the *auctoritas patrum*, mentioned above, should be interpreted.

Membership of the senate was formalised by the *lex Ovinia*, passed between 339 and 318.[84] It also allowed plebeian access to the censorship, and may be seen as part of the general compromise, which established the senate as a permanent institution, independent of the consuls, for the newly formed aristocracy of patricians and plebeians. It laid down new rules for the *lectio senatus*, the censors' selection of senators, and according to Festus (290L), senators should now be drawn 'ex omni ordine' to ensure proper representation for plebeians. In principle, all citizens might have been eligible but the poor were, of course, never considered. In theory, the censors ought to pick the best men from every rank, while in practice only aristocrats were selected. However, the senate's formal openness remained important to the elite ideology that evolved during the middle republic, as we shall see in the next chapter. At this stage the tribunes may not have been regularly enrolled into the council, which counted fewer than 300 members. Cornell has argued that the senate would have been a much weaker body prior to the *lex Ovinia*, which 'emancipated' it from the magistrates by ensuring that senators could no longer be expelled for political reasons.[85] Exclusion now required a special written justification,

---

[81] Linderski 1990: 41. In Badian's formulation the plebeian office holders became 'honorary patricians', 1996: 210.

[82] Brennan 2000; Bergk 2011.

[83] Most scholars hold that *plebiscita* were beyond the senate's influence, leaving aside the issue of religious legitimacy that might have been bestowed on these resolutions by the *auctoritas patrum*.

[84] Cornell 1995. In 339 plebeians had gained access to the censorship by the *lex Publilia*, while 318 was the last census before Ap. Claudius' controversial census in 312.

[85] Cornell 2000, who suggested the early senate had little independence or authority.

a censorial *nota*. In reality, however, the *lex Ovinia* may have changed little, since membership of the senate had probably already become relatively stable before its passing.[86]

Another important outcome of the 'Struggle' was the creation of a tribal assembly, the *comitia tributa*, convened by consuls or praetors to pass *leges* and elect curule aediles. Since the tribal division of the voters appears to have been first introduced in the *concilium plebis*, we are faced with the paradox of a 'state' institution apparently modelled on an 'alternative' plebeian one. The existence of a *comitia tributa* has therefore been called into question by scholars, who argue that the *concilium plebis* remained the only assembly entirely based on the *tribus* until the Sullan reform.[87] However, the reported instances of consuls convening the tribes undermine this hypothesis. The paradox of the *comitia tributa* might be solved by rethinking what a Roman assembly was. It may be a misconception to see them as 'institutions' in the modern sense of permanent constitutional bodies. They had no existence independently of the magistrates, who – quite literally – created them *ad hoc* to ratify a specific proposal, deliver a verdict or approve of/elect his successors. According to context and purpose the magistrates would call up the *populus* in one of its various divisions: the centuries primarily for military and foreign matters, the *curiae* for religious purposes and the tribes for most domestic affairs. Therefore, rather than being separate bodies these assemblies were simply the *populus* convened in one configuration or another. This point is illustrated by the famous assembly in 45 when the consul first convened the *populus* as a *comitia tributa* to elect the quaestors, then changed his mind and decided to call a consular election, in turn reconfiguring the crowd into a *comitia centuriata*.[88] Although the case is exceptional, the procedure was perfectly legal since it was the magistrate who constituted the assembly for a task which he himself defined.

The appearance of tribally organised *comitia* reflected the growing importance of the tribes during the early republic. The process is obscure and much disputed, but we can observe how these geographically defined units came to replace the *curiae* as the basic division of the Roman people. From the late fourth century this role was assumed by the tribes, which became the units used for both the census and for

---

[86] Cf. Hölkeskamp 2011: 143–6; hypothetically accepted by Cornell 2000: 85.
[87] Sandberg 1993; 2000; 2001; 2004; cf. Develin 1975; 1977a; convincingly refuted by Humm 2005: 419–29; Pina Polo 2011: 100–21.
[88] Cic. *Fam.* 7.30.1–2 (SB 265).

conscription (perhaps from 332).[89] Membership of a *tribus* eventually came to signify Roman status and identity, to the point that it even entered the standard nomenclature of male citizens. Following this shift the tribunes began to organise the *plebs* into these, presumably more authoritative, units when calling a *concilium*. Viewed against this background it should come as no surprise if the consuls chose to convene the people along similar lines. In doing so, they may not necessarily have taken their cue from the tribunes; most likely their actions reflected a general trend which accorded ever greater prominence to the tribal divisions of the Roman people and, as we shall see, eventually would affect also the military assembly, the *comitia centuriata*.

The nature of this development is difficult to gauge, and there is no agreement as to the origins and significance of the *tribus*.[90] The question has long been approached from a 'political' perspective and placed within a discourse on 'democratic' and 'aristocratic' values in early Rome. Historians have focused on the significance of the tribes as a potential means of promoting the people's interests, but that assumes the assembly actually served as a vehicle of popular influence. As we saw, this cannot be taken for granted and the growing prominence of the tribes may therefore not be indicative of any real shift in power. It has been speculated that the tribes had greater 'democratic' potential since they in principle offered all citizens an equal vote, while the *curiae* remained dominated by patrician *gentes*. Supposedly, the tribes were originally groupings of landed estates, some of which were also held by plebeians, thereby making them the natural choice of unit for their assembly.[91] On this interpretation the tribes replaced the *curiae* by the late fourth century as a result of Rome's expansion, since newly enfranchised citizens could not be inscribed in *gentes* and hence in *curiae*. However, the identification of *curiae* as 'aristocratic' and tribes as 'democratic' is questioned by evidence suggesting that all citizens – patricians as well as plebeians – were members of a *curia*, although many did not know which one they belonged to.[92] If membership of the *curiae* was universal in Rome, there was no reason why newly enfranchised citizens might not be inscribed in them.

---

[89] Humm 2000: 92–5 on tribes and the census. The link was first introduced in 332 according to Lo Cascio 1997, but not certain until 304.

[90] Rieger 2007 recently argued they primarily were administrative units, directly comparable to Greek demes, though rightly critical Linke 2010.

[91] Sceptical Linke 1995: 156.

[92] Cf. above n. 58 The ancient tradition stating that the earliest *concilium plebis* was organised in *curiae* also becomes meaningless if plebeians were not even members of these units.

What distinguished the *tribus* from the *curiae* was their geographical definition, often seen as yet another 'democratic' quality. Indeed, it has been argued that they gave rural voters a relatively greater say by compensating for their longer travel and allowed them to be represented despite the practical obstacles they faced.[93] The *tribus*, however, had no defined political interests, and no internal organs, local assemblies or elected representatives, which questions the – in itself quite anachronistic – notion of tribes as means of 'representation'. There is, moreover, little evidence that the Romans were concerned with geographical representation or ever contemplated introducing a fairer system that, for example, correlated the size of tribes with their distance from Rome. Their only concern was that members of all tribes be present and take part in proceedings.

The general shift towards tribal voting does not lend itself easily to a 'political' reading and the rationale behind it effectively escapes us. But the trend was so universal that the military configuration of the Roman people, the *comitia centuriata*, would also eventually be affected by it. The development of this assembly is crucial for our understanding of the Roman political system as a whole.

The *Comitia Centuriata*

The *comitia centuriata* was the Roman people organised as an army and divided into military units, centuries. As a military assembly it met outside the *pomerium* on the Campus Martius, and originally the gathering may simply have marked the occasion when the army formally swore an oath of loyalty to its new commander, while later it delivered verdicts in capital cases, approved declarations of war and peace settlements, and passed other legislation, although to what extent remains uncertain.[94] Its internal structure and division into *centuriae* reflected the same economic distinctions that determined military service. Therefore, since conscription remained closely linked to property ownership, the assembly had a built-in social bias in favour of the better-off. Initially, the property distinctions may have been quite basic and directly mirrored the primitive organisation of the army. Thus, the centuries were at first divided into *equites*, the *classis* – hoplite-type legionaries – and those placed below the *classis* (*infra classem*) the light-armed infantry or *velites*. The original number of centuries in each of these categories is not known, but later this simple organisation was turned into a far more complex timocratic structure consisting of

---

[93] Hackl 1972: 137.   [94] See Paananen 1993.

193 centuries arranged in an intricate hierarchy. At the top and voting first came the eighteen centuries of *equites*, including the six 'sex suffragia' (probably the senators – originally just the patricians). Then came the eighty first-class centuries, twenty centuries for each of the second, third and fourth classes, thirty for the fifth, followed by four non-armed military units, and finally the single century of *proletarii* who were too poor to serve in the army. Although ascribed to Servius Tullius by the ancient sources, this elaborate structure seems to have been introduced in the late fourth or early third century.

The purpose evidently was to grade the influence of individual voters according to rank and social standing, and its introduction may have been a response to a functional change which transformed the elective assemblies from acclamatory into decision-making bodies faced with real choices between multiple candidates. This development cannot be traced in any detail or even approximately dated.[95] An early date may seem difficult to reconcile with the monopoly on the chief magistracy which the literary sources insist the patricians held during that period. A limited selection of patrician candidates might, of course, have been put before the assembly, but it is perhaps more likely that the succession was arranged informally in advance before receiving the approval of the assembly. Similarly, the appointment of mostly patrician colleges of 'consular tribunes' in the fourth century can hardly have been the result of open elections which offered a – predominantly plebeian – electorate a broad choice of patrician and plebeian candidates.

After the plebeio-patrician settlement it was, in any case, no longer possible to regulate the succession internally within the elite. The political class had not only become much broader but probably also less cohesive. It may therefore not have been until the later fourth century that elections with several candidates contesting each post became the norm. A number of features might support this idea. The new constitutional arrangement reserved one consulship for the plebeians, which almost certainly must have become the object of competition; presumably there was no well-defined plebeian 'inner circle' able to organise the succession, comparable to the heads of the old patrician families. The decision was therefore left to the assembly, a solution that held numerous advantages for the elite and may have been instrumental in securing the long-term future of the aristocratic government. Not only did it strengthen the inclusive construction of the *res publica* that became central to the identity of the emerging

[95] Cf. Rilinger 1976: 87–8.

plebeio-patrician *nobilitas*, but the *comitia* also provided the vital external factor which ensured that the procedures regulating access to executive office remained public and transparent. In addition, leaving the choice to the 'people' may have helped address the problem of electoral failure; as Bleckmann noted with reference to Thucydides, defeats are borne more easily when they are not inflicted by one's peers but by an outside body.[96] In Rome this adjudicatory role was passed to the *populus*, i.e. the abstract and highly formalised version of the people that constituted itself in the assembly.

The changes to the elite thus had a knock-on effect on the role of the assemblies, and particularly the *comitia centuriata*, which in turn explains the reorganisation of this institution in the late fourth century – the moment when the plebeio-patrician compromise became effective. The traditional Roman practice of block voting offered a unique opportunity for giving votes different weight, a practice later praised by Cicero as embodying the specifically Roman version of citizen rights, which managed to be simultaneously equal and unequal (*Rep.* 1.43). The restructuring of the *comitia centuriata* was an attempt to ensure that it conformed more directly to traditional aristocratic ideals by guaranteeing men of substance a greater say in the decision-making. As such the reform was a practical response to wider political changes and reflected concerns similar to those expressed in the regulations on the calling of judicial *comitia*. As we saw, the *commentarium vetus anquisitionis* sought to ensure not just a substantial turnout but also the presence of the 'right people', and this preoccupation with the maintenance of traditional social hierarchies also dictated the transformation of the *comitia centuriata* into a stratified timocratic body.[97]

The political implications of this move should not be overstated, however, and there is little reason to perceive it as a concerted attempt to assert oligarchic control over elections. The elite were already in full command of the process through the powers of the presiding magistrates and the senate. Moreover, the political content in elections was probably always negligible; indeed there is no evidence that they were ever the focus of any sustained conflict between elite and populace. The massive under-representation of the poor, confined to just a single unit in the

---

[96] Bleckmann 2002: 230; Hölkeskamp 2010: 98–106. Cf. Thuc. 8.89.3. Likewise, in 311 a plebiscite introduced popular election of the *IIviri navales* and the *tribuni militum*, important first steps of a public career, Liv. 9.30.3–4; cf. Hölkeskamp 2011: 150–3. The move may not reflect increased political influence of the people as much as the need to regulate appointments externally after the settlement.

[97] For the property qualifications for the *classes*, see Rathbone 1993; *pace* Yakobson 1992.

centuriate assembly, has struck modern observers as extreme in its near-disenfranchisement of the lower classes, but the most interesting aspect of the proletarian *centuria* is perhaps its very existence. Excluded as they were from service in the army, the poorest had logically no place in a military assembly. The presence of the *proletarii* in the *comitia centuriata* may therefore be understood in symbolic terms as an inclusive gesture reflecting traditional Roman concerns that the entire citizen body take part in proceedings which confer legitimacy within the *res publica*. Rather than a 'trick' to deceive the masses, as it is often presented, the proletarian century is a reminder of the 'ritual' dimension to public proceedings in Rome.

Placing the decision in the hands of the propertied classes automatically reduced the incentive for candidates to campaign widely at elections, which may have been one of the major benefits of the reform. Since open competition poses a threat to the stability of aristocratic systems, it is crucial that the electoral structures and procedures are designed to minimise the potential for clashes. These concerns may also have provided the spur for the next reform of the *comitia centuriata*, which casts a revealing light on the politics of the middle republic and therefore will be considered in some detail.

The Reform of the *Comitia Centuriata*

The evidence of Cicero and Livy implies a change to the structure of the *comitia centuriata* during the later third century. The former indicates a reduction in the number of first-class centuries from the eighty previously recorded to seventy, while Livy adds more detail, informing us that the ancient system of Servius Tullius had since been modified and in his day the centuries had been combined with *tribus* so that each *tribus* contained two centuries, one of *seniores* and one of *iuniores*.[98] The reduction of first-class centuries reflected this co-ordination, the seventy centuries matching the thirty-five *tribus*. This figure in turn allows us to date the reform, which must have taken place after 241 when the expansion of the tribes ended and they reached their final total of thirty-five. Moreover, since no reform is mentioned in the surviving books of Livy, it probably predates 221, when the Livian text resumes. It is unclear whether all classes were co-ordinated with the tribes or just the first. The problem was a practical one – how to

---

[98] Cic. *Rep.* 2.39; Liv. 1.43.12–13: 'qui nunc est post expletas quinque et triginta tribus duplicato earum numero centuriis iuniorum seniorumque ... '.

combine thirty-five units with twenty or thirty units. A highly complex solution was suggested by Mommsen, but as other historians have pointed out, there is in fact no explicit evidence that the centuries outside the first class were co-ordinated with the *tribus*.[99] The reform probably also involved a change in the voting order, although much remains uncertain. Still, it seems likely that the *equites* were moved from their traditional position as the first voters and came to vote after the first class.[100]

The reform has often been interpreted as 'democratic', shifting power from the elite to the populace.[101] The view is based on the fact that the number of first-class centuries was reduced and the second class now had to be called in order to reach a majority, and on the reversed voting order of the *equites* and the first class.[102] We are, however, dealing with very minor adjustments to the distribution of voting power. Only about 5 per cent of the centuries were reallocated in favour of a few slightly less wealthy *assidui* of the second class. The change had no impact on the overall timocratic structure of the assembly. Moreover, the loss of the joint majority of *equites* and first class was only really significant if we assume that they had previously voted unanimously and effectively kept the second class away from voting, which seems unlikely.[103]

The basic difficulty with 'democratic' interpretations of the reform lies with the premise that elections were inherently 'political'. But not only was the field of candidates restricted to the elite, but there is also no evidence that Roman elections – even in the polarised climate of the late republic – were ever driven by programmes or policies that turned them into

---

[99] Mommsen 1887: 3.275–8, cf. Taylor 1966: 88–91. Mommsen's theory seemed to find confirmation in rules laid down in the *Tabula Hebana* for the selection of fifteen centuries which nominated praetorian and consular candidates during the early Empire, *Roman Statutes* no. 37. But see Develin 1978c: 366; Grieve 1985.

[100] See Develin 1979; Grieve 1987.

[101] E.g. Grieve 1985; Yakobson 1993; Rathbone 1993: 150. *Contra* Meier 1956: 581; Staveley 1953: 32–3; Taylor 1957; Hackl 1972; Develin 1978c: 371.

[102] Further support for this view has been drawn from a comment by Dionysius of Halicarnassus, *Ant. Rom.* 4.21.3, who states that the *comitia centuriata* had been changed in a more democratic direction 'in our times', 'en de tois kath emas kekinetai kronois', which makes it unlikely that it refers to the third-century reform, *pace* Nicholls 1956: 234; Grieve 1985: 298 n.94; Yakobson 1993. Dionysius specifically mentions the voting order, but that may, as Grieve 1985: 309 n.145 suggested, relate to changes following the *plebiscitum reddendorum equorum*, *c.* 129 (Cic. *Rep.* 4.2), when the (senatorial?) *sex suffragia* were separated from the *equites* and perhaps moved to a position just before the second class, cf. Cic. *Phil.* 2.82.

[103] Livy, 1.43.11, implies that prior to the reform voting rarely reached the second class, but we may doubt the accuracy of this information, since it is predicated on complete unanimity. Yakobson 1993 speculated that the reform greatly enhanced the voting power of the poor but there is little evidence for that.

'political' events in a modern sense. Some historians have attempted to gauge the political character of the reform by comparing the number of 'new men' in the consul lists before and after the changes, assuming that an increase would indicate a strengthened 'democracy'. Since none could be traced, it was concluded that the reform must have been oligarchic.[104] The equation of 'new men' with democracy is dubious, however, since there is no reason to believe the newcomers generally would have been any more responsive to the people's needs than the old elite, whose ranks they joined. A 'democratic' assembly need not in principle have elected more 'new men' than an aristocratic one.

If the reform is unlikely to be 'political' in the sense that it shifted power from one section of society to another, we will have to look for an explanation elsewhere. The central feature was undoubtedly the integration of tribes and centuries, since it was the introduction of a tribal element that triggered the reduction of first class units. And while the political consequences of this change may have been limited, it was highly significant on a formal level. The *comitia centuriata* was historically the people assembled in its military configuration, but its units, the centuries, no longer represented the *populus* under arms. As army units they had been replaced by maniples sometime between 340 and 280, thereby removing the correspondence between military units and voting units.[105] Meanwhile the *tribus* had, as we saw, acquired a status as the primary division of the Roman people, used for a wide range of administrative and political procedures. Therefore, by co-ordinating tribes and centuries the formal authority of the centuriate assembly – as well as the mandate it delivered – would be strengthened. This approach does not, however, clarify the likely change in voting order; that requires a different explanation. Moving the *equites* from their prestigious and influential position as first voters might seem a 'demotion', but since their place was taken by the first class, evidently also men of substance, it is perhaps better understood as a result of another innovation, which is the introduction of the so-called *centuria praerogativa*, itself one of the most intriguing features of the Roman electoral process.[106]

---

[104] Hackl 1972: 145.

[105] Stemmler 2000: 124 n.98. The *centuriae* could not simply be abolished, since they appear to have a permanent identity and were led by a *centurio*, Fest. s.v. *niquis scivit* 184L; Var. *L.* 6.93; *Comm. pet.* 18. Grieve 1985: 301–4.

[106] The date of the change is, as noted, uncertain since the two components of the reform are not intrinsically connected. Most scholars take the connection for granted, however, e.g. Meier 1956: 568; Taylor 1957: 345 n.21; Hackl 1972: 162, 166; Rosenstein 1995: 61.

The *Centuria Praerogativa*: Lottery and Elections

After the reform one century from the first class, the *centuria praerogativa*, would be chosen by lot to cast its vote before the rest.[107] Only when its results had been announced could the voting of the first class commence. The rationale behind granting one unit a privileged role as 'pre-voters' must have been to provide a lead for the rest of the centuries. And according to the ancient sources the example set by the *centuria praerogativa* was indeed followed by the other centuries, to the extent that the outcome of the election could be predicted as soon as its vote had been declared.[108] The nature of the influence of the *centuria praerogativa* is not entirely clear. Some have seen it as a 'bandwagon' effect, where voters keen to support a winner backed the most promising candidates. The idea may seem plausible but does not fully explain how a single unit could create such momentum that it effectively decided the election. Its vote must have carried a very particular significance, and others have therefore interpreted the *centuria praerogativa* in religious terms. Cicero describes its vote as an omen, i.e. a sign from the gods, and the use of the lot is probably important in this context. If so, that might explain its impact on the rest of the voters.[109]

In a challenge to this interpretation, Rosenstein noted that the Romans sometimes used the lot simply as a practical means of selection and argued that if it had been an omen it must have been binding, whereas in practice the vote of the first century could be disregarded, seemingly without religious misgivings.[110] Thus, in 215 and 211 the presiding magistrates intervened after its vote had been announced and asked it to change its mind, which it obligingly did. Rosenstein is right to argue that the vote of the *centuria praerogativa* was not a formal impetrative omen, i.e. Jupiter's response to a specific question, but that does not deprive it of religious significance. Although not every lot was regarded as a sign from the gods, in some situations it was employed for divinatory purposes.[111] The context

---

[107] It has traditionally been assumed that the *centuria praerogativa* was chosen from among the *iuniores* only, since all three explicit references mention *iuniores*, Liv. 24.7.12; 26.22.2; 27.6.3. But that information would be superfluous if that was always the case, cf. Ryan 1995. In theory it could, as Meier 1956: 572–3 suggested, have been drawn from the first class and the equestrian *centuriae*, assuming they voted together but this is unlikely for a number of practical reasons, cf. Mouritsen 2011a: 233–5 nn.12, 19, 24.

[108] Cic. *Planc.* 49: 'una centuria praerogativa tantum habet auctoritatis, ut nemo umquam prior eam tulerit, quin renuntiatus sit aut iis ipsis comitiis consul aut certe in illum annum'. Jehne 2000a: 665 n.19 noted that 'prior' must mean the first to be announced by the *centuria praerogativa*, cf. Meier 1956: 593.

[109] *Mur.* 38; *Div.* 1.103, 2.83.　　　[110] Rosenstein 1995; followed by Jehne 2000a.

[111] Cf. Stewart 1998: 12–51. A lot could also be taken within a *templum* to decide military strategy.

must therefore be taken into account, and here the 'religious' dimension of the occasion seems undeniable. Jupiter was a constant presence and partner in Roman public life and never more so than at a *comitia*. Before the assembly could begin prayers were said and auspices taken. The augurs remained in attendance throughout, and the physical setting for the vote was that of a *templum*, a formally inaugurated space, freed of extraneous spiritual forces. It therefore seems unlikely that a lot taken at the assembly, presumably within the *templum* itself, could be regarded as purely practical and 'secular'.[112]

The two instances where the *centuria praerogativa* was asked to reconsider its vote may be less conclusive that it might first seem. In 215 the consul Fabius Maximus recalled the *centuria praerogativa* and invited it to review its choice of his son-in-law, instead putting himself forward as a candidate (Liv. 24.7.10–9.3).[113] In 211 one of the candidates chosen by the *centuria praerogativa*, Manlius Torquatus, approached the presiding consul and asked him to recall the *centuria*, excusing himself because of his poor eyesight. The *centuria praerogativa* then conferred with the *seniores* of its tribe and two new consuls were elected; it is not clear whether they had been among the original candidates from the first round (Liv. 26.22.3–13). In this case there had been a flaw in the first vote, since the consul was in fact incapacitated. A second vote could therefore go ahead, which was later fully vindicated when it shortly afterwards transpired that the other chosen candidate, T. Otacilius, had actually died (Liv. 26.23.2).

An omen was not an inflexible dictate that could not be circumvented without sacrilege. Signs from the gods were always subject to interpretation and negotiation. In this case it worked through the selection of one unit which would make a choice between the available candidates. Changes to the list of candidates therefore allowed a new vote to be taken without violating the initial omen. In 215 the two eventually elected, Fabius and Marcellus, had not been candidates, and that may also have been the case in 211. The events in 215 also indicate that the authority of the *centuria praerogativa* went beyond the purely conventional. Thus, when Fabius

---

[112] On *templa* see Vaahtera 1993a. The authority of the *centuria praerogativa* may also have been bolstered by a general tendency among the Romans to view beginnings as in/auspicious. In legislative assemblies the first voter of the first *tribus* was considered so important that his name was included in the actual law text, as demonstrated by epigraphically preserved laws, *Roman Statutes* nos. 2, 14, 22, 63; Cic. *Planc.* 35; *Dom.* 79–80. Originating in the period of oral voting, it was continued after the introduction of written ballots, when the first voter would declare his (affirmative) vote to the whole assembly. Cicero's description of him as the 'auctor', 'creator' of the law, underlines his ritual significance. Staveley 1969; Linderski and Kaminska-Linderski 1973.

[113] Since Fabius was one of Livy's heroes, the absence of any suspicion of impiety is less surprising.

Maximus tried to prevent the election of his son-in-law, he did not simply address the remaining 192 centuries, recommending a different choice to them, but insisted that the first century change its vote. His actions highlighted not just the power of the *centuria praerogativa* as a determining influence on the *comitia*, but also its ritual importance; ideally there should be no discrepancy between the vote of the *centuria praerogativa* and the final outcome.

The voting procedures did not require a randomly chosen unit of 'pre-voters' and the Romans had managed without until the reform.[114] The purpose of the *centuria praerogativa* was therefore not practical but political. Randomly selecting a single unit to provide a lead to the other centuries helped minimise divisions and generate a clearer, more unanimous electoral outcome.[115] But merely asking one unit to vote before the others would not in itself have produced that result; it must have been – tacitly – endowed with a much more fundamental authority most likely derived from a perceived divine aspect to its selection. The reform reinforced the ritual element of Roman elections by involving the gods more closely in the process, but it was done indirectly for the simple reason that the actual decision never could be taken out of the hands of the *populus*. The ingenious solution was to let 'divine fortune' choose a single unit which would then decide the election by its example. It was, in short, the use of the lot that gave the *centuria praerogativa* its special status.

There were real political benefits for the elite since it retained the principle of 'popular choice' while largely reducing the outcome to a matter of chance. Open contests over public office and executive power always pose a risk to aristocratic systems, and the Roman senate, concerned with the collective interests of the elite, therefore tried to put a lid on electoral campaigning and other means of gaining competitive advantages. From an elite perspective the ideal distribution of public office happens either through a closed rotational system or by pure chance, neither of which allows interference in the selection process. The former is a largely theoretical possibility in most societies – and would have been politically unacceptable in Rome – and the introduction of the *centuria praerogativa* may be seen as an attempt to move the process towards the latter.

---

[114] Staveley 1969: 519 assumed that before the reform the *equites* performed this function and Livy refers to the *equites* as *praerogativae centuriae*, 5.18.1; 10.22.1. But the terminology may not be authentic, since they were 'first voters' not 'pre-voters', cf. Meier 1956: 568. The equestrian *centuriae* were also unlikely to present a unanimous choice capable of providing a clear guide to the rest.

[115] According to Meier 1956 the aim was to focus the vote, maintain *concordia*, and avoid a split vote which left the decision to the lower classes.

The reform combined election and lottery, entrusting the decision to a small, randomly chosen subsection, which would have represented an unpredictable and elusive target for electoral campaigners. In order to maximise this effect the pool of *centuriae* from which the deciding one was chosen had to be as large as possible, which explains in purely practical terms why the first class replaced the *equites* in the voting order. Lobbying the *centuriae* of the first class would have been more difficult simply because of its size, and perhaps even more so after additional complexities had been introduced with the co-ordination of tribes and centuries.[116]

The reform can be understood as an attempt to manage the aristocratic republic more efficiently by reducing the incentive for open campaigning. The lottery element also militated against undue concentration of power in the hands of a few elite families, since each of them maintained close links to their own *tribus* and could normally rely on their support at elections; the random selection of the *praerogativa* therefore automatically ensured a degree of rotation. Finally, the reform strengthened the formal authority of the assembly as a representation of the *populus Romanus*.

While the reorganisation of the *comitia centuriata* may strike us as eccentric in its combination of lottery and election, it does in fact have interesting parallels in the constitutions of later Italian city-states, suggesting that Rome was responding to basic structural problems facing aristocratic republics in general. Venice and later also Genoa devised methods for electing their public officials which bear a remarkable similarity to the Roman system, although no direct inspiration can be traced. In Venice a complex procedure was introduced in 1297 to elect the Doge, which involved multiple rounds of elections and drawings of lot in order to produce a final selection of random electors who would choose the new head of state.[117] The aim was to create a system that precluded electioneering, officially forbidden, and maintained stability within the closed but highly competitive Venetian elite.

The Roman reform probably shared similar objectives, responding to the new situation created by the plebeio-patrician settlement that had placed the centuriate assembly in a decision-making role. The question is how effective the measure was.[118] As we shall see, electoral campaigning

---

[116] Grieve 1985: 309, perceptively noted that the *centuria praerogativa* was 'a more elusive target for canvassers and whips'.

[117] For a fuller exploration of Venetian parallels, see Mouritsen 2011a.

[118] Jehne 2013a: 128–31 doubts whether the measure was aimed at campaigning, pointing to continued attempts to curb electioneering after the reform. However, lack of efficacy does not necessarily invalidate its original purpose. Lottery by its nature puts the outcome beyond outside interference

appears to have become more intense in the following century, and there are signs that the role of the *centuria praerogativa* may itself have been redefined over time. In the two instances, discussed above, where the presiding magistrate called upon the first century to reconsider its vote, he asked them to change both their choices. But later Cicero implied that only the first candidate to be announced by the *praerogativa* carried the particular authority that guaranteed his election.[119] The implication is a significant reduction to its influence, and Cicero further noted that the chosen candidate would be elected at that *comitia* or 'certainly that year', 'in illum annum', which usually has been taken as a reference to *comitia* that overran and had to be completed the following day. It is not obvious, however, why Cicero would highlight such a minor technicality, and Mommsen therefore suggested the attractive reading 'alium annum', which would imply that if the candidate had failed that year he could still expect to be elected if he stood again.[120] If the emendation is accepted, the passage would reflect a further weakening of the power of the *centuria praerogativa* during the later republic.

The institution may have sought to regulate elite competition and 'streamline' elections, but with the growth of empire and increased competitive pressures the scope of the first unit's influence was redefined to allow for wider choice and hence greater opportunities for influencing the outcome. Thus, having once provided a definite guide to the other centuries, only one consul would later be decided by this century. And towards the end of the republic the *praerogativa* may have given little more than a general boost to the authority of its chosen candidate, improving his chances now or in the future, but no longer able to settle the election as originally intended. It was possible to loosen the electoral 'strait-jacket' of the *centuria praerogativa* in this way because its vote had never been formally defined as an impetrative omen; its authority was established through the collective perception of the assembled voters.

The elite's attempt to manage the elections appears to have been confined to the *comitia centuriata*, undoubtedly because it chose the most

---

and thus militates against campaigning. The reason further measures were needed was that the Roman reform remained a half-way compromise between lottery and election.

[119] *Planc.* 49. Some scholars have taken Cicero's comment as indicative that the example of the *centuria praerogativa* always had been limited to one of the consulships, but that is difficult to reconcile to Livy's accounts. It also seems unlikely that an institution which sought to randomise and homogenise the vote should limit itself to just one of two posts.

[120] Mommsen 1887: 3.398.

important magistrates and was the focus of the fiercest competition. Whether the non-elective *comitia centuriata* operated with a *centuria praerogativa* is uncertain, but events surrounding the declaration of war on Macedon in 200 do not suggest so.[121] Presumably, these occasions were seen as acts of ratification rather than choice. In the tribally organised assemblies the first *tribus* to vote was known as the *principium*, but there is no evidence that it functioned as a '*tribus praerogativa*'. It was chosen by lot, but so were presumably all the units that followed during the process of successive block voting.[122]

The use of the lot is again significant, since it draws attention to the fact that Roman elections were not determined simply by the number of block votes each candidate gained but also by the order in which he received them. In theory, more candidates could gain a majority than there were posts to be filled, and the ones chosen would be those who gained a majority first. Therefore, also after the tribal assemblies had moved from successive to a single contemporaneous vote – probably after the introduction of the written ballot in 139 – the announcement of the votes was still done successively and after drawing lot. Electoral assemblies thus had a basic element of lottery to them, which underscores the fundamental point that they were not conceived primarily as vehicles of 'popular power'. No effort was ever made to ensure that the results reflected the 'Will of the People'; on the contrary, the outcome was as far as possible left to fortune. The assemblies were part – an essential part, it must be stressed – of the symbolic construction of the Roman state as a community of free citizens, acting in partnership with the gods under the guidance of its leaders. But they were not 'political' bodies in the modern sense. They conferred legitimacy, but a legitimacy that was not derived from democratic principles – hardly compatible with the lottery aspect – but from the observance of correct procedure, since the assemblies essentially expressed the 'Will of the People' in symbolic form. This point is further illustrated by the rules regulating competition, which suggest a very different conceptualisation of the people's role.

---

[121] Liv. 31.6–8.1.

[122] In the *lex Malacitana* 57 the lot decided the order in which each individual result was announced, a system likely to reflect Roman practices. Cicero, *Agr.* 2.79, refers to an established *ordo tribuum*. Staveley 1969 suggests that the *principium* indicated the starting point in the list of tribes, which would then be called in a fixed order. But the *ordo tribuum* might have been relevant only at the census, where there was no point in drawing lot, while in the *De lege agraria* the context is land distribution. See also Rieger 2007: 602–10.

Breaking the Rules: *Ambitus*

If the introduction of the *centuria praerogativa* ever had any substantial impact on the level of electioneering among magisterial candidates, it does not seem to have lasted long. Already in the early second century we find signs of growing competition, as a number of measures were passed to curb electoral malpractice. Regulating campaigning is entirely normal in participatory systems based on general election, but in Rome the underlying concerns appear to have been quite different from those shaping modern legislation in this area. The Roman terminology is itself revealing, since *ambitus*, usually translated as electoral malpractice, simply refers to candidates going around asking voters for support, an act which from a modern perspective would seem to be an entirely natural part of canvassing.[123]

Although the earliest recorded measures may be of doubtful historicity, they still provide a valuable hint of the nature of the concerns we are dealing with. In 432, Livy reports that a plebiscite banned the use of the *toga candida*, the whitened toga intended to attract attention to the candidates (4.25.13–14). Perhaps more authentic may be the *lex Poetilia* from 358, which curbed campaigning on market days and outside Rome (Liv. 7.15.12–13), suggesting that the mere soliciting of votes might have been considered problematic. Later in the fourth century the dictator C. Maenius issued an edict against *coitiones* (314, Liv. 9.26.9), which is particularly interesting as an electoral offence, since it merely describes a compact between two candidates running for the same offices. *Coitiones* continued to be a source of concern as documented by, for example, Cicero's defence of Plancius against the charge of collusion, although the precise legal status of such agreements during this period remains unclear.[124] Still, the fact that alliances could be seen as an issue suggests we consider the nature of electioneering more broadly and in particular the question of payment, which became highly controversial during the middle and later republic.

In 181 the *lex Cornelia Baebia de ambitu* first addressed the question of payment to voters (Liv. 40.19.11). The previous year the *lex Orchia de cenis* had laid down rules for private expenditure, while the games of the aediles were regulated in 179 (Liv. 40.44.10–12). In 159 yet another

---

[123] Cf. e.g. Var. *L.* 5.28; Fest. s.v. *ambitus* 5L, 15L. For an overview, see Lintott 1990; Wallinga 1994; Mouritsen 2001 ch. 5; and most recently Rosillo-López 2010: 49–85.

[124] *Planc.* 53. Accusations of *coitio* were often associated with charges of bribery, e.g. Cic. *Parad.* 46; *Q. fr.* 2.15.4.

ambitus law was passed (Liv. *Per.* 47), only to be followed in 149 by the *lex Cornelia Fulvia de ambitu.* A permanent *quaestio de ambitu* may also have been established, perhaps in 122, to deal with this offence.[125] During the first century further measures were implemented. In 67, a *lex Calpurnia* targeted *divisores*, the agents organising the payment, while in 63 the *lex Tullia* cast the net even wider and included games and other forms of spending such as hospitality. In 55 the *lex Licinia de sodaliciis* again dealt with aspects of the organisation of payment.[126] Another attempt was made in 54 to limit the practice and in 52 the *lex Pompeia* sharpened the penalties for *ambitus*.

The issue of payment, typically described as 'bribery', tends to be evoked as a sign of 'corruption' and general political decline. Whether this interpretation is necessarily correct remains debatable, and there is a risk that we project modern notions onto republican Rome. In contemporary polities, paying voters for their support counts as an obvious transgression, but in Rome the situation may have been more complex. Not all forms of payment were, for example, illegal. When candidates confined it to their own *tribules*, it could be described as a time-honoured tradition, suggesting it functioned as a kind of *sportulae*, small gifts which patrons traditionally presented to their clients.[127] *Ambitus* was committed only when candidates paid voters indiscriminately; or, in other words, the offence happened when candidates tried to subvert the position of their competitors within their *tribus*.

Nowadays the basic objection to electoral fraud is the damage it does to the democratic process by distorting the free expression of the 'popular will'. The politicians competing for popular favour are, of course, affected when that happens but this is an incidental side-effect of the interference with the democratic choice; the real casualty is ultimately the sovereign people and its right to self-government. In Rome, on the other hand, the primary 'victims' of *ambitus* seem to have been the competitors who lost out.[128] Thus the overriding aim was to maintain a level playing field between the candidates. In this context, the ban on *coitiones* is particularly telling, since there was nothing inherently 'undemocratic' about candidates pooling their resources to support each other; only their fellow candidates suffered when that happened.

---

[125] Wallinga 1994: 423–4.   [126] Mouritsen 2001: 149–51.   [127] Cic. *Mur.* 72; *Planc.* 44–5.

[128] Jehne 2010: 29 also noted that the term 'bribery' anachronistically implies that voters were paid to suppress their true political convictions. In reality, however, there was little to distinguish one aristocratic candidate from another – and hence little 'democratic' choice to be made, cf. Jehne 1995b.

In a system like Rome's the selection of new magistrates was ideally managed with as little involvement by the electorate as possible. To that end the scale of the proceedings was, as we shall see in the next chapter, kept deliberately small and unrepresentative. Attempts were also made to limit the candidates' ability to reach larger sections of the *populus* – through personal contact, public largesse or the direct purchase of votes. It was crucial that electioneering did not spin out of control, creating friction within the elite or leading to mass mobilisation of the electorate. *Ambitus* laws served to prevent precisely these outcomes. For that reason they included measures that went far beyond what is today perceived to be 'malpractice' and covered forms of electioneering now considered entirely innocent. For example, at some point before 68 the use of *nomenclatores* was prohibited, although their role merely was to help candidates remember the names of people in the Forum (Plu. *Cat. Mi.* 8.2). Likewise, in 64 the *lex Fabia* limited the number of *sectatores*, the personal supporters who followed the candidate around during the campaign (Cic. *Mur.* 71).

Ambitus legislation addressed the distortions caused by uneven distribution of resources and influence in the Roman elite by seeking to prevent the rich and powerful from gaining unfair advantages. It was essentially aimed at maintaining the equilibrium of the ruling class – rather than ensuring the purity of the 'democratic' process. As such it reminds us that what happened in the elective *comitia* was something more complex than simply the *populus Romanus* choosing its leaders. The assembly performed a key role as an 'independent' arbiter in the elite's ongoing struggle for power and public *honores*. But to fulfil that function it must ideally be beyond outside interference. Hence the attempt to randomise the outcome as far as possible and, when that failed, the repeated measures to stop the candidates from reaching the voters.

CHAPTER 2

Leaders and Masses in the Roman Republic

While no Roman ever disputed that power belonged to the *populus*, it does not necessarily follow that the Roman assemblies were conceived of or intended as vehicles of direct popular influence. As argued above, their peculiar structures hint at a formalistic, almost ritualised notion of legitimacy in Rome. The *res publica* may, as Schofield argued, have belonged to the *populus* but it was always managed by leaders to whom the people had entrusted its care. The question is how this paradoxical construction worked in practice, and in this section we will look more closely at the influence the people exercised after the *res publica* had been handed over to its chosen leaders. The highly formalised structure of the assemblies in principle does not exclude the possibility that they could have served the interests of the *populus*, thereby making the constitution more 'democratic' than it might otherwise appear. If so, that might explain the broad social and political stability which scholars have identified as a defining feature of the 'classic' middle republic.

Confronted with these issues historians have in recent years increasingly turned from traditional constitutional history towards the study of 'political culture', a concept which also comprises the attitudes and beliefs that inform and give meaning to the political process. Thus the ideology, 'style' and self-representation of the elite as well as its interaction with the *populus* have been widely identified as key elements in forging the apparent consensus, which impressed even Polybius. In addition, there is now much greater awareness of the symbolic and 'performative' aspects of politics – monuments, spectacles, processions, and festivals – as factors contributing to civic inclusion and a shared sense of community. This approach has greatly advanced our understanding of the Roman republic, and we will return to some of the new insights it has generated later in the chapter.

It is vital, however, that the 'nuts-and-bolts' of Roman politics are not forgotten; indeed one might argue that it is through a combination of 'hard' and 'soft' political history that further progress may be made. Let us therefore start by considering politics at its most basic: how many people took part, who were they, why had they turned up, and how did they vote? When looking at the popular assemblies from this perspective, one is struck by two remarkable features: first, the small scale of the proceedings which automatically limited participation to a tiny minority of the electorate; and second, the fact that those who did take part virtually never rejected any of the proposals they were asked to decide upon. These two aspects are intimately connected, and looking more closely at the scale of participation may help to explain the voting patterns.

Popular Participation

Ancient authors provide no hard figures for voter turnout or go beyond even the vaguest indication of scale. This is itself unsurprising given that turnouts were irrelevant to the question of political legitimacy. But it means that the issue of participation will have to be approached indirectly through the venues used and the procedures followed. While these may give us a broad sense of voting capacity, we should bear in mind that the figures, themselves mere guesstimates, all indicate *maximum* attendance.

The Romans voted in a number of different locations: the tribally organised assemblies, which passed most laws and elected the tribunes and lower magistrates, convened in the Comitium, in the Forum by the Temple of Castor, and on the Capitol, while the centuries, responsible for declarations of war and peace and the election of praetors, consuls, and censors, gathered in the Saepta on the Campus Martius. Some of these venues allow us to assess their scale and capacity.

The Comitium, the ancient meeting place of the Roman citizens, was located in the north-eastern corner of the Forum Romanum and incorporated the speaker's platform, the Rostra, as well as other structures. Little remains of this building but the surviving fragments seem compatible with a roughly circular structure consisting of a central open space surrounded by a stepped *cavea*, perhaps similar to the Comitia that have been uncovered in Latin colonies across Italy.[1] The Comitium probably covered an area of around 46 metres in diameter but since the available meeting space was reduced by various structures we are left with *c.* 1300 square metres. If we assume a crowd density of four per square metre, we get a maximum capacity of 5200 citizens. However, since they also had to be organised into

---

[1] Cf. Mouritsen 2001. On the archaeological remains most recently, Amici 2005. On Comitia in Latin colonies, see Mouritsen 2004.

voting groups and be able to move around when called forward, an
estimate nearer 3900 is probably more realistic, a figure far below that of
the male citizen population of Rome, even during the middle republic.
In 145, the tribune C. Licinius Crassus proposed a law on popular election
of priests without senatorial backing, on which occasion he 'was the first
to lead the people, for the hearing of laws, from the Comitium to the
voting area (or expanse) of the Forum'.[2] Rather than a response to space
constraints in the old venue, this move appears to have been a political
gesture of defiance towards the senate, whose building, the Curia, visually
and symbolically dominated the 'people's' meeting space.

Irrespective of the turnout normally expected, it obviously made good
practical sense to organise the voters in the larger open space that was
available in the Forum Romanum, and in the later republic that became
the norm for legislative assemblies; tribal elections, on the other hand, were
transferred to the Saepta on the Campus Martius. Although voters were
now lined up in the Forum, the votes still had to be cast within an
inaugurated space, a so-called *templum*, and for that purpose the Temple
of Castor was used. The space in front of the temple might have been able
to hold a substantial crowd of around 15,000 to 20,000 people, but that
tells us little about actual participation. A closer look at the procedures
followed and the space where the voting took place may be more instructive. We are reasonably well-informed about the size and layout of
the republican Castor temple, allowing some cautious estimates of its
capacity.[3] Even on the most optimistic assumptions a figure of 10,000
voters becomes quite unrealistic given the length of time it would have
taken for a crowd of that size to complete the vote. Indeed, Cicero hints
that attendance could be much lower; in an attack on Clodius he refers
to the practice by which members of other *tribus* would be transferred to
the empty ones where no one had turned up.[4]

Although this chapter will mostly be concerned with legislative
assemblies, we may for the sake of comparison briefly consider the
Saepta and its capacity. This extensive structure is known to us almost
exclusively from fragments of the Severan plan of the city of Rome, the

---

[2] Var. *R* 1.2.9: 'primus populum ad leges accipiendas in septem [saepta?] iugera forensia e comitio
eduxit', cf. Cic. *Amic.* 96.
[3] See Nielsen and Poulsen 1992.
[4] Cic. *Sest.* 109; cf. Mouritsen 2001; Jehne 2013a: 134; 2013b: 150. Kaster 2006: 334–5 dismisses the
passage as rhetorical hyperbole. But although Cicero obviously tried to portray the assembly that
exiled him as wholly unrepresentative, not least when compared to the one that recalled him, the
reference to voters transferred from one *tribus* to another makes sense only if such a mechanism
existed to cope with low turnouts – and if his audience were familiar with the procedure.

Forma Urbis, which depicted Caesar's monumentalised version of the voting enclosure, the Saepta Iulia. The location and scale are therefore reasonably certain. It was shaped as a rectangular enclosure measuring 310 by 120 metres, making it substantially larger than the facilities available in the Forum. The internal structure, on the other hand, is entirely a matter of conjecture. Taylor envisaged a single open space divided into thirty-five long aisles (one for each *tribus*), which at one end led to a platform where the votes would be cast, and suggested that it might hold 70,000 voters. This reconstruction is not based on any concrete evidence, leaving it open to doubt.[5] When MacMullen reconsidered the *Forma Urbis* fragments he noted that part of the space must have been taken up by a substantial forecourt. Procedurally, it follows that the crowd would have assembled here before being called to vote and separated into their various units. In that case we are dealing with a considerably lower capacity of perhaps just around 20,000.[6]

All the indications we have for the scale of political participation suggest that only a tiny proportion of the citizen population could ever be present on these occasions. In principle this tells us little about the political role of the *populus*, since in any participatory system there is bound to be a disparity between those entitled to vote and the ones making use of this right. Even in modern democracies, where voting is decentralised and easily accessible, not all citizens cast their vote – without the democratic nature of the process thereby being called into question. There are fundamental differences, however; nowadays non-participation is 1) purely a matter of personal choice since all citizens can cast their vote in both theory and practice, and 2) generally considered unfortunate and at variance with prevailing democratic ideals. In Rome, on the other hand, the discrepancy between *populus* and voters appears to have been an integral and, it would seem, intended feature of the political system. There is no recorded attempt to allow the assemblies to become more representative – in fact the opposite rather seems to have been the case. Venues were not expanded to accommodate the growing electorate

[5] Taylor 1966: 47–58. The internal layout, including the long aisles and the platform envisaged to the south, is little more than conjecture and many other configurations are possible: indeed, the features on the *Forma Urbis* fragments that have been interpreted as the corners of the platform are placed off-centre.

[6] MacMullen 1980; Mouritsen 2001; Jehne 2013a: 115–16. Phillips 2004 questioned the idea of a separate space for the waiting citizens, referring to recorded instances of interaction between candidates and voters. The argument is not compelling, however, and none of the examples are incompatible with a forecourt structure, Var. *R* 3.2.1; Val. Max. 4.5.3; 8.15.4.

and the arcane and time-consuming procedures remained in place despite the huge increase in the number of citizens. No effort was made to encourage *rustici* to take part; decentralised voting was never considered and the market days, on which they might have visited the capital, were explicitly designated as non-comitial.[7]

The limited turnout did not give rise to concerns about the validity of any given law or appointment, which may be explained by the particular Roman conceptualisation of popular legitimacy, explored in the previous chapter. As we saw, the people's involvement carried a unique element of abstraction, which subsumed individual votes into blocks and effectively eliminated conventional quantification of turnouts. In doing so it also removed any incentive to increase participation or promote popular representation. Since it was an abstract version of the *populus Romanus* that granted its consent on these occasions, mass participation was practically, as well as ideologically, irrelevant. For that reason the situation we encounter in the late republic should not be seen as a 'degeneration' of a system that had once aimed at greater representation or an inadvertent side-effect of expansion and population growth.[8] There is no reason to believe that Roman assemblies were ever intended as political fora for the citizen body in a concrete physical sense. We must therefore distinguish between the *populus* as a constitutional concept and source of public legitimacy and the actual people who took part in voting. Indeed this separation seems fundamental to understanding Roman politics and may offer a basic structural framework for analysing the assemblies and their voting patterns.

'Saying Yes': Voting in the Popular Assemblies

Our next question concerns the – small number of – people who did turn up for the assemblies. Did their behaviour conform to the 'ritual' interpretation of the assemblies suggested above? Or put differently, did the political reality differ from the constitutional theory of leadership and 'entrustment'? Since the people's constitutional powers, at least in terms of legislation, were purely 'responsive', the only way they could influence the political process was by withholding formal consent. A simple but effective means of measuring the degree to which the assemblies displayed any independence and functioned as decision-making bodies is therefore to look at the frequency with which that happened.

---

[7] Taylor 1966: 18, 118.   [8] Cf. Flaig 2003: 158–64; *contra* e.g. Bleicken 1975a.

Egon Flaig investigated comitial rejections in the greatest detail and his list of recorded instances forms a useful starting point.[9] Livy mentions four instances from the fourth century but given their doubtful historicity they will not be considered here.[10] That leaves us with the following five (possibly six) cases, dating to the period between 209 and 104. In 209 the tribune C. Publicius Bibulus attempted to have the *imperium* of M. Claudius Marcellus abrogated, attacking not just the general himself but also the entire nobility for its inability to drive Hannibal out of Italy.[11] Marcellus defended himself vigorously and the assembly rejected Bibulus' proposal, 'rogatio . . . antiquaretur'. The most famous instance followed in 200 when the declaration of war against Macedon was rejected by the *comitia centuriata*. The consul, however, strongly urged by fellow senators, called a *contio* at which he addressed the centuries, before asking them to repeat the vote. At the second attempt the motion was approved.[12] Almost half a century passes before another unsuccessful *rogatio* is recorded; in 149 a proposal to set up an extraordinary court to try Ser. Sulpicius Galba was rejected.[13] It was followed by two bills which according to Cicero were defeated by Laelius and Scipio Aemilianus (*Amic.* 96). The first, in 145, was the aforementioned proposal of C. Licinius Crassus to transfer the election of *pontifices* to the people; the second was C. Papirius Carbo's attempt to allow the re-election of tribunes in 131/30, which Aemilianus is said to have thwarted, albeit without explicitly stating that it was formally rejected. Finally, in 104 an agrarian law of the tribune L. Marcius Philippus was voted down by the tribes.[14]

When these instances are looked at more closely certain patterns emerge. In 209 and 149 we are dealing with *ad hominem* measures which used the assembly to settle personal scores. As such they are directly comparable to the attempt to block Aemilius Paullus' triumph in 167, when the tribune Ser. Sulpicius Galba, supposedly driven by personal *inimicitia*, stirred up

---

[9] Flaig 2003: 175–80; cf. Bleicken 1975b: 273–9; Nippel 1988: 55; Eder 1991: 179; Jehne 2001: 104; Tiersch 2009: 40–1.

[10] Liv. 5.30.7; 5.55.2; 6.39.2; 8.37.11. These also predate the *lex Hortensia* of 287, by which plebiscites first gained the status of law.

[11] Liv. 27.21.1–4; Plu. *Marc.* 27.1–3.

[12] Liv. 31.6–8.1. cf. Rich 1976: 75–87; Warrior 1996: 37–89; Vishnia 1998.

[13] Liv. *Per.* 49; Cic. *Brut.* 90, cf. *Mur.* 59; Val. Max. 8.1.2. Gruen 1968: 12–13.

[14] Crassus: Cic. *Amic.* 96, *Brut.* 83, Var. *R* 1.2.9. Carbo: Cic. *Amic.* 96, Liv. *Per.* 59; Philippus: Cic. *Off.* 2.73. Flaig 2003: 176 suggests all three rogations were withdrawn in the face of opposition rather than defeated, but Cicero explicitly says about Carbo's bill: 'suffragiis populi repudiata est', 'rejected by the people's votes', *Amic.* 96, and uses the term 'antiquari' about Philippus': *Off.* 2.73, cf. Ferrary 2012: 20 n.63. Hiebel 2009: 152–4 argues that other rejections happened in 119 and 62 but the evidence is weak.

discontent among disgruntled soldiers and persuaded them to vote the motion down (Liv. 45.35–9). The attempt eventually failed, but only because of the last-minute intervention by leading senators. Similar methods appear to have been used in 200, when we are told that the initial rejection was instigated by a tribune, who exploited widespread disaffection over the prospect of another major war. This particular bill stands out as the only one that enjoyed the full backing of the senate and whose rejection, unsurprisingly, was quickly reversed. The other proposals were all presented by 'maverick' tribunes, who apparently acted without elite support. During this period it would therefore seem that bills enjoying the senate's approval were virtually certain of becoming law, while those without on rare occasions might suffer defeat.

A fragment of C. Titius' speech on the *lex Fannia* from 161, which regulated public and private banquets and distributions, mentions boys who apparently were being sent to the Forum to inquire: 'who speaks for it, who argues against it, how many tribes support it, how many reject it'. The implication is that the outcome, at least in this instance, was considered in the balance and that the tribes realistically could have turned the proposal down.[15] The situation may well be untypical, however. The law was highly controversial, directly affecting the lifestyle of the propertied classes and probably generating considerable debate and agitation on both sides. Opposition to the measure is therefore plausible both within the political class and among affluent voters in general (who may have dominated the assembly on this as well as most other occasions, see further, below pp. 70–72). It was in other words, a prime example of a bill likely to split the assembly.

This brief survey suggests that laws were rejected extremely rarely and usually as a result of exceptional circumstances. Some scholars have argued that there may have been many unrecorded instances of proposals failing to get onto the statute book supposedly not making it into the history books either.[16] The logical implication is that rejections happened so frequently that they attracted little or no attention. However, the instances we do hear of all appear to have been highly contentious and caused considerable stir at the time. The rejection of a bill, especially one that carried the senate's *auctoritas*, can hardly have been a trivial matter. As the examples show, it typically happened as the result of internal divisions within the elite when

---

[15] *Suasio legis Fanniae* 161 (Malcovati *ORF* 1.51): 'qui suaserint, qui dissuaserint, quot tribus iusserint, quot vetuerint'.

[16] Bleckmann 2002: 228–9 n.4.

dissenting factions and individuals mobilised opposition in advance. Ideologically, they represented glaring exceptions to the dominant *concordia* ideal and in practical terms the disputes would often have produced their own written record, with speeches being delivered – and published – by both sides. If rejections had been a regular occurrence, we would expect far more passing references to failed bills, not least during the late republic when the record is exceptionally rich and detailed. The fact that no securely documented rejection has reached us from the entire first century therefore suggests that we are not dealing with an accident of transmission but a genuine feature of Roman politics.

The inescapable conclusion is that the Roman *comitia* cannot be understood in conventional terms as decision-making bodies. Following the example of Keith Hopkins, Flaig therefore argued that legislative assemblies functioned as what he called *Konsensorgane*, suggesting that instead of making decisions they provided political legitimacy on a purely symbolic level.[17] No actual preferences were expressed, since the role of the assembly was to confirm the *rogatio* put before it. On this interpretation the people's involvement in legislation directly matches the constitutional model explored above, since the contribution of the *populus* was reduced to ratifying proposals put forward by magistrates and tribunes, who usually – but not always – acted on behalf of the senate. As such the proceedings seem to reflect a peculiarly Roman constitutional mentality that perceived the *populus* as a vital but also essentially passive source of public legitimacy.

From *Comitia* to *Contiones*: the Rise of a New Paradigm

Although the small scale of the popular assemblies as well as their habit of passing virtually every bill placed before them have been widely accepted, that has – perhaps surprisingly – done little to settle the long-running debate about the 'power of the people', let alone put the notion of a Roman 'democracy' to rest. Indeed, the most common response has been to shift the popular 'input' into the political process from the assemblies onto the *contiones*, the public meetings which preceded them.[18] As a result there is now an overwhelming emphasis in modern scholarship on the communication and direct face-to-face interaction that took place between politicians and *populus*. Paradoxically, the public meetings, which were long

---

[17] Hopkins 1991; Flaig 2003: 167.
[18] Pina Polo 1996 remains fundamental on the *contio*. See also Mouritsen 2001; Morstein-Marx 2004; and the papers in Steel and Van der Blom 2013. For an overview of recent literature, see e.g. Tiersch 2009: 40.

treated as secondary precisely because they took no decisions, have after the 'communicative turn' become the primary, indeed pivotal, political fora.[19]

In accordance with this new paradigm, *contiones* are identified as the crucial testing grounds for new ideas, as any proposal that proved unpopular when presented to the public was supposedly quietly withdrawn before it could be put to a potentially disastrous vote, especially if popular feeling appeared openly hostile. In this way, the meetings tested the 'will of the people', or 'Volkswille' as Flaig put it, and the ongoing consultation process ensured that leaders and people remained in broad agreement and affirmative comitial votes stayed the norm. The 'power of the people' was, in other words, both real and tangible, even if it was expressed informally through spontaneous responses to politicians at *contiones* rather than through formal votes in the assemblies. On this line of reasoning the effectiveness of the consultation is demonstrated precisely by the rarity of comitial rejections. Almost through the backdoor the argument thus restores the status of the *populus* to that of an active and decisive player in republican politics: at *contiones* the people exercised a power, which no magistrate could afford to ignore.[20]

The new understanding of *contiones* as focal points of the political process has become so entrenched that it is fast turning into a new 'orthodoxy'. And *prima facie* it is not without plausibility, explaining as it does not just the compliance of the *comitia* but also the remarkable frequency of *contiones*, especially during the late republic, and the attention they seem to have attracted. But as soon as we consider how this 'consultation' might have worked in practice doubts start mounting and we have to ask whether *contiones* were really suited to serve as fora for political debate. A *contio* was a public meeting called by an official with *potestas contionandi*. He retained total control over proceedings and could decide who was allowed to speak and on what topic. In principle, any issue could be discussed. Some were linked to legislation and hence part of the statutory process, by which proposals had to be presented at three separate meetings over a period of three market days, *trinum nundinum*, before being voted upon.[21] These assemblies were preceded by a final *contio* at which both sides could argue their case, and as we shall see, this meeting differed in nature from 'ordinary' *contiones*. Many *contiones*, it should be noted, were unrelated to legislation and simply served as a platform for attacks on political opponents, who might respond by calling counter meetings of their own. Finally, some *contiones* were used to make routine public announcements and hence entirely uncontroversial.

The audiences were there to listen – and only to listen. Formally, they played no active role in the proceedings, where their input was reduced to shouting and cheering. As a means of testing 'popular opinion' these occasions would have been less than perfect.[22] What would a prospective legislator, for example, do if the message from the crowd was mixed? Or if the audience seemed indifferent, would he then abandon his carefully prepared plans? His dilemma went deeper, however, since the logistical and practical constraints meant that only a minute proportion of the electorate could be present at a *contio*.[23] There was no guarantee therefore that the audience a politician addressed at one *contio* would necessarily be the same as the one that would turn up for the following meetings and, crucially, for the decisive vote in the *comitia*.

The 'consultation' model assumes that the people who had first listened to the arguments presented at *contiones* would later pass the bill in the *comitia*. But since these were separate events, held several weeks apart, and each accommodated only small subsections of the voters, there was no direct or necessary identity between the crowds attending them. In other words, the crowd that turned up for the *comitia* might have been quite different from the one that had given the bill an upbeat reception at the *contiones*. To restore the link between *contiones* and *comitia* we would therefore have to revive Mommsen's theory of the '*plebs contionalis*', a group of shopkeepers and craftsmen active around the Forum who regularly turned up for meetings and assemblies and de facto impersonated the *populus Romanus* on these occasions.[24] The evidence for this hypothesis is limited, however, and it also implies that a few hundred traders, belonging to a class for which the Roman elite normally had nothing but disdain, effectively were allowed to control the legislative process.[25]

---

[22] As Moreau 2003 showed, the examples from the late republic of audiences being encouraged to respond to rhetorical questions put by the speakers were departures from the norm, since this type of *rogatio* rightfully belonged to the *comitia*.

[23] We have no concrete evidence for the scale of attendance at *contiones* but the venues used were all relatively small and, crucially, acoustically quite difficult spaces with obvious implications for audibility. Cf. Betts 2011: 124–9.

[24] Mommsen 1854–5: 2.94; Meier 1980: 114; Eder 1996: 443; Jehne 2006a; 2013d; 2014b: 127–8.

[25] If such small, compact groups really did control Roman legislation, we might also wonder why the opponents of a bill never mobilised counter crowds, which should have been a relatively easy task given the scale of the urban population.

The closer one looks at these meetings the more problematic the notion of *contiones* as foci of popular power becomes. Wilfried Nippel, for example, accepted that 'The composition of the assembly was different every time', but explained the largely affirmative role of the assembly by suggesting that 'the supporters of a particular proposal were likely to appear in numbers, with the result that the tribune taking the initiative has a very good chance of obtaining the majority of the tribes' votes'.[26] However, the opponents of a given measure held counter *contiones* of their own, which in principle would neutralise the efforts of those in favour. With competing meetings being held – usually for different but equally supportive crowds – it would have been impossible to tell who would prevail at the final vote. This situation is illustrated by the struggle over the *rogatio Servilia* in 63, when both Rullus and Cicero organised separate meetings, apparently with similarly positive responses. Conversely, it could be argued that a negative reception did not exclude the possibility that among the vast Roman electorate other citizens might be more sympathetic; it could simply be a question of failed mobilisation which could be improved next time round.

The feedback received from a *contio* was, in other words, an uncertain guide to 'popular opinion' – if such a thing ever existed. The underlying assumption seems to be that the *contio* served as a Roman equivalent of modern focus groups, which are used by politicians and marketers to test the waters before launching new policies, products or advertisements. The parallel does not work, however, for whereas participants of focus groups are carefully selected to ensure that they are representative, based on sophisticated models and demographic profiling, Roman *contiones* were filled with self-selecting, in principle unpredictable, crowds. They were potentially also unstable and fluctuating, with different people turning out for different meetings and in different numbers. Persuading a *contio* to support a given bill would therefore not have guaranteed its smooth passage through the final assembly.

Some scholars have tackled the logistical problem by envisaging the existence of a single, measurable 'popular opinion' or 'will of the people', which would render the question of turnouts obsolete since most citizens held broadly similar views on most issues.[27] The notion of 'the People' as a monolithic entity seems indebted to the constitutional fiction which

---

[26] Nippel 1995: 47. Tiersch 2009: 48 assumes greater attendance at *comitia* than at *contiones*, which would be odd since the former almost invariably said yes.

[27] Flaig 2003: 155–231; Morstein-Marx 2004.

defined the *populus* in abstract terms, e.g. in the famous pairing with *senatus*. Needless to say, however, the social and demographic landscape of republican Rome must have been far too complex and varied to be reduced to a simple model of 'senate' and 'people'. The degree of unanimity implied in the concept of the 'popular will' seems unrealistic given the size and diversity of the non-senatorial population. Speakers always addressed a symbolic *populus* as well as a concrete audience, and whichever opinion may have been expressed by the latter is by definition unlikely to have been that of the *populus Romanus*. At the heart of the Roman *contio* lies a fundamental ambiguity – between the *populus* and the actual crowds present at the meeting – which will have to be disentangled if we are to understand the communication that took place there.

The notion of a 'popular will' expressed at *contiones* and assemblies has paradoxical political implications. If we assume that the 'People' voted for proposals they liked and had been persuaded to endorse, we find ourselves confronted with a remarkable degree of inconsistency, given the wide range of laws and measures that were passed, pursuing very different aims and policies. The assembly, as Morstein-Marx noted, approved numerous laws opposed by most of the senate and its leaders.[28] But on other occasions it abrogated these very same measures or passed laws seemingly contrary to the people's own interest.[29] Brennan, for example, identified 'a volte face on the part of the people', when the assembly first deprived the disgraced C. Hostilius Mancinus of his citizenship in 135, only to restore him again shortly afterwards.[30] Does the fact that the assembly adopted measures diametrically opposed to each other imply that the 'People' had suddenly changed its mind on Mancinus' culpability? We are left with a strikingly fluid and malleable 'will of the people', for which the small, self-selecting crowds at *contiones* nevertheless managed to provide such an effective barometer that not a single proposal failed in the *comitia* during the late republic. This is all the more surprising since contional crowds, as far as we can judge from the first-century evidence, were generally favourable towards those who had called the meetings. If the audiences supported the organisers – who consulted them precisely in order to gauge public opinion – that would have undermined their ability to act as 'focus groups' even further.

---

[28] Morstein-Marx 2013 listed thirty laws passed against senatorial opposition between 140 and 50.
[29] E.g. the abrogation of C. Gracchus' grain law, Cic. *Brut.* 222. The assembly also gave Sulla's *voluntas* the force of law, *Ver.* 2.3.82, cf. App. *BC* 1.99; Plu. *Sull.* 33.1. Cf. Vervaet 2004.
[30] Brennan 2014: 41.

Taking account of this feature, Robert Morstein-Marx gave the 'contio-model' a new twist, since he interpreted the acquiescent crowds as a sign of asymmetrical communication taking place at contiones, where speakers always held the upper hand and were able to shape opinion through their superior knowledge and skill.[31] The argument seems to overlook the fact that in the competitive world of Roman politics different contiones would have sent different messages, in theory cancelling each other out. This affects Morstein-Marx' 'pars pro toto' model of participation, which implies that small groups attended the contiones and then through a seemingly osmotic process spread the message to the rest of the population, thereby shaping the 'popular will'. But if the messages they received at contiones were mixed, so was their input into 'public opinion'.

Recently, the examples of laws passed against 'significant senatorial resistance' led Morstein-Marx to modify his earlier thesis of an aristocratic 'cultural hegemony', partly based on contiones.[32] However, instead of seeing these bills as 'successful assertions of popular sovereignty' one could argue that the assembly simply conformed to established norms and ratified all measures put before it. What we observe in the later republic may be a growing willingness of tribunes to defy the senate and go ahead with proposals opposed by its majority, rather than any shift in voting behaviour. Viewed from that perspective the assembly remained entirely consistent, even when they, as in the Mancinus case, ratified bills that contradicted each other.

In formal and ideological terms the contio formed an essential part of the 'inclusive' construction of the res publica, its procedures reflecting the ideals of popular rights and 'sovereignty' combined with magisterial leadership and aristocratic oversight. But as a practical means of consulting the electorate it was not a viable institution, especially during the later republic when Rome had far outgrown the 'village-format' on which the model relies. In that period the small-scale meetings can hardly have performed the role which they have been accorded in the recent debate. Finally, and perhaps most detrimental to the theory, there is in fact no solid evidence that proposals were ever withdrawn in the face of contional discontent. And given the rarity of comitial rejections it is indeed hard to see why any would-be legislator would abandon his bill for that reason; during the first century the possibility was largely hypothetical, few Romans being able to remember when it had last occurred. Many proposals failed to become law, but that happened for a variety of reasons, popular hostility at contiones not

[31] Morstein-Marx 2004.   [32] Morstein-Marx 2013.

being one of them. The most common factors were tribunician veto and physical obstruction, but peer pressure and general elite opposition probably also played an important part.

If *contiones* are unlikely to have generated such all-embracing popular consensus that ratification became the standard outcome, we are back where we started with regard to the *comitia* and their apparent rubber-stamping of laws, which still requires an explanation. Moreover, we will also have to ask why Roman magistrates kept calling public meetings if their impact on the success and failure of bills remained so limited.

Comitia as 'Civic Rituals'

Confronted with a procedure that formally represented an act of decision-making but in practice functioned as an expression of consensus we may follow the example of Keith Hopkins, who first approached the comitial procedures as 'rituals', i.e. highly formalised actions, performed according to strict rules and invested with a significance that extended beyond the acts themselves.[33] Through their regular performance rituals have the potential to become essential and necessary elements of the collective identity of a community. They do, however, have to be accepted as such by the participants, especially in cases such as this, where the assembled citizens were presented with an open question that in principle could have been answered negatively. The fact they largely abstained from exercising the choice put to them implies that the participants agreed to the formal terms of the ritual. How that happened must remain conjecture. Still, some possible factors may be identified, including the strong sense of hierarchy which characterised these occasions. The presiding official exercised full authority over the assembled crowd, literally there at his personal request. When he asked for its sanction, the logical response was one of compliance and conformity; in formal terms the *comitia* had one and only one function and that was to express the consent of the *populus*. Crowds gathered for a *comitia* adopted the mantle of 'the People' and in doing so became participants in a highly formalised and carefully choreographed ritual which had as its expected, almost inevitable, outcome the ratification of the proposal.

---

[33] Hopkins 1991. The approach was further developed by Flaig 1995a; 2003; Jehne 2001; 2013a: 118; cf. Timmer 2008: 313–14. Flaig's suggestion that they served as means of 'Sozialdisziplinierung' is doubtful, however, since attendance would have been so limited that most citizens never experienced the ritual first-hand.

The shaping and conditioning of participant behaviour through institutional structures and social conventions are not specific to Rome but can be encountered also in modern societies. John North noted, for example, that while the Council at British universities formally has the final say on all important matters, in reality its hands are tied by the logic of the decision-making process; for when a proposal reaches the Council – after long planning and several committee stages etc. – it is generally considered too late to change course and reverse the policy.[34] The process has at that point gained a momentum which in effect neutralises the choice that is supposed to be exercised on that occasion. Similarly, the Annual General Meeting of large corporations in theory offers shareholders the opportunity to hold the board and executives to account, but in practice tends to be a mere formality; when annual reports and proposals reach the AGM they are virtually certain of approval, since the crucial negotiations with major shareholders have already taken place beforehand. In fact, it is generally seen as inappropriate to let internal divisions surface in public or to use the shareholder meeting for actual decision-making. Tellingly, when smaller shareholders try to do that, it is often presented as a 'revolt' rather than the exercise of legitimate voting rights.

The Roman assemblies appear to have been imbued with similar expectations of consent which only concerted outside campaigning could reverse. It might even have been considered improper to use these 'ritual' occasions for 'political' ends, although from an ideological point of view it remained hugely important that the vote *could* go against the organiser; otherwise the meaning of the event – and the popular legitimacy derived from it – would be lost. Still, the voting patterns we can observe suggest this was a largely theoretical possibility – and intentionally so. In fact, it is a moot point whether the assembly had ever functioned as a decision-making body. Since the assembly in effect was *some* people symbolically representing *the* People, it could hardly have been allowed to behave as if it were the *populus Romanus*. Regular rejection of bills would have exposed the gap between the two, undermined its role as a formal representation of the *populus* and made the assembly a focus of contention rather than consensus.

The ritual status of the assembly was challenged only in exceptional instances, when dissident members of the elite brought their disagreements into a realm that was normally insulated from political strife. In those instances it was a question of politics 'spilling over' into the ratification

---

[34] North 2002.

procedure, which was usually kept separate. The taboo associated with such behaviour is underlined not just by the rarity with which it happened but also by the consternation it appears to have caused. The implication is that opponents of a bill generally accepted that when it finally – even after much debate, perhaps even acrimony – was put before the assembly the battle to prevent it becoming law was over – and effectively lost. Despite the small numbers required to change the outcome there seem to have been virtually no attempts to mobilise counter-crowds to block contentious bills. Even during the turbulent – and exceptionally well-documented – first century there are no recorded rejections, suggesting the assemblies retained their traditional role as purely affirmative bodies, passing laws of widely different political colouration and intent with almost mechanical predictability.[35]

In 58, Cicero wrote several letters to Atticus from his exile, discussing the campaign for his recall and the obstacles it faced. Among them were the *sanctio* clauses included in Clodius' law, which sought to prevent even the discussion of Cicero's restoration, as well as the risk of a tribunician veto, which appears to have been his primary source of concern.[36] What is strikingly absent from these deliberations is any worry that the assembly might turn the bill down.[37] Similarly, a few years later in 56, Cicero discussed the various proposals to restore King Ptolemy of Egypt in letters to Lentulus Spinther, noting that 'As for the role of the people [i.e. the assembly], I think we have so managed that no proceedings in that quarter are possible without violation of the auspices and the laws, in fact without violence', which suggests that the preferences of the 'people' were entirely marginal to the discussion.[38] The question was which proposal managed to get before the assembly, not what the assembly thought about them.

Violence and disruption, along with tribunician intervention, became the common means of preventing proposals from becoming law – rather than comitial rejections. An imaginative alternative to this strategy is recorded in 61, when the senate compelled the consul Pupius Piso, despite his support for Clodius, to put forward a bill regarding the latter's trial for sacrilege, which suspended normal rules for juror selection. To sabotage

---

[35] *Pace* Morstein-Marx 2013.

[36] *Att.* 3.15.6 (SB 60), Cicero wondered whether the abrogation could go through without the unanimous approval of the tribunes, 'ac si per populum, poteritne nisi de omnium tribunorum pl. sententia?'. Cf. 3.23.1–5 (SB 68); 3.24.1 (SB 69).

[37] Cf. Cic. *Q. fr.* 1.4.3 (SB 4), where he expresses concerns about Clodius' gangs and a possible tribunician veto, but not about getting the bill through the *comitia*.

[38] *Fam.* 1.2.4 (SB 13): 'Quod ad popularem rationem attinet, hoc videmur esse consecuti, ut ne quid agi cum populo aut salvis auspiciis aut salvis legibus aut denique sine vi posset', cf. *Fam.* 1.4.3 (SB 14).

his own bill Piso allegedly distributed voting ballots without any yes signs (or only no-ballots), suggesting this was the safest, perhaps the only, way to prevent its routine ratification in the assembly. As it happened, leading senators intervened before it came to a vote.[39]

But if legislative assemblies were civic rituals invested with an intrinsic logic that was hardly ever challenged by those taking part, the question is why anyone took the trouble to turn up. What was the point of investing time and effort, if, as it seems, the result was entirely predictable? The issue must be put into perspective, since numbers are likely to have been quite small, for practical as well as political reasons. As we saw, there are indications that attendance might be extremely low, so low that some *tribus* might not even be represented (Cic. *Sest.* 109). Nevertheless, some citizens obviously did turn up, and although their motivation can only be conjectured, we cannot exclude the possibility that participation in civic rituals of this kind may have conveyed a sense of community and shared citizenship.[40] Performing one's role as a Roman citizen made sense as a re-enactment of the basic values of the *res publica*, providing a collective, civic experience, irrespective of the outcome. Still, whatever attraction the assemblies may have held, comitial attendance never became a regular part of daily life in the capital, or one that attracted large sections of the populace; for the bulk of the city's inhabitants the assemblies must have remained outside their normal field of experience.

If those who voted in assemblies by necessity represented a small sub-section of the urban population, the question is who they were. In formal terms the assembled crowds always represented the *populus Romanus* and the sources consistently describe them as such, which means we have little concrete evidence to go by. Still, the fact that Roman assemblies were both frequent and time-consuming, and no effort was ever made to encourage mass participation, practically, politically or financially, would *a priori* militate against substantial 'working-class' turnouts.[41] In many cases, participation would have meant personal sacrifices of time and income, for which the celebration of citizenship and *libertas* is unlikely to have provided adequate compensation.

It follows that the politically active section of the population was most likely the one with sufficient time and resources, which should come as no surprise since typically that has been the case in most polities. Rome was,

---

[39] *Att.* 1.14.5 (SB 14): 'operae Clodianae pontis occuparent; tabellae ministrabantur ita ut nulla daretur "uti rogas"', cf. Luisi 1995; Flaig 2003: 188–91. Nicolet 1970: 125 suggests that voters received two ballots, one for and one against, and Piso failed to distribute any of the latter.

[40] As suggested by Jehne 2013a: 119–21.   [41] *Pace* Jehne 2006a; 2013a.

like other pre-modern societies, characterised by a vast distance between rich and poor, and the existence of a substantial, middling group of 'ordinary Romans' somewhere between these extremes cannot be taken for granted.[42] Roman society was not just deeply polarised but also in many respects divided and layered along lines very different from those of later Western societies. The extensive use of slaves and freedmen in all parts of the economy would have prevented the emergence of an educated, professional, urban class comparable to those constituting the middle classes of the early modern period.[43] At the same time, large-scale population movements – and the absence of any social safety net – must have provided fertile ground for the emergence of a substantial underclass.[44]

In the city of Rome the differentiation would have been particularly complex. Economically, we must envisage a social scale which included the structurally poor, who lacked stable income and/or residence; dependent as well as independent skilled workers; residents with modest businesses that relieved them of manual work; and finally more substantial property owners ranging from the affluent to the super-rich. The economic scale was intersected by legal distinctions (citizens/non-citizens, free/unfree, freed/freeborn), and ethnic descriptors (native Romans, Romans of Italian origin and provincials). Residency also played a role, given the likely scale of immigration, where we must distinguish between seasonal workers, immigrants and long-term residents. Finally, there were questions of social relationship and connections, since some Romans enjoyed elite patronage, while others did not; some were embedded in local social networks, whereas others, perhaps recent arrivals, were socially more isolated. Given these multiple social, economic, legal, and ethnic subdivisions of the Roman population the search for the elusive 'man in the street' faces insurmountable obstacles. Certainly, the simple equation of 'ordinary Romans' with independent and reasonably comfortable shopkeepers and artisans will no longer do.[45]

---

[42] Scobie's 1986 study of poverty in Rome remains a classic. Scheidel and Friesen 2009: 62 suggested a wide gap between rich and poor, concluding that: ' . . . the vast majority of the population lived close to subsistence . . . '. They also identify a separate 'middling group', distinct from the elite, but such a category is likely to have been quite fluid, economically as well as socially, cf. Mouritsen 2015b.

[43] As already Finley 1983: 11 observed: ' . . . we must sedulously avoid the modern corollary of a substantial middle class with its own defined interests'. For the recent attempts to invent such a class, e.g. Veyne 2000 (whose 'plebs media' is adopted by Courrier 2014: 299–421) and Mayer 2012, see Mouritsen 2012; Wallace-Hadrill 2013. On the impact of slavery on Roman social structure, see Mouritsen 2011b; 2015b; 2017.

[44] Morley 2009; Scheidel and Friesen 2009; Holleran 2011.   [45] See also Holleran 2012.

Politics would logically have been the preserve of the *boni*, who enjoyed the leisure, interest, and information required to take part. As John North observed: 'All theories have to reckon with the possibility that the voters were in fact only a slightly wider section of the political elite than the senatorial class, and that the whole political process had little or nothing to do with the poorer classes in Roman society.'[46] Most likely, comitial participation was considered a natural part of the lifestyle of the Roman gentlemen who frequented the Forum on a regular basis.[47] When a bill was to be ratified, they probably obligingly performed their civic duty and spent some hours in the voting pens, conversing with their fellow *tribules*.[48] The attendance of these groups must have contributed to the conformity of the *comitia*, since the participants broadly belonged to the same propertied classes as the politicians themselves, with whom many would have been personally acquainted. They were, in other words, not just those with the greatest ability and motivation to be there; they probably also were those with the least inclination to assert themselves against the office-holding class. A broad community of interest would have linked politicians and voters.

This understanding of the *comitia* as political and to some extent social rituals brings us back to the role of the *contiones*. The centrality of these meetings is well documented, although their connection with the legislative process has turned out to be tenuous at best. There is little evidence that they served as crucial testing grounds for new policies, whose fate depended on a positive reception at the preceding *contiones*. We may therefore look for their significance elsewhere.

Audience and Communication at *Contiones*

The Roman *contio* presents us with a fundamental paradox: their importance to the political process seems beyond doubt, but we cannot pinpoint precisely what made them so important. They were held with great frequency and treated as occasions of genuine significance. Indeed, politicians addressed the small, in principle arbitrary, audiences as if they really

---

[46] North 2007: 274–5.

[47] On the clearing of the Forum of traders and its transformation into a formal, representative space during the republic see Morel 1987; Hölscher 2001: 190–202. On the remaining trades, see Papi 2002.

[48] Paradoxically, the Roman elite were expected to know their *tribules* personally, despite the fact that each *tribus* counted thousands of widely-dispersed members, cf. e.g. Cic. *Att.* 1.18.4 (SB 18); 1.19.5 (SB 19); *Fam.* 13.23.1 (SB 289); 13.58.1 (SB 140); *Comm. pet.* 17, 24. Most likely, however, they were directly acquainted only with the small circle of prominent *tribules* that regularly participated in *comitia*.

mattered – despite the fact that they took no decisions. In recent years the *contio* has taken centre stage in discussions about the nature of Roman politics and has, depending on approach, come to represent either democracy in action or – less commonly – democracy subverted. For many historians, *contiones* stand as incontrovertible manifestations of basic democratic principles expressed through regular communication between leaders and masses and the public testing of political arguments.[49] As we saw, modern interpretations of the *contio* have tended to focus narrowly on the link between *contiones* and legislative assemblies. This connection is, of course, irrefutable, at least at a strictly procedural level, but it could be argued that the two types of meetings were essentially different in nature and served very different purposes.

As a starting point for exploring the *contio* we may consider the simple questions: 'who was talking to whom – and why?' Recent scholarship has paid relatively little attention to practical issues of attendance, concentrating more on the communicative process itself, the rhetorical strategies and the debates performed in front of this audience. Most often the Romans' own definition of political crowds as the *populus* has been accepted at face value.[50] In formal terms, that is, of course, perfectly true; any gathering of people, no matter how small and unrepresentative, convened by a magistrate according to the established rules, *did* represent the *populus*. However, as a description of the actual crowds, their social composition and economic profile, it is evidently of little use. The challenge is therefore to move beyond this constitutional fiction, which is so pervasive in our sources that we have almost nothing to go by when trying to discern who were actually there. Still, the scarcity of evidence does not allow us to ignore the issue, let alone to reduce the complex social reality of republican Rome to a binary division of leaders and masses, mirroring the constitutional duality of *senatus populusque Romanus*.

There are good reasons for doubting the conventional image of socially inclusive events filled with crowds of 'ordinary Romans', or at least a broad cross-section of all classes and orders. Already by the middle republic Rome had become a metropolis where the Forum Romanum no longer

---

[49] The extent of this communication should not be overstated. Most senators never addressed a *contio*, and many reached high office with minimal contional experience, cf. Mouritsen 2013.

[50] E.g. Flaig 2003; Tiersch 2009: 58, who referred to 'Kommunikation zwischen Senat und Volk'; Yakobson 2010. Beness and Hillard 2012: 279 described the crowd as 'a broad cross-section'. Even Hölkeskamp 2010: 72 refers to participants as 'the mass of ordinary citizens', and suggests that the 'audience represented . . . the *populus Romanus* and its *res* – and by no means only in an abstract and detached ideological sense'.

functioned as the local village green. As Rome outgrew the boundaries of a simple, face-to-face society, the notion of the Forum as a shared space where high and low mingled with each other becomes increasingly anachronistic. Not only were there fundamental logistical obstacles, but the socio-economic logic of Rome's growth also led to spatial differentiation and a concentration of elite activities in and around the central square, including court proceedings, financial transactions, high-end shopping and, of course, politics.

It should come as no surprise therefore if it was the leisured classes, with time, interest and resources, who attended the *contiones* as well as the *comitia*. This would conform to a typical pattern observed in many societies across time; as Kostas Vlassopoulos noted: ' ... Athens was exceptional in the degree it decided to use communal resources to enhance the participation of ordinary citizens. For most other political communities, from antiquity until modern times, the fact that the largest part of the population had to devote their time to making a living, provided a natural justification for confining the "political nation" to an elite of leisure and wealth, which was able to devote itself to public affairs.'[51] In Rome, no steps were ever taken to promote participation, neither were any financial rewards offered as compensation to the working population. It is therefore not obvious why Rome, uniquely among known polities, should have bucked what otherwise appears to be a universal trend.

The notion of diverse crowds with a substantial 'popular' presence raises a number of practical and political issues. How did the small plebeian minority that might have attended a given *contio* constitute itself? Were they simply passing by the Forum and somehow lingered to listen to speeches? Or did they go there specifically to hear more about a political issue that interested them? As we saw, Nippel suggested they were 'supporters of a particular proposal'. But how would they know about the proposal when the topics of *contiones* were not advertised in advance? And what about the meetings that were held by opponents of a proposal or dealt with quite uncontroversial issues? Moreover, if people generally turned up to endorse a politician, the character of *contiones* becomes more akin to partisan gatherings than the open communication between leaders and masses envisaged by modern historians.

---

[51] Vlassopoulos 2010: 81. Among Roman historians the new paradigm is now so well established that my own attempt (2001) to restate what used to be the conventional position has been described as 'the most controversial contribution to the discussion', Beness and Hillard 2012: 279. Cf. e.g. Tiersch 2009: 46–7 n.42.

Alternatively, as we saw, it has been suggested that the meetings were filled by a regular '*plebs contionalis*', composed of shopkeepers and artisans from around the Forum. Such a crowd would not, of course, have represented the '*populus*' any more than the men of leisure, who tend to dominate participatory politics, and the theory also raises issues of practical and economic feasibility. Some *tabernarii*, as Jehne noted, may have been able to put slaves and relatives in charge when they wished to attend *contiones*.[52] However, the notion of a distinct '*plebs contionalis*' implies regular participation in events held almost daily over extended periods. In that case their political activity becomes a full-time occupation rather than an occasional pastime. The '*plebs contionalis*' presents an insuperable paradox; not only would these small traders seem to be those with the least time to spare, but the theory also implies that the Forum was largely empty apart from them. But in reality they would, of course, at any time have been outnumbered by the affluent customers who frequented their shops and by all those who came to do business and politics in and around the Forum. In his speech for Flaccus, Cicero noted the difference between Greek and Roman assemblies, the latter being characterised by a more elevated social profile; indeed the Forum was 'full of courts, full of magistrates, full of the most eminent men and citizens'.[53] Did these crowds suddenly vanish from the Forum whenever a *contio* was called, leaving the political centre to small traders and craftsmen who rushed to take their place?

A further question concerns the motivation of the putative '*plebs contionalis*'. What would have induced these relatively humble citizens to spend so much time at meetings where their role was limited to that of passive listeners? It has been suggested that members of the lower classes might have been drawn to *contiones* by the attraction of hearing aristocratic leaders of state addressing them in elevated terms as the *populus* and pleading for their support.[54] It is not difficult to imagine how such performances, however formalised, of the basic tenets of the *res publica* – and the reversal of social hierarchies it involved – may have appealed to disadvantaged Roman citizens who otherwise had little to feel proud of in their lives. But in that case we are dealing with a general motivation, in

---

[52] Jehne 2013a: 121. Cf. p. 63 above.

[53] *Flac.* 57: 'plenum iudiciorum, plenum magistratuum, plenum optimorum virorum et civium'. There are plenty of references to politicians and their followers occupying the Forum, e.g. Cic. *Div. Caec.* 50; *Mur.* 21, 44; *Att.* 1.18.1 (SB 18); 2.1.5 (21); *Comm. pet.* 2, 54, and to wealthy businessmen filling the space, Cic. *Man.* 19; *Comm. pet.* 29.

[54] Jehne 2013a; 2013b; 2013d.

principle shared by most Roman citizens, which only a very small minority acted upon – and indeed did so with remarkable frequency. If people generally enjoyed listening to their social superiors extolling the greatness of the *populus Romanus*, why did only members of the '*plebs contionalis*' turn up? There seems to be an incongruity between the universality of the impulse and the very limited response it triggered, effectively restricted to those running small businesses within short walking distance. And while the theory may explain popular participation from a psychological perspective (if not its localised nature), it leaves other questions open; why did the elite attach such importance to the events if they merely involved addressing the same (humble) crowd of regular meeting-goers? What was it about these traders that made the elite invest such time and effort into persuading them of their case?

Studies of (published) speeches delivered at *contiones* have concluded that they assume a surprisingly detailed knowledge of a wide variety of subjects ranging from history to law and politics.[55] When reading Cicero's surviving contional addresses one is struck not just by their considerable length but also by the complexity of the arguments and the scope of their cultural references. This takes them well beyond the rousing 'pep talks' one might have expected if he had been addressing a heterogeneous crowd composed of people from all walks of life. Most Romans had probably received little formal education and enjoyed limited access to reliable information about politics and current affairs.[56] The preserved speeches therefore suggest an audience belonging to the relatively narrow social stratum whose background and social connections enabled them to grasp their content and implication. Most historians nevertheless assume relatively broad popular involvement in Roman politics, albeit on a paradoxically small scale. The suspension of the class distinctions and economic constraints that normally govern political participation places Rome in a unique historical position. The departure from the norm which that represents would seem to put the onus of proof on the proponents of this theory. However, looking more closely at the evidence reveals remarkably little support for the idea of widespread lower-class participation.

---

[55] Morstein-Marx 2004: 117 concluded that: ' . . . the audiences of public speeches were expected to be quite aware of the Roman past and present, and were treated as involved and regular participants in political affairs', which hardly sounds like a description of the urban masses of a pre-modern metropolis. Cf. Williamson 1990: 271; Van der Blom 2010: 118; Jehne 2011: 123 n.25.

[56] On literacy, Harris 1989 is fundamental, cf. Mouritsen 2015c. On political information, see Laurence 1994.

The most famous reference to the social profile of contional crowds comes from July 61, when Cicero pondered the benefits of friendship with Pompey. Among the advantages was the support of – or at least peace with – the crowd that adored the great general, which Cicero dismissed as 'that miserable and starving mob that goes to *contiones* and sucks the treasury dry'. In the same context he even called them 'sordem urbis et faecem'.[57] While this passage would at the very least suggest a socially diverse crowd, there are also occasions where the audiences at *contiones* are associated with the elite. Thus, when describing Pompey's troubles in 56, Cicero mentions that the 'contionarius populus' was practically estranged from him, the nobility hostile, the senate unfair and the youth wicked.[58] The close link between the 'contionarius populus', the *nobilitas*, the senate, and the *iuventus*, a term normally used to describe younger members of the aristocracy, suggests we are here dealing with a far more elevated section of the *populus* than the mob dismissed by Cicero in 61.[59] His comments on the whole-hearted support for Bibulus and Curio in their stand against Caesar in 59 also suggest a Forum crowd dominated by the well-to-do. For example, he notes the popularity of Curio in the Forum, where Caesar's man Fufius is pursued by the *boni* with shouts and hisses, while also stressing the popularity of Bibulus, whose edicts and *contiones* are written down and read by the Forum crowd.[60]

Given the scarcity of ancient evidence, the theory of broad popular participation ultimately seems to rely on the assumption that contional crowds would not have been described as the *populus Romanus* unless they bore some relation to the populace as a whole. But here we have to bear in mind that in Roman political discourse any formal gathering automatically assumed the status of the *populus*. Although it would have been evident to

---

[57] *Att.* 1.16.11 (SB 16): ' . . . illa contionalis hirudo aerari, misera ac ieiuna plebecula'. Cicero's reference to 'imperitissimi' attending *contiones* is not a generalisation about contional crowds but a hypothetical scenario where 'even the most ignorant' are able to see through the populism of some speakers, *Amic.* 95: 'contio quae ex imperitissimis constat'. Cicero therefore never characterises contional crowds in general terms as 'imperiti', *pace* Jehne 2011: 115; 2013a: 121; 2014b: 130. The oratory aimed at 'auribus imperitorum', mentioned in *Brut.* 223, relates specifically to *contiones* of *seditiosi*, whose crowds are often denounced as such. Moreover, even jurors, all belonging to the elite, could be described as 'imperiti' in some contexts, Cic. *Fin.* 4.74, and in *Brut.* 184–9 Cicero distinguishes between 'imperiti' and 'docti', the latter being experts in oratory.

[58] *Q. fr.* 2.3.4: 'contionario illo populo a se prope alienato, nobilitate inimica, non aequo senatu, iuventute improba'.

[59] *Pace* Wiseman 2009: 2, who took these two passages as proof of the plebeian profile of political crowds. He also invoked Cicero's reference to 'turba et barbaria forensis', *De orat.* 1.118, which describes rowdy crowds attending trials and therefore is unrelated to the question of political participation, cf. Mouritsen 2013.

[60] *Att.* 2.18.1 (SB 38); 2.20.4 (SB 40); 2.21.4 (SB 41).

any observer that speakers in the Forum did not address 'the people' but 'some people', the Romans consistently used the abstract term *populus* to describe them. Cicero could, for example, publicly declare that in 63 'populus Romanus universus' had been present at the *contio* which unanimously approved his actions (*Pis.* 7). Despite the obvious hyperbole it was from a constitutional perspective perfectly true. The problem arises when this convention is taken at face value as a description of the actual crowds.

The willingness to accept the constitutional fiction of the *populus* is in many respects puzzling and may deserve closer consideration. It probably reflects the new emphasis on the 'power of the people' in Rome, which can itself be seen as part of a broader cultural shift in Western academia over recent generations. There is now much greater interest in writing history 'from below', focusing on the lives of 'ordinary' people, with a view to recovering their experiences and voices. In the study of ancient Rome this trend has revived the study of, for example, slavery and gender, while in the field of republican political history we have seen a reaction against the attitudes prevalent in much older scholarship and expressed, for example, in concerns about the dangerous urban 'mob'. Following this change in outlook historians have become more inclined to present 'the people' as a valued and responsible participant in the political process, no longer an apathetic, let alone irresponsible, underclass, but informed agents with views and interests actively pursued in public fora. This retrospective 'empowering' of the Roman plebs raises some historical as well as ethical issues, however. Attributing to the masses an influence they did not have adds little to our understanding of Roman politics, and there is a further risk that by 'rehabilitating' the plebs in this way we may end up downplaying the poverty and deprivation which large parts of the urban population must have suffered.

The picture of an almost modern 'middle class' attending the Roman assemblies – broadly educated, financially comfortable, politically engaged – may be an understandable response to the 'fickle mob' stereotype that once dominated modern historiography. Restoring the dignity of the much-maligned Roman masses has indeed been long overdue but we should at the same time not overlook the abject destitution many of them experienced. The social landscape of the metropolis must have been dominated by a wide gap between rich and poor, and the former's extensive reliance on unfree and tied labour probably left little room for an independent and secure, 'middling' social category to emerge. Viewed from this perspective it may be more realistic to assume that the bulk of the urban citizens were absent from political events. Their very poverty alienated them from the world of the governing classes, for whom they remained a marginal and largely undifferentiated mass, usually described in generic, derogatory terms as the *vulgus* or *multitudo*. This marginality was only in part due to aristocratic snobbery, although that, of course, was manifest; the main reason the masses – as opposed to the abstract *populus* or the hugely important *boni* – feature so little in elite discourse was precisely their limited ability to shape political events through the formal channels.

Doubting how much real power the Roman plebs exercised is therefore no different from acknowledging the limited influence of other under-privileged classes throughout history. These may well develop rich 'political cultures' of their own, but we rarely hear about them, and by necessity they tended to remain separate from the world of official politics. Accepting the political marginalisation of the plebs does not, in other words, make them 'apolitical'; it merely implies that their interests and concerns were distinct from those of the elite and probably pursued through different means. These means were primarily direct action, informal gatherings and riots, their strength lying in superior numbers and in the latent threat that posed to the elite. As Finley rightly observed: ' . . . it would not be far from the truth to say that the Roman *populus* exercised influence not through participation in the formal machinery of government, through its voting power, but by taking to the streets, by agitation, demonstrations and riots, and this long before the days of the gangs and private armies of the civil-war century'.[61] The fact that the people lacked effective constitutional representation did not entail that the people had no objective political interests or that power in the Roman state was not being constantly negotiated; but their part in this negotiation took place largely outside the official framework.[62]

Why Did the Romans Hold *Contiones*?

This conclusion takes us back to the purpose and function of *contiones*. Understanding Roman *contiones* presents modern historians with a very particular challenge, since they operated on a symbolic/ideological level while at the same time fulfilling an important practical role in the political process. The two sides are closely entwined and any interpretation must seek to accommodate both. *Contiones* were an essential part of Roman

[61] Finley 1983: 91.
[62] In *Ver.* 2.5.143, Cicero stresses that the people exercise its influence through *existimatio* (public opinion) and *frequentia* (numbers).

political life, which no politician could entirely ignore. They were not simply
instruments of persuasion used to prepare new legislation. The *contio* embodied the fundamental principles of the free *res publica*, founded on *libertas*
and popular 'sovereignty'. This premise automatically lent the political
process a strong public aspect, since the *populus* formally had to be consulted
and informed on all issues, and the ideological significance of the *contio* lay
precisely in the fact that it represented the public side of the political process.
It could therefore be hailed as one of the basic institutions safeguarding the
republic against tyranny. In Cicero's long letter to Quintus on provincial
governorship it is, for example, the *contio* rather than the *comitia* that
features among the pillars of freedom and security.[63]

The *res publica* as a political system based on the sharing and devolving
of power was entirely dependent on the observance of open, transparent
procedures. The senate, for all its influence on foreign and domestic policy,
did not function as a parliament and could never do so. Not only did
it have limited formal powers, but it was also an exclusive body whose
proceedings remained inaccessible to the *populus*. Roman politics, on the
other hand, was by definition public in the sense that it had to take place in
the open and in principle be available to all citizens. For that reason,
debates could never be confined to the Curia, and it was the *contio* that
formally constituted the principal guarantor of the people's *libertas*. All
matters of state, including routine transactions, had to be announced
before the *populus* (however notional) in order to gain validity, and all
new initiatives had to be presented to successive *contiones* before they could
be ratified in the *comitia*. *Senatus consulta* were read out at *contiones*, and
in 59 the candidates were obliged to pronounce a curse clause, *exsecratio*, at
a *contio* for the simple reason that otherwise it would not have been
public.[64] Cicero therefore also renounced his province at a *contio* and
could refer to a letter read out in a *contio* in the sense of being brought to
the public's attention.[65]

---

[63] *Q. fr.* 1.1.22 (SB 1), on the situation in the provinces where governors rule supreme, and 'nullum
auxilium est, nulla conquestio, nullus senatus, nulla contio'. Similarly, the famous fragment of
Fannius' speech against the extension of citizenship to the Latins, Malcovati *ORF* 1.32.3 = Iul. Vict.
41.26, warned that the old citizens would be crowded out of the *contiones* (not the formally much
more important *comitia*) and their games and festivals, presenting the public meetings as one of their
essential civic privileges.

[64] Cic. *Att.* 2.18.2 (SB 38). In *Att.* 2.24.3 (SB 44) he also mentions that Vettius was presented at a *contio*
to give his version of the nebulous affair named after him, cf. *Sest.* 132; *Vat.* 24.

[65] *Fam.* 5.2.3 (SB 2); *Att.* 8.9.2 (SB 188). In *Att.* 15.15.2 (SB 393) fit for being 'read out in a *contio*'
('in contione dicere auderem') means suitable for public knowledge. For that reason Cicero could
also mention a letter that contained nothing that could not have been read out at a *contio*, i.e. cause
any embarrassment, *Fam.* 7.18.4 (SB 37).

Some *contiones* famously became the scene of heated exchanges and confrontations, but by focusing too closely on these incidents we may miss the real significance of the *contio* as the public face of the political process in general, providing a stage for all kinds of events ranging from humdrum announcements to dramatic debates. The convention that public actions must take place in full view of the *populus* was vital not just to the ideological construction of the *res publica*, but also to the political process itself, which required openness and consultation with groups outside the office-holding class. Thus, if we move beyond the simple equation of the constitutional *populus* with the actual people, it becomes apparent that outside the ranks of the senate there existed a substantial affluent stratum, which in many respects constituted the senators' political 'hinterland'. As already noted, Roman society had become far too complex and stratified to be captured by the simple duality *senatus populusque Romanus*. The senators were not identical with the elite; neither did they exist in a social vacuum. The politically active section of the elite was embedded in a broader class of the well-off, whose opinions could not be ignored.

Alongside the senators we find *equites*, whose wealth often exceeded that of their formal superiors, and even below the two highest *ordines* there would have been many with considerable means that relieved them of the need to work. Our sources typically refer to them as the *boni*, that is, respectable well-to-do pillars of society who commanded the respect and attention of the rulers of the Empire. These were people who mattered to the political class. Many of them had personal contacts with those in power, and through their domination of the first census class they held a controlling stake in the distribution of the highest offices. They probably also represented an important constituency in what might vaguely be called 'public opinion(s)', the sentiments and views heard when people met in the Forum, at morning receptions and at private social gatherings.[66] Communication between office holders and *principes* and this social and political 'hinterland' remained vital, and it may partly be the need for winning their hearts and minds that gave the *contio* its key role in Roman politics. As Cicero's speeches make clear, 'consensio omnium bonorum' remained a central value in political arguments, and it was above all at *contiones* that it was solicited and claimed.

Contiones were essential parts of an ongoing public dialogue about state affairs and policy, but they also served an important function in regulating

---

[66] For example, in *Att.* 7.13.3 (SB 136) Cicero expresses his concerns about 'opiniones' in Rome, in this case clearly those of the *boni*.

the legislative process. 'Public opinion' (however socially restricted) was a powerful tool in political negotiations and manoeuvrings, not necessarily because opposition might lead to rejection in the assembly (virtually unheard of, as we saw), but because it put real pressure on the key players. The Roman practice, by which the assemblies gave almost automatic approval to new proposals, may have succeeded in limiting direct popular input into decision-making, but it also left the magistrates with dangerous amounts of personal power. To prevent officials from making laws at will, a range of safeguards were developed, including the convention that proposals be approved by the senate beforehand, the principle of magisterial collegiality and the ability of tribunes to block each other's bills. Finally, when all these instruments had failed, the possibility remained that the law might be subsequently annulled on procedural grounds. Ideally, however, proposals that proved controversial and unacceptable to substantial sections of the elite would be quietly dropped. It is in this context that public speeches become significant as means of shaping 'public opinion' on any given issue.

The statutory, pre-comitial *contiones* held over a period of three market days were important because they offered a breathing space which allowed opponents to intervene and mobilise 'public opinion' against a bill. But rather than the mechanical scenario of audiences rejecting proposals that were then withdrawn to avoid defeat, we may envisage a more subtle process where meetings were called in order to build up momentum in public opinion for or against a proposal. Ideally, the magistrate would abandon the idea when faced with sufficiently strong opposition. Alternatively, a tribune might be persuaded to intervene and bring a swift end to the initiative, as happened in 63 when Cicero opposed Rullus' agrarian bill. Both sides made their case at competing *contiones*, and eventually the tribune L. Caecilius threatened a veto that forced Rullus to withdraw.[67] Whether Caecilius had been so impressed by Cicero's arguments that he felt compelled to intercede we cannot tell. But if Cicero's alarmist revelation of hidden dangers in Rullus' scheme had swayed opinion among important sections of society, it might well have encouraged the tribune to act. Much of the politicking would undoubtedly have taken place behind closed doors; still, the *contio* was where these issues were officially brought to the attention of wider sections of the elite.

---

[67] Cic. *Sul.* 65. Despite the doubts of Jehne 2013d: 51, it is difficult to see why Rullus otherwise should have withdrawn his carefully prepared *rogatio*, which – like any other bill – must have been virtually certain of ratification had it reached the *comitia*.

The potential link between *contiones* and tribunes draws attention to the intriguing pre-comitial debate known in modern literature as the *suasio-dissuasio*.[68] This was a formalised debate for and against a proposal held just before the *comitia* was about to vote. Some ancient authors, above all Livy, present it as a constituent part of the legislative process, the final opportunity for opponents and supporters of a bill to make their points before the assembled voters. The institution poses interesting questions given the voting patterns observed above, which imply that counter-arguments invariably failed. However, if this debate was merely another part of the 'ratification ritual', and in effect a piece of political theatre, the decision of opponents to speak up, sometimes with great fervour, becomes inexplicable. It suggests that despite the absence of comitial rejections they may have been politically significant at a different level.

The so-called *loca intercessionis* are particularly interesting in this context, since they indicate a connection between the *suasio-dissuasio* debate and the tribunician veto.[69] This rule referred to the particular moment in the proceedings when a tribune could legally submit his veto.[70] The sources indicate that a tribune had to wait until the formal debate had come to an end and all interested parties had had the chance to make their case. The implication is that the tribunes were a primary – and entirely logical – target of the arguments presented; at this late stage the fate of a bill effectively lay in the hands of these officials who decided whether to withdraw or maintain a veto.[71] For that reason tribunes were required to wait and listen to both sides before blocking a proposal or allowing it to become law. This function explains the apparent urgency of some reported debates, which may have been less about swaying the minds of voters than persuading tribunes one way or the other. Rhetorically, they were, of course, shaped as addresses to the *populus Romanus*, to whom all public oratory in principle was directed.

One of the fullest accounts of a *suasio-dissuasio* debate comes from Livy's description of the repeal of the *lex Oppia* in 195 (Liv. 34.1–8). The speeches

---

[68] Mommsen 1887: 3.394–6.

[69] As already noted by Mommsen 1887: 394 n.3. The pivotal role of the tribunician veto is illustrated by Cicero's comment that one can always find a compliant tribune to obstruct a bill, 'quod enim est tam desperatum collegium, in quo nemo e decem sana mente sit?', *Leg.* 3.24.

[70] In 169, tribunes blocked the praetor who tried to declare war on Rhodes without the senate's approval but violated the *loca intercessionis* rules by interceding too early in the proceedings, Liv. 45.21.6–8. The issue was also raised at the trial of C. Cornelius, Asc. *Corn.* 71C. Meier 1968; Rilinger 1989.

[71] Illustrated by the case from 137 when Scipio Aemilianus persuaded a tribune, M. Antius Briso, to abstain from vetoing the *lex Cassia tabellaria* on secret balloting at trials, Cic. *Brut.* 97, cf. *Leg.* 3.37.

may be Livy's own invention, but they adhere to the format and conventions followed on such occasions.[72] Two tribunes, M. and P. Iunius Brutus, had announced their intention to veto the bill. Nevertheless, both sides of the debate ostensibly sought to persuade the *populus* to endorse or reject the repeal, despite the fact that their voting intentions would have been irrelevant if the interceding tribunes persisted. Therefore, whatever form the argument may have taken, the real target must have been the tribunes who decided the outcome. A similar subtext is apparent in one of the best recorded debates of the late republic, which concerned the *lex Manilia* of 66. In Cicero's *suasio*, he explicitly warned any tribune contemplating a veto against Pompey's appointment, suggesting that they may have been the actual focus of the heated exchanges, rather than the large crowd which had clearly turned up to demonstrate their support for the popular general (*Man.* 58).

Although it may be possible to construe these debates as events of real political import, it does not follow that they were always part of the proceedings. If a proposal was uncontroversial, there was no obvious reason to go through the motions of a formal debate. And while they feature with some regularity in our sources, they are not nearly as common as one might expect. The *lex Oppia* episode belongs to the second century, from which most recorded instances seem to derive. Despite ample evidence from the first century, accounts of *suasio-dissuasio* debates are comparatively rare. A few attracted considerable attention, such as the passing of the *lex Gabinia* in 67 and the *lex Manilia* in 66, mentioned above. But the latter was also the only known occasion where Cicero, the pre-eminent orator of his day, appeared at such an event. The question is therefore how common the debates really were during this period. For example, *suasiones* and *dissuasiones* seem strangely absent from the surviving rhetorical literature as well as from the record of published speeches, fragmentary as well as complete.[73] Moreover, on several occasions during the first century no debate appears to have been held.[74] Most strikingly, in 58 it seems clear from our detailed record that the passing of Clodius' bill sending Cicero into exile was not preceded by formal interventions on his behalf; had that been the case, Cicero would undoubtedly have mentioned it along with the speakers on either side.[75]

---

[72] Interestingly, in the entire corpus of Cato's rhetorical fragments there is no trace of his speech against the repeal of *lex Oppia*, cf. Perl and El-Qalqili 2002.

[73] *Contra* Russell 2013: 107. Exceptions include *Rhet. Her.* 3.4, 6; Cic. *Part.* 85.

[74] Hiebel 2009: 150–6 lists *suasiones-dissuasiones* in the late republic but fails to distinguish between 'ordinary' *contiones* and the final debate preceding the vote.

[75] Mommsen 1887: 395 n.4. *Pace* Hiebel 2009: 155.

So what had happened to this – supposedly essential – part of the political process? The powers of persuasion of the 'great and the good' may have become less effective in regulating tribunician activities than they used to be. The rise of the dynasts also upset traditional patterns of negotiation, providing a counter-weight to the authority of the *principes*. A veto, if submitted, was also less decisive than before, since the tribune in question could be deposed or his intervention ignored. At the same time, controversial bills might now be accompanied by violence and intimidation, rendering the safe conduct of formal debates more difficult. Presumably, it was now accepted that unless a bill could be prevented by force or religious obstruction it was destined to become law – which left annulment or repeal as the only remaining options.[76]

The *Contio* in the Late Republic

The political changes of the late republic did not leave the *contiones* unaffected. The works of Cicero allow little doubt as to the continued importance of public meetings, which were held with great frequency, sometimes daily. It is evident too that they were general talking points and objects of considerable attention in political circles. Their value was two-fold: providing vital public exposure for politicians, including young aspiring tribunes who wished to raise their profile, and mobilising 'public opinion' for or against new legislation. By garnering public goodwill among the wider political class, momentum could be created behind – or against – an initiative which would further or impede its progress. Finally, the ability to claim the full support of a contional audience, formally representing the entire *populus Romanus*, was intrinsically valuable and provided a considerable political boost.

As competition intensified in the late republic and political conflicts became more embittered, the senate's ability to maintain consensus gradually weakened. The effect on the *contiones* was probably a growing tendency towards more 'managed' meetings along with an attendant 'disintegration' of the institution as a political factor. In order to ensure a positive reception and a constructive outcome, organisers seem to have relied more and more on supportive crowds organised in advance. Public appearances could propel careers and programmes, while failure meant embarrassment or even humiliation. *Contiones* also became practical tools in the political struggles of the late republic when office holders would

---

[76] See Heikkilä 1993.

summon opponents to *contiones* and interrogate them in front of hostile audiences. Politicians therefore preferred holding their own *contiones*, rather than turning up for those of their opponents. A rare glimpse of this dynamic comes from the speeches which Cicero delivered in 63 on Rullus' land reform. Rullus had first presented his complex and detailed bill to a *contio* towards the end of 64, the initial reception apparently being quite positive.[77] Cicero, however, denounced the plans, first in the senate and then at his first consular address to the 'people'. Rullus responded by calling another *contio*, to which he invited Cicero. The consul understandably declined, preferring instead to organise a meeting of his own, which he used to launch another attack on Rullus' proposal.

Therefore, despite the large number of meetings reported during this period we paradoxically find very few examples of open dissent or disagreement; audiences by and large seem to have endorsed the magistrate who had called the *contio*.[78] A large turnout could therefore be emphasised as a source of pride, since it indicated a strong level of support.[79] The political significance attached to the scale of meetings underlines this presumption; it also poses a problem for the theory of a *plebs contionalis*, which assumes the same regular crowd turned up for most meetings, irrespective of organiser.[80] Only in a few instances do we hear of *contiones* that failed in their aims, which, given the antagonistic climate of the late republic, suggests that they were indeed very rare. And even then it was more a case of crowds that remained lukewarm rather than turned against the organiser. For example, in 90 the audience of the tribune C. Curio simply deserted him in the Forum, while in 59 Caesar failed to rouse his audience to march on Bibulus' house.[81] Cicero (admittedly not an unbiased source) also claims that when Clodius addressed his brother Appius' *contio* even the *infimi* laughed at him.[82]

While these instances stand out for their rarity, it is nevertheless clear that *contiones* retained an element of unpredictability. However supportive the crowds may have been, much still hinged on the speaker's performance

---

[77] As implied e.g. by Cicero's comment that they had not understood what the bill was about, *Agr.* 2.13.

[78] Walter 2009: 48 noted that after the Ides of March 44 popular expressions were 'alles anders als einheitlich' and following Morstein-Marx 2004: 151 he assumes a 'fundamental indeterminacy of the Popular Will'. Still, contional crowds, while politically inconsistent, were entirely dependable in their support for whoever had called the meeting.

[79] *Fam.* 11.6.2 (SB 356); *Phil.* 1.32; 4.1; 6.18; 14.16; *Agr.* 2.103; *De orat.* 1.225; *Sul.* 34.

[80] In *Agr.* 3.2, Cicero seems to imply that his audience had also attended Rullus' latest *contio* and been swayed by his arguments. Most likely, that is a rhetorical trope playing on the notional *populus Romanus* which all speakers formally addressed at *contiones*.

[81] Cic. *Brut.* 192, 305; *Att.* 2.21.5 (SB 41).   [82] *Att.* 4.2.3 (SB 74); *Har.* 8.

on the day. Speeches were carefully designed to elicit vocal support and to rouse the crowd to full enthusiasm, and what had been said at *contiones* and how individual speakers had fared were topics of general interest.[83] A successful appearance could enhance one's reputation, whereas a less glittering performance became an embarrassing talking point, as famously happened to Pompey at his first *contio* after his return from the East.[84] It showed that the strategy was not without risk – and explains the temptation to organise supportive crowds in advance.

How crowds assembled for *contiones* in the late republic can only be conjectured. Most likely we should envisage a range of different scenarios and types of mobilisation, from the tightly stage-managed to the purely spontaneous. Since Cicero is our main source we know more about the former, particularly those organised by his opponent Clodius and other so-called *seditiosi*. Cicero describes in detail how Clodius brought crowds into the Forum which had been raised in the neighbourhoods of Rome, the *vici*, through a network of local associations with intermediate leaders. This allowed him to call up followers at short notice and establish himself as a powerful presence in Roman politics, even as a mere *privatus*. It is in this context that we hear of working people being drawn onto the political scene, as happened when Clodius ordered the *tabernae* to be closed in 58.[85] The need for such radical measures to ensure wider popular participation is a striking reminder of their general absence.[86]

A well-known passage of Cicero's *Lucullus* also indicates that the masses had to be mobilised and drawn into the world of official politics. The speaker first asks: 'Why then, Lucullus, do you bring me into public disfavour and summon me before a *contio*, so to speak, and actually imitate seditious tribunes and order the *tabernae* to be shut?' He then goes on to accuse Lucullus of trying to stir up the craftsmen but warns that 'if they come together from every quarter, it will be easy to stir them on to attack your side'.[87] The description of this imaginary *contio* suggests it was not

---

[83] Cf. Mouritsen 2013.   [84] *Att.* 1.14.1 (SB 14), cf. 2.21.3 (SB 41).

[85] *Dom.* 54, cf. 89–90. Similar steps were considered in 52 when the verdict in Milo's murder trial was to be announced, Asc. *Mil.* 52C, cf. 41C. It deprived traders and craftsmen of a day's income and can therefore hardly have been well received among members of this class.

[86] References to overcrowding at public meetings are extremely rare, the notable exception being Cicero's description of the passing of the *leges Gabinia* and *Manilia*, when Pompey's personal popularity undoubtedly played a part, *Man.* 44, 69.

[87] *Ac.* 2.144 (*Luc.*): 'Quid me igitur, Luculle, in invidiam et tamquam in contionem vocas, et quidem, ut seditiosi tribuni solent, occludi tabernas iubes?'; 'Qui si undique omnes convenerint, facile contra vos incitabuntur'.

a question of swaying the minds of a crowd of *opifices* who routinely turned up for meetings. Rather it indicates that they took part when politicians targeted them directly and encouraged them to do so.[88]

The rhetorical tropes associated with *contiones* are typically couched in dramatic language that gives the impression of lively mass events attended by broad sections of the population. This creates a peculiar dissonance between the ancient accounts of the meetings and the structural and socio-economic framework we are able to reconstruct. Cicero is fond of stressing the stormy and unpredictable nature of *contiones*, but again things may not always be what they seem.[89] For example, in the *Pro Cluentio* Cicero dwells on the *contiones* of the 'seditious' tribune Quinctius, who stirred up crowds against C. Iunius, notorious for his involvement in judicial corruption in 74. We are told that Quinctius, after reviving the *contio* in the aftermath of Sulla, became popular with 'a certain type of people', 'cuidam hominum generi', whose goodwill he later forfeited. The scale and force of these crowds are repeatedly stressed, but Cicero at the same time consistently describes them as 'stirred up'.[90] The political context also suggests 'top-down' organisation in this case; for the target of all this activity was the senate's control over the courts, an issue unlikely to be a major concern of the urban plebs, who were probably relatively unaffected by the senatorial juries. So, while Quinctius' *contiones* may have been rowdy and 'popular', they also appear to have been more or less staged-managed demonstrations aimed at intimidating political opponents.

How one organised a contional crowd must remain a matter of speculation. Clodius' local networks of personal supporters were clearly exceptional, but we do have scattered references to men who acted as semi-professional organisers of contional crowds. In the *Commentariolum petitionis*, Quintus Cicero mentions an intriguing group of people who 'contiones tenent', 'control *contiones*', probably individuals with a network of contacts that allowed them to influence the turn-out for meetings. Later, in his speech for Sestius, Cicero also refers to 'contionum

---

[88] Cf. the designation of Clodius' man L. Sergius as 'concitator tabernariorum', *Dom.* 13. The same verb is used by Cicero to describe politicians who stir up *opifices* and *tabernarii*, *Flac.* 18.

[89] The broadly supportive crowds, noted above, are difficult to reconcile with the rhetorical trope of the orator calming and controlling the excited *populus*, e.g. Cic. *De orat* 1.31; *Mur.* 24. In practice, such a situation is highly unlikely, given the problems a speaker would have faced trying to make himself heard against a hostile audience. The unpredictability is implied in e.g. *De orat.* 2.339, on the avoidance of negative reactions.

[90] *Clu.* 110, cf. 'contiones cotidianas seditiose ac populariter concitatas', 93, 'incursionem potius seditionis', 'vim multitudinis', 103, 'per multitudinem concitatam', 108.

moderatores', who appear to have had a hand in managing crowds.[91] Sallust mentions 'organisers of crowds who were used to disturb the community for pay'.[92] Apparently, this was not a new phenomenon; already Scipio Aemilianus had been accused of using political organisers who loitered in the Forum and were able to drum up supportive crowds when called upon (Plu. *Aem.* 38.2–4).

The pre-organised – or even hired – crowds which we sometimes hear about probably belong at the extreme end of the scale. Most likely they were used predominantly by politicians who cultivated a more radical image that might alienate them from the usual Forum crowds. Thus at the opposite end of the continuum there may still have been *contiones* which conformed to conventional patterns and addressed anyone who happened to be present in the Forum. That would, as argued above, typically have been politicians, candidates and their retinues, businessmen and those with time and leisure to shop, socialise and watch court cases. The latter must have provided a primary source of entertainment for this constituency, supplemented by the regular *contiones* that offered a different type of oratory and the occasional taste of political drama. Given their ability to spend time in the Forum, these audiences probably shared a basic commonality of interest with the political class, which may have ensured a relatively sympathetic hearing for most speakers. Here the concept of 'weak preferences', which Flaig used to explain the general compliance of the *comitia*, may be most relevant, although it does not necessarily mean crowds were always calm and placid.[93] As Cicero noted in the *Pro Flacco*, Roman *contiones* were not free of rowdiness despite the elevated social standing of their audiences, and the crowds making up the *corona* at trials were also known for their unruliness, reminding us that the Roman elite did not always follow modern middle-class norms of polite public conduct.[94]

Even speakers appealing to these broadly 'friendly' crowds may therefore have done so with a degree of trepidation; it is perhaps not by chance that Cicero capitalised on the opportunity offered by his inaugural consular address to deliver his long speech against Rullus before an influential and

---

[91] *Comm. pet.* 51; cf. *Sest.* 125: 'Ubi erant tum illi contionum moderatores, legum domini, civium expulsores? Aliusne est aliquis improbis civibus peculiaris populus, cui nos offensi invisique fuerimus?' The existence of such organisers is also difficult to reconcile to the idea of a '*plebs contionalis*'. If the crowd was a relatively constant group of local *tabernarii*, what would be the role of these middlemen?

[92] *Cat.* 50.1: ' . . . duces multitudinum qui pretio rem publicam vexare soliti erant'.

[93] Flaig 2003: 173; inspired by Veyne 1990: 223–8.   [94] *Flac.* 57; cf. *Att.* 2.19.2 (SB 39).

sympathetic audience which had turned up specifically to celebrate his accession. On other occasions, speakers may have instructed friends and clients in advance, asking them to offer vocal support should the reception be less warm than hoped for or should opponents try to hijack the meeting. Still, *contiones* never became entirely predictable. In principle, anyone could turn up and speeches might fall flat or even backfire, giving every *contio* an element of uncertainty. The trend in the late republic therefore appears to have been for political battles to be fought through separate, competing *contiones*, in order to enhance the positive effect and minimise the risk of failure.

The general polarisation of late republican politics affected the ability of the *contio* to fulfil its traditional role in the regulatory system that kept office holders in check. If, as it seems, organised – perhaps even paid – crowds often filled the meetings, from which opponents stayed away, the opportunity for real debates and communication must have been much reduced. As a result, the Roman elite, defined broadly as the propertied classes, in a sense lost the public space where ideas were tested, popularity measured – and troublemakers reined in. And as 'public opinion' (among those whose views carried weight with the political class) became more elusive and difficult to gauge, so it also became less politically effective.

As the public aspect of Roman politics became more distorted, the logistical context also changed profoundly. With Rome outgrowing the format of a city-state and reaching an unprecedented scale and degree of complexity, many of those who mattered politically became unable to attend public meetings, either because they resided outside the capital, for instance the municipal elites, or had temporarily retreated to country estates, served in the provinces or were away on business. In response to this increasingly diffuse elite, speeches delivered at *contiones* began to circulate in written form as a means of reaching those who had not been present – whether deliberately because of political opposition, or due to practical obstacles. The importance of the meeting itself was thereby relativised along with the traditional face-to-face character of Roman politics.[95] In the end we are faced with yet another paradox; for as the *contiones* became more and more frequent and turbulent, they may also have become less efficient in terms of shaping political events. In fact, Cicero's repeated comments about how one captures the views of 'the people' can be seen as symptomatic of the fundamental elusiveness of

[95] For a discussion of this phenomenon, see Mouritsen 2013.

'public opinion' in a large-scale society without print media, opinion polls or effective general elections (see further below pp. 153–54).

As regards lower-class participation, there can be little doubt that the changes to the *contio* drew wider sections into the world of official politics. The question is whether that also caused a 'politicisation' of the plebs. As noted above, our references to the 'common people' at *contiones* suggest it usually happened as a result of prior (elite) mobilisation, which even included the enforced closure of their business premises. But whatever the driving forces were, it probably involved at least some of them more closely with individual politicians than had previously been the case. Morstein-Marx argued that meetings served as an instrument of control, small crowds turning up, listening to speeches by their social superiors and returning to their neighbourhoods with messages that shaped opinion among wider sections of society.[96] The model assumes a kind of politicisation by 'osmosis', which also presupposes that messages received at *contiones* were clear and unambiguous. But not only did politicians hold competing meetings, the use of mobilisation also implies that crowds were broadly sympathetic when they turned up and therefore had little need of further persuasion. Finally, we find ourselves confronted with the basic question of whether 'politics', as practised by the office-holding class, held such popular attraction to members of the wider population that they were prepared to spend a day in the Forum listening to speeches, most of which dealt with issues of limited relevance.[97]

In their influential work *The Civic Culture,* the political scientists Almond and Verba identified three ideal types describing the relationship between citizens and the world of government and politics: 1) 'participant', in which citizens understand and take part in politics, 2) 'subject', where citizens are largely compliant but participate little, and finally 3) 'parochial', in which citizens have little awareness of or interest in politics.[98] Applying this taxonomy to the Roman republic would suggest we are dealing with a mix of 'parochial' and 'subject' relationships. For the large majority of citizens, politics probably represented a remote and separate sphere which had little bearing on their daily lives, while the minority that did take part seem to have displayed what can only be described as 'subject' behaviour, largely conforming to the agenda set by the political class.

---

[96] Morstein-Marx 2004; cf. Mouritsen 2005.
[97] As Wiseman, 1985a: 2 rightly noted: 'Politics was a subject of absorbing interest, at one particular social level. But it was not the only one, and for most of the population of Rome probably not the most interesting'.
[98] Almond and Verba 1963.

The fundamental paradox is that the institutional and ideological structures were in place for a 'participant' relationship between citizens and government to have evolved in Rome, as illustrated by the public discourse, which was entirely predicated on the people as a participant. But the practical constraints as well as the intrinsic limitations to the scope of politics meant that these potentials were never realised.

The events of the late republic offer one important lesson: they vividly illustrate the ability of small, dedicated crowds to capture the political process and dominate the public stage. It was possible at any moment for a group of citizens to turn up and spontaneously make their views heard in front of members of the ruling class. What is striking therefore is the rarity with which that seems to have happened. An exceptional instance that proves the rule is recorded in Cicero's *Pro Flacco*, where we are told that 'Jewish crowds on occasions set our public meetings ablaze', clearly to assert their collective interests.[99] It shows how susceptible to any concerted popular initiative the system was, and the real question is why the disaffected masses of Rome did not exploit this feature to a greater extent. Riots may, as already noted, have been more frequent than often assumed, but importantly they never seem to have 'spilled over' into the world of official politics. Usually, they were triggered by specific complaints, often linked to material concerns, and at no point do we hear of crowds calling for substantive social and political change; the politics of the street – like Roman politics in general – appears to have been entirely issue related, which is perhaps less surprising when we consider the ideological context; how could demands for a more 'democratic' system be formulated when the 'people' formally already held the power? Still, the extent to which the official political process appears to have been divorced from any genuinely popular agenda is remarkable. Most glaringly, the urban masses even allowed measures to be passed that were directly detrimental to their own interests. For example, C. Gracchus' grain law was abrogated by a vote of the *populus*, seemingly without the beneficiaries of the scheme making any attempt to prevent its repeal; Cicero even stresses the popular backing it enjoyed.[100] Such compliance is surprising, not because

---

[99] *Flac.* 67: ' ... multitudinem Iudaeorum flagrantem non numquam in contionibus ... '. In a puzzling passage of the same speech, 17, Cicero refers to Phrygians and Mysians interrupting *contiones*, presumably with the implication that they are former slaves.

[100] Cicero claims the *lex Octavia* was passed 'populi frequentis suffragiis', Cic. *Brut.* 222, cf. *Off.* 2.72. The law is generally dated to the 90s, Schovánek 1972; Garnsey 1988: 198; Ungern-Sternberg 1991: 39; Bleicken 1981: 101–5. Conversely the *comitia* rejected Philippus' agrarian law, which presumably supported the *commoda populi*, Cic. *Off.* 2.73.

populations necessarily rise up against their rulers, but because the political institutions and procedures in Rome allowed any group with a modicum of organisation to assume control. Examples such as Paullus' troops, who almost succeeded in blocking their general's triumph would, however unusual the circumstances, have demonstrated the ease with which the political initiative could be seized by relatively small numbers. That, however, happened only at the instigation of dissenting members of the elite, be they office holders or *privati*.

How do we explain the apparent consensus and general acquiescence displayed by the mass of the Roman population? Polybius, as we saw, was in no doubt that the secret of Rome's stability lay in its 'mixed constitution', which offered the people a share of power and ensured that their interests were accommodated. However, given the general absence of the '*populus*' from political proceedings and its inability to set – or even influence – the agenda, we might ask whether there were other channels through which the masses could feel represented. Alongside the popular assemblies, Polybius listed the tribunate as part of the 'democratic' foundations of the People's power, thereby adding a 'representational' element to Rome's political system, which was otherwise based on direct participation (6.16.5). In formal terms, however, tribunes were not defined as 'representatives' any more than other Roman magistrates were. They may historically have presented themselves as 'defenders of the plebs', but with the plebeio-patrician settlement this polarity became obsolete and thereafter the tribunes were no longer associated with any specific social group.[101] And while some tribunes may have proposed bills which furthered the interests of the poor, most of them did not – or even obstructed those who did. Moreover, since tribunes and other magistrates were not appointed on the basis of particular programmes or promises for which they could later be held accountable, there was in effect no political choice and very little opportunity for voicing popular concerns at elections. Still, we should not lose sight of the symbolic dimension of the tribunate, which endured long after the 'Struggle' had been settled and a new aristocracy had come to power; for while it hardly justifies Polybian notions of a 'mixed constitution', the tribunate, with its rich historical baggage, may still be significant as part of a particular Roman identity which encompassed rulers as well as ruled and shaped their mutual

---

[101] Cicero could describe their responsibilities in vague terms as subservience to 'voluntas civitatis', *De orat.* 2.167. Elsewhere he famously declared that it was the duty of the consuls to protect the *salus populi*, *Leg.* 3.8.

relations. Thus the remarkably stable political order we find especially during the so-called classic republic can only be properly understood if we broaden our perspective and go beyond the realm of conventional politics.[102] The political system was embedded in, and reflected, wider socio-economic as well as ideological structures, which all contributed to the formation of a long-term accommodation – one might almost say 'social contract' – between masses and elite.

Leaders and Masses: the 'Political Culture' of the Republic

Attempts to explain the political stability of the middle republic in social rather than political terms have a long and distinguished history, beginning with Gelzer's identification of clientelistic networks as a central feature of Roman society.[103] Through a dense web of personal ties and obligations the ruling class was supposedly able to keep the masses in check, in effect turning the 'democratic' institutions into instruments of aristocratic control. The theory, long dominant in Roman historiography, has in recent decades been challenged by historians who have pointed out the scarcity of concrete evidence to support it.[104] On a basic logistical level the idea of an all-encompassing system of *clientela*, linking top and bottom of society, is difficult to reconcile with the scale of republican Rome, especially during the later periods. Moreover, the fact that most members of the plebs never could be politically active removes the political imperative for the elite to maintain comprehensive social networks in order to stay in power. Given the fluidity of the urban population, that would also have been extremely difficult to achieve. *Clientela* was undoubtedly important as a distinct type of reciprocal, while at the same time asymmetrical, social relationship that revolved around an ongoing exchange of favours and obligations. It is unlikely, however, to have translated into a solid structure of social and political control underpinning the elite's ascendancy. Clients were appreciated and cultivated but not indiscriminately so, and it remains doubtful

---

[102] The concept of a 'classic' republic is, of course, partly the result of hindsight, cf. below pp. 106–8, but the period nevertheless appears to have been largely free of major social disruption. A considerable degree of acceptance of the prevailing social and political order seems likely, especially since the absence of armed forces to control the masses left the ruling class highly exposed to collective popular action; despite the presence of guards and attendants, the Roman elite ultimately depended for its personal safety on the existence of a broad social consensus.

[103] Gelzer 1912.

[104] Sceptical Meier 1980: 24–45; Beard and Crawford 1999: 68; Develin 1985: 127–31; Brunt 1988: 30–2, 382–442; Morstein-Marx 1998; Wallace-Hadrill 1989; Johnson and Dandeker 1989; Mouritsen 2001. *Contra* Eder 1996: 443; cf. Deniaux 1993. A balanced assessment in Garnsey 2010.

how often the poor were admitted to the *clientelae* of the rich and powerful; after all, we have no evidence that Cicero personally knew a single poor person.[105]

With the realisation that *clientela* may not have been the *arcana imperii* previously envisaged, the focus of recent scholarship has shifted onto what has become known as the 'political culture' of the republic.[106] The concept, originally inspired by political science, represents an attempt to capture the manifold aspects of the political process usually not covered in traditional accounts of constitutional and institutional history despite their importance in shaping political mentality and behaviour. They include issues of identity, ideology, rhetoric, and what might be called 'style of government'. It also comprises the various forms of interaction that took place between politicians and citizens, ranging from direct personal contact to symbolic, 'performative', and 'monumental' communication.[107] These innovative approaches, particularly fertile in German academia, have added an important dimension to our understanding of republican politics and have also laid the basis for a new understanding of the middle republic and its social and political stability.

The self-image of the political class and the way it formally constituted itself are essential components of this 'culture' and key to understanding the particular relationships that developed between leaders and masses.[108] After the plebeio-patrician settlement in the fourth century the ruling elite ceased to be hereditary, with the exception of certain priesthoods still reserved for patricians. As the old families lost their birth-right to power and prestige, they were forced to compete with plebeian newcomers who joined the new plebeio-patrician ruling class that became known as the *nobilitas*. As Hölkeskamp noted, the creation of the *nobilitas* was more than a quantitative expansion of the elite; it involved the formation of a new type of ruling class with a distinct ideology and identity and a different kind of relationship with the *populus*.[109]

---

[105] It is telling that Cicero noted that no man known to his *nomenclator* of any *ordo* had not come to greet him on his return from exile – apart from his enemies, *Att.* 4.1.5 (SB 73). The reference to *ordo* and *nomenclator* suggests we are dealing with affluent *boni*. Goldbeck 2010: 90–7 seems to overestimate the scale of *salutationes* and the numbers attending them.

[106] As Stemmler 2001 observed, this trend continues a shift away from Mommsen's legal positivism, which identified the formal structures of the state as the solid framework which maintained Roman society. Gelzer 1912 challenged that model by introducing informal power relations and explaining social stability by reference to the elite's value system, especially the elite's cardinal virtues of *virtus, pietas, fides,* and *dignitas*, which in turn underpinned the *clientela* networks.

[107] Hölkeskamp 2006 gives a broad overview of this 'school'.   [108] Hölscher 1978.

[109] Hölkeskamp 1993; 2010.

Public office, defined as *honos*, became the source and measure of *dignitas* and *auctoritas*, and crucially it was the *populus* that assumed the role of external arbiter in the elite's ongoing contest over power and influence, dispensing the vital *honores*. The Roman elite could therefore justify its ascendancy in meritocratic terms by reference to popular mandates and services to the community, rather than conventional aristocratic claims to birth right or innate superiority. Public honours thus conferred not just legitimacy and status but also obligations, which went far beyond the 'noblesse oblige' of later aristocracies.[110] A striking illustration of the link between status and duty comes from the famous *laudatio* of L. Caecilius Metellus (cos. 251, 247), which lists his numerous achievements and personal qualities while maintaining a 'civic' reference point and perspective, by stressing his bravery, public honours, and great services to the *res publica* (Plin. *Nat* 7.139–140). The community dimension is even more pronounced in the Scipionic *elogia*. The two LL. Scipiones Barbati, father and son (cos. 298 and 259 respectively), are described in their epitaphs as having been consul, censor, aedile 'apud vos', 'among you', i.e. the Roman people, thus directly invoking the audience which had granted their honours.[111]

The elite's focus on 'office-holding as the decisive criterion for high rank' shaped its outlook and encouraged regular interaction with the public.[112] Since the power of the ruling elite was not defined in contrast to the *populus* but derived from it, we look in vain for a Roman oligarchic discourse – in sharp contrast to the Greek world. Instead we find a consensual construction of the state as identical with the *populus* and the elite as its dutiful guardian. This unique definition of the elite was not without contradictions, however. The elevated status and renown associated with the *nobilitas* soon became a hereditary quality, specifically claimed by those who could count a consul among their ancestors.[113] It always remained an informal status, never recognised in law, but by widening the concept of merit beyond the individual and applying it to entire family lines an important new distinction between *nobiles* and *novi* was created, which was to become a source of considerable tension within

---

[110] Cf. e.g. Cic. *Off.* 1.124. Walter 2014b: 101.
[111] *CIL* I² 6.7 = *CLE* 7 = *ILLRP* 309; *CIL* I² 8–9 = *CLE* 6 = *ILLRP* 310. Kruschwitz 2002: 32–57, esp. 44, and 58–70. Cf. Hölkeskamp 1993: 30; 1995: 32; 2010: 122 on the ideology expressed in the *elogia*.
[112] Hölkeskamp 2010 31.
[113] The precise definition of *nobilis* is long debated; cf. Gelzer 1912; Burckhardt 1990; Shackleton Bailey 1986; Goldmann 2002. A good overview in Van der Blom 2010: 34–59, who noted that it was not an absolute or precisely defined category but apparently negotiable and to some extent relative. It also follows that *nobilitas* and *novitas* were not binary distinctions.

the elite. But although parts of one's *dignitas* could now be passed on to descendants, it did not carry any formal entitlement as much as a vaguely defined moral advantage over competitors who were unable to boast of a similar family record of public service.

As importantly, the concept of *nobilitas* left the role of the *populus* as the ultimate source of *honor* and *dignitas* unchallenged. Indeed, it could be argued that the definition of *nobilitas* bound the elite even more tightly to the aristocratic code of public service and obligation, since every noble invoking illustrious ancestry would invariably be measured against the achievements of his *maiores*. For example, the elogium for Cn. Cornelius Scipio (Hispanus?) proudly states that 'I upheld the praise of my ancestors, so that they rejoice that I was born to them. My (public) honour ennobled my family'.[114] Conversely, failure to match these expectations became a source of shame. In the elogium for the early-deceased P. Cornelius P. f. Scipio we are therefore assured that ' ... you would easily have outshone the glory of your ancestors', thus pre-empting any criticism.[115] The claims implicit in the concept of *nobilitas* thus laid its members open to accusations of falling below the high standards expected of them, and in some contexts '*nobilis*' could be used almost derogatively as a reproach implying unearned privilege and arrogance. But although many fared poorly in this comparison, voters nevertheless seem by and large to have accepted their claim to preferment. As the *fasti* reveal, members of the same noble families kept being returned to the highest offices, presumably on the assumption that these over time had developed a particularly strong ethos of service as well as a degree of practical leadership experience that made them the safest choice.[116]

The fact that membership of the ruling class was now determined solely by a vote of the *populus* had a profound impact on the political 'culture' of the republic. The conceptualisation of the *res publica* as founded on the partnership of *senatus populusque Romanus* created an ideological bond between the masses and their leaders, who adopted a style and demeanour which contrasts with that of most other aristocracies. Respect for the *populus*, even deference, became hard-wired into rhetorical strategies and political arguments. And the elite were not just deferential to the abstract concept of the *populus Romanus* but also seem to have displayed

---

[114] 'Maiorum optenui laudem, ut sibei me esse creatum laetentur. Stirpem nobilitavit honor', *CIL* I² 15 = *CLE* 958 = *ILLRP* 316.

[115] *CIL* I² 10 = *CLE* 8 = *ILLRP* 311, cf. Kruschwitz 2002: 70–89, esp. 86–9. Cf. *CIL* I² 11 = *CLE* 9 = *ILLRP* 312; Kruschwitz 2002: 90–107.

[116] Badian 1990c on the nobility's near monopoly on the consulship.

a remarkable degree of restraint in their direct dealings with social inferiors. In an important study Martin Jehne drew attention to the many anecdotes and stories which exemplified the ideal conduct of a Roman *nobilis* and noted the particular 'jovial' stance expected of him in those situations.[117] Appearing haughty or superior to the 'common man' was considered a social faux-pas, as illustrated by the oft-cited anecdote about P. Scipio Nasica, cos. 138, who failed in his attempt at the aedileship after he had jokingly asked a *rusticus* with rough hands whether he walked on them. The comment spread to bystanders, and members of the rural tribes felt they were being taunted with poverty.[118]

The unique identity of the Roman elite did not, of course, obliterate class divisions but it probably softened the edges of oligarchic rule by presenting a consistent image of selfless dedication and duty – even a degree of mutuality between elite and masses. These values were widely advertised and reinforced in public rituals and gestures which emphasised the elite's devotion to the common good.[119] Collectively the political class demonstrated its contribution to society through a variety of media, including public manifestations such as funerary orations and processions, the so-called *pompae funebres*.[120] Rome also witnessed a remarkable growth in aristocratic monumentalisation of public spaces, with the erection of columns, statues, and other structures commemorating the deeds of great men, past as well as present.[121] The triumphal route became lined with votive temples, which showed Rome's piety and success while also providing lasting memorials to the victorious generals.[122] In parallel, the private houses of great families were also turned into memorials to the ancestors, displaying trophies and other *monumenta*. During the middle republic, numerous statues of *maiores* were put up in public, eventually causing such overcrowding that the Forum had to be cleared in 158, when statues put up without public sanction were removed (Plin. *Nat.* 34.30).

---

[117] Jehne 2000b defined 'Jovialität' as a particular friendly stance and approachable demeanour by superiors towards commoners.

[118] Val. Max. 7.5.2, cf. Jehne 2000b: 216–17. Significantly, the other voters took offence at Nasica's implication that they were poor and worked with their hands. The story therefore does not indicate that poor *rustici* filled the *comitia*, as much as the code of polite conduct which candidates were expected to observe.

[119] During the earlier and middle republic the message may have been further underpinned by the elite's relatively modest lifestyle, which gave the impression of a more egalitarian society than the distribution of power indicates.

[120] Flaig 1995b; Stemmler 2001: 233–9; Hölskeskamp 1996; 2008. Polybius 6.53 linked aristocratic funerals to the canonical stories of great men of the past, the so-called *exempla* tradition.

[121] Gruen 1996; Hölscher 2001; Walter 2001; 2004.

[122] Ziolkowski 1992; Hölscher 2001: 194–201.

The beginning of this process coincided with the end to the 'Struggle' and the creation of the new 'meritocratic' nobility, and, as Tonio Hölscher observed, the monumentalised *exempla* served to demonstrate that the commitment to public service was not just an abstract ideal but was actually practised.[123] In the end the citizens of Rome became literally surrounded by the elite's monumental and performative celebration of themselves and their ancestors. The influence on the wider population is, of course, difficult to gauge; the sheer volume and monotony of the message conveyed may well have weakened the impact. Nevertheless, the fact that the ruling class presented itself in this particular mode remains significant, and even more so when we consider that the process of memorialisation took off at the very moment when Rome started to expand beyond the confines of the city-state in the late fourth and early third centuries. Not by chance were the services rendered to the *res publica* – and so extensively celebrated – overwhelmingly of a martial nature. When searching for the structural causes of the relative stability of the middle republic one should not lose sight of the fact that this was also a period of extraordinary military success. The continuous engagements abroad played a vital role in shaping the relations and attitudes between elite and masses, while also transforming the character of the Roman state itself along with its citizenship.

Epilogue: Politics and Military Expansion

It is impossible to grasp the nature of the middle republic without factoring in the expansion of Roman power and territory during this period. This is not the place to discuss the origins and character of the process by which Rome grew from medium-sized city-state to world power, but the profound militarisation of Roman society which accompanied this transformation must have played an important part. The relentless drive towards further conquest became integral to her civic structures, many of which were shaped around continuous warfare, and apart from the ritual distinction between *domi* and *militiae* there was no clear separation of military and civilian spheres.[124] The soldier-citizen identity affected all aspects of Roman society, the ethos of the elite, the attitudes of the serving population, and not least the interaction between leaders and masses.

---

[123] Hölscher 2001: 199: 'Das Exemplum hat die Aufgabe, die Konvergenz von ideal und Wirklichkeit zu demonstrieren'.

[124] Harris 1979; North 1981; Rüpke 1990. On popular support for expansion, see Gabba 1984.

With the exception of the very poorest, male citizens became habituated to prolonged military service, and at elite level the militarisation was equally profound. Extended service became part of the public career structure, the pinnacle of which was the intensely coveted triumph.[125] Military values were thus firmly embedded in the lives and outlook of the Roman aristocracy, which has often been described as a 'warrior elite'.[126] Competition gained a strong martial aspect and claims to military prowess became a fundamental factor underpinning the power of the elite. As Hölkeskamp has shown, it is no coincidence that it was during the period of rapid Italian conquest that the *nobilitas* established itself so decisively as Rome's ruling class. It drew immense prestige and authority from its successful management of Rome's external wars, thereby strengthening its political claim. In the early period after the 'compromise' the rise of plebeian leaders was closely linked to personal ability in the field against Rome's Italian opponents, as was e.g. M. Popillius Laenas and C. Marcius Rutilus, while military prowess was also instrumental in the rise of patricians such as Q. Fabius Maximus Rullianus and P. Decius Mus.[127] These men embodied the ideals of sacrifice and competence which helped entrench the position of the new elite at home.

As noted earlier, military success became the object of extensive memorialisation, to the extent that part of Rome's cityscape was reshaped as more and more votive temples and other victory monuments were being built. They served as permanent reminders to the public that the remarkable expansion of Roman power took place under their auspices and leadership. The elite's extensive self-celebration defined the bond between *populus* and nobility in military terms as one of soldiers and commanders, with all the attendant values of loyalty and obedience. Thus the expansion did not just strengthen the elite through the prestige and 'proven record of success' it conferred upon them; the extensive conscription and prolonged military service may also have imbued Roman society with a military ethos that shaped relations between leaders and masses in the field as well as in the civilian sphere.

Rome's militarisation led Moses Finley to suggest that 'obedience to the authorities became so deeply embedded in the psyche of the ordinary

---

[125] Military service: Brunt 1971; Hopkins 1978.
[126] At least until the late republic when, according to Blösel 2011, the elite underwent a remarkable 'demilitarisation'. Still, despite fewer opportunities for conquest and military glory, the elite nevertheless retained its ideological attachment to martial values, cf. Walter 2014b: 103.
[127] Hölkeskamp 1993: 22.

Roman citizen that it carried over into his explicitly political behaviour'.[128]
While there can be little doubt that warfare had a pervasive impact on
Roman mentality and social dynamics, the shared military experiences may
have encouraged not just respect for superiors but also recognition among
the elite that men under arms must be treated equitably and rewarded for
their service. The military offered by far the most intense social contact
between citizens from all backgrounds. During extended campaigns, soldiers, officers and generals faced the same hardship and dangers, which
may have helped forge bonds across class boundaries. Such bonds might be
carried over into the civilian sphere, instilling military values of discipline,
leadership and common purpose into Rome's political culture. Among the
ruling class this mentality seems to have expressed itself in a particular
approachable style, and the 'joviality' mentioned above had a distinctly
military aspect to it. Thus, while a friendly demeanour might not disguise
manifest inequalities of power and resources, it should nevertheless be
recognised as a contributing factor towards generating political consent.

Military expansion changed Roman society beyond recognition. Rome
grew into a territorial state, albeit one which paradoxically retained the
political structure of a city-state. A unique policy of incorporating defeated
peoples and granting them formal political rights was adopted, which was
possible because in practice they had little chance of exercising them.
The remarkable growth of her citizen body, to which the enfranchisement
of freed slaves also contributed, reinforced the non-political definition
of the Roman citizenship. The 'non-participatory' nature of the People's
constitutional role became further entrenched by the fact that only
a vanishingly small proportion of the citizen body could now take part in
the proceedings. Collective political activity was never a unifying factor in
the new territorial state. That function was instead performed by military
service, which, as Jehne demonstrated, remained the single most cohesive
element in the Roman republic.[129] It did so by generating a shared soldier-
citizen identity but also more practically by bringing together citizens from
different parts of the country. Military units were deliberately composed of
soldiers drawn from a cross-section of the tribes, thereby creating a regional
mix which encouraged integration and militated against the formation of
strong local identities and the separatism to which that might give rise.

---

[128] Finley 1983: 130; cf. Schofield 1995: 65; Raaflaub 1991: 580. The political implications of the soldiers'
subjection to military discipline is illustrated by the Roman recognition that a serving soldier could
not act politically while under oath to his commander, cf. the controversial cases when laws were
passed in the field, e.g. Liv. 7.16.7–8.

[129] Jehne 2006b.

The militarisation of the Roman republic not only created a social environment conducive to promoting internal stability on a number of levels; as importantly, expansion also provided the opportunities which allowed the elite to claim that its leadership brought concrete benefits for the soldier class. The most obvious reward came in the form of spoils distributed among the soldiers, and in continuation of this practice the senate also carried out an extensive programme of colonial foundations on conquered territory across Italy and Cisalpine Gaul. Large numbers of Roman citizens were settled on confiscated land through a variety of colonial and viritane schemes, which were usually drawn up and approved by the senate rather than the tribunes.[130] Rome's victories abroad also led to huge imports of war captives, and, in a move that cannot have been unrelated to the newly abundant manpower resources, the *lex Poetilia de nexis* was passed in 326, abolishing debt bondage.[131] Later examples of grain provision from the provinces for the urban poor are also recorded, presumably aimed at defusing social tension and preventing unrest (e.g. Liv. 31.50.1).

Expansion brought access to resources which, at least during certain periods, were remarkably evenly shared, although differences in rank and status were scrupulously observed in the distribution process. It allowed social problems to be, at least in part, 'exported', which may have further entrenched the position of the ruling class. Political stability may therefore not have been, as Polybius insisted, the precondition for Rome's external success; rather it was her military expansion that laid the foundations for the political consensus and created the conditions for the relative social peace that seems to have characterised the period. It may explain why the *populus*, despite its circumscribed political role and limited means of expressing its views and preferences (apart from the riots which were usually sparked by specific grievances), nevertheless appears to have accepted the status quo.

The formation of the *nobilitas* as a martially defined elite may, directly and indirectly, have strengthened civic cohesion through the pursuit of continuous expansion combined with broadly inclusive social policies

---

[130] Harris 1979: 60–5. The politically sensitive land schemes were generally initiated by the senate rather than tribunes, Hölkeskamp 2011: 33, 155–62, 172–82, 184, 200–3. For example, in 200 (Liv. 31.49.5) veterans were settled on land with no reported dispute, cf. Liv. 38.36.7–9. The opposition to Flaminius' scheme in 232 represents a rare exception. For the scale of population movements entailed by this policy, see Brunt 1971: 28–32, 53–5, 190–3; Scheidel 2004; De Ligt 2012: 150–4.

[131] Liv. 8.28; Var. *L.* 7.105; Cic. *Rep.* 2.59; Dion. Hal. *Ant. Rom.* 16.5.2–3. On war captives, see e.g. Oakley 1993: 22–8.

which it encouraged and facilitated. Its emphasis on personal merit rather than birth helped justifying the elite's overall position in relation to the people. In addition, the formal openness it entailed allowed the admission of gifted newcomers to its ranks. The composition of the republican senate has been much debated and traditional notions of a closed, almost hereditary, aristocracy shown to be unsubstantiated. At no point were the highest offices simply passed on from fathers to sons – partly for purely demographic reasons, although that does not mean that the pool of families occupying these posts was not highly restricted.[132] At the lower rungs of the senate the turnover of families is likely to have been greater; after all, what made the careers of men like Marius and Cicero so exceptional was their attainment of the consulship, not their entry into the senate. The dynamic structure of the ruling class ensured that the senate at any time encompassed those capable of and interested in pursuing public careers and attaining power and status, thereby preventing the emergence of oppositional groups outside the established elite; in other words, it produced an elite with an extraordinary ideological and structural cohesiveness.

Since personal ability can never be passed on, a 'meritocratic' aristocracy is also a contradiction in terms. As a class the elite justified their position on merit and service, but to maintain internal stability it was paramount that all nobles formally be considered equally qualified.[133] Otherwise the system of power sharing – and the delicate balancing act on which it relied – could not be sustained. If meritocratic ideals were to prevail in full, unacceptable concentration of power in the hands of a few individuals of outstanding ability would ensue, threatening the very foundations of the aristocratic republic. Individual talent poses a problem to any system predicated on power being divided evenly among a number of persons and families with equal entitlement. But in Rome, this quandary was aggravated by two factors: on the one hand, the nobility's self-definition as an open, office-based elite, and, on the other hand, the historically strong powers of the executive. The latter entailed that tenure be restricted as far as possible in order to maintain equilibrium; the most able could never be allowed to dominate the chief offices at the expense of their less gifted peers. This concern became particularly pressing in relation to military commands because of their superior prestige and potential to destabilise

---

[132] Hopkins and Burton 1983 ch. 2; cf. Beck 2005. Badian 1990c analysed the consuls in considerable detail. A project to produce a digital prosopography of the Roman republic currently under way at King's College London seeks to refine our picture of the Roman elite even further.

[133] Cf. Rosenstein 1990b: 255–6.

not just the elite but the entire *res publica*.[134] It follows that, while the ascendancy of the *nobilitas* as a whole may have been relatively secure, it remained vulnerable to challenges from within. The meritocratic ethos it espoused and which in many respects was one of the secrets of its success made it more difficult to contain the power of 'great men', as would become apparent during the later republic.

---

[134] Already in 342, the first attempt to regulate iteration of the consulship was made, albeit flexibly implemented, Liv. 7.42.2; Zon. 7.25.9. The relationship between military ability and office holding has been much debated; cf. Rosenstein 1990a; 1990b; Hölkeskamp 1994; Cavaggioni 2010; Waller 2011; Rich 2012.

CHAPTER 3

Consensus and Competition

The history of the Roman Republic is in many respects that of an immensely successful ruling class which managed to share power for hundreds of years, before eventually descending into decades of internecine warfare that led to the rise of monarchy. Historians used to wonder at the republic's spectacular collapse, but – perhaps more pertinently – we might ask how the system lasted so long, given its many contradictions and the tensions intrinsic to all oligarchic systems. The fact that aristocracies are based on competitive power sharing creates an essential conflict between the interests of the collective and the individual. As a result, oligarchic republics tend to be fundamentally unstable. They rely for their survival on the elite's ability to maintain internal cohesion while balancing competing claims to power and influence. Some of the most successful oligarchies in history devised sophisticated and highly complex safeguards against undue concentrations of influence. In Venice, for example, public office was restricted to a closed elite, terms of office were kept short and individual families were prevented from holding several offices simultaneously or sitting on multiple state committees.[1] The allocation of posts was, as we saw in the previous chapter, highly randomised to avoid campaigning and political interference. The greatest restrictions were naturally placed on the Doge, who despite being the formal head of state, had limited ability to dictate policy or extend influence and patronage.

In Rome, such mechanisms of aristocratic 'self-preservation' were for a number of reasons not politically feasible. Chief among them was the historical division of powers within the republic, which acknowledged the *populus* as the basis for public legitimacy, and invested the magistrates with extensive executive powers, while at the same time reducing the formal authority of the senate, the collective voice of the elite. Furthermore, the elite was far more fluid in its composition than was the case in Venice,

[1] For a useful survey, see Finer 1997; cf. Mouritsen 2011a.

defined as it was through office-holding rather than birth, which put even greater strain on the system by increasing competition for the *honores* that held the key to rank and status. The structural challenges to the long-term survival of the Roman aristocratic system were, in other words, even more daunting than in later oligarchies, which were able to formalise the ascendancy of the elite – and enforce internal discipline and cohesion – to a much greater extent than was possible in Rome.

The final section of this study will look in some detail at the factors that helped keep the system together in the face of these challenges as well as those that eventually tore it apart. But before entering into this discussion we may briefly consider the question of periodisation and chronology, which have a direct impact on the way these issues are conceptualised.

Narrative and Periodisation: the Making of the 'Classic' Republic

The end of aristocratic government has typically been framed in a tripartite narrative that divides the republic into an early formative period, followed by a 'classic' age that marked its zenith. Then, as if mirroring a biological cycle, gradual decline set in, leading almost inexorably to its final collapse. This 'rise and fall' narrative has chronologically been pegged to a set of canonical dates and events. The resolution of the 'Struggle of the Orders' in 367 and the formation of the new *nobilitas* it signified have marked the transition from the early to the 'classic' middle republic, which lasted until 133 when the tribunate of Ti. Gracchus brought it to an abrupt end and ushered in a new age of political instability. The 'late' republic in turn lasted around three generations, although the precise cut-off date is debatable – 49, 43, 31?[2]

No understanding of the past is possible without identifying distinctive eras and tracing and explaining the transition from one to the other. But while periodisation is an essential part of writing history, it is also intrinsically problematic. Not only is there a risk of over-simplification, since all aspects of society obviously do not change simultaneously, but the labels applied may themselves carry unhelpful connotations. Here the 'organicist' model poses particular problems in terms of ideological 'baggage'; for while 'early' may imply a somewhat unformed and embryonic stage, it is nevertheless associated with promise and youthful energy. By contrast, 'late' signals ageing, a certain over-ripeness, and in some cases even decadence.

[2] For an interesting attempt to challenge the conventional periodisation of the Roman Republic, see Flower 2010.

Between these two stands the 'classic' age that represents the pinnacle of maturity and experience and in a sense embodies the 'ideal type' of a given civilisation.[3] These categories have important implications. In Rome it follows that the middle Republic over an extended period presented an almost perfect example of a well-functioning aristocracy sustained by internal discipline and effective power-sharing. Furthermore, the existence of this 'classic' age in turn throws into sharper relief the subsequent breakdown, since it implies that an otherwise stable system suddenly stopped working. However, we may wonder how helpful the distinction between 'middle' and 'late' republic is in terms of understanding the driving forces behind the political changes we can observe in this period.

The 'late' republic arguably gains its meaning from the notion of a preceding 'classic' period, which in turn implies that the political system in principle was sound and viable. It follows from this premise that the causes of the eventual 'decline and fall' will have to be sought in factors external to the political system, be they moral, socio-economic, military or geo-political. The question is, however, whether the 'classic' republic ever existed in the form imagined by later writers. Scholars have begun to question the ancient vision of a smooth-running aristocratic republic, suspecting it may be an idealised gloss on what was probably a far more messy reality; for what is striking about the 'classic' Roman republic is the extent to which it – like many other periods invested with similar nostalgic qualities – is the product of hindsight. Indeed, one of the main differences between the 'middle' and 'late' periods is the almost complete absence of contemporary records for the political life of the former.

Therefore, when studying the 'middle' and 'late' republics we are in some respects not comparing like with like. While the former is based almost entirely on later sources, for parts of the latter we have – through the works of Cicero – extensive first-hand, contemporary evidence that gives us direct insight into everyday politics and current affairs. As a result, the 'middle' republic – as well as its dramatic conclusion in 133 – comes to us through a process of retrospective 'post-rationalisation' carried out by observers who knew all too well what was to follow. By contrast, the eye-witness perspective of Cicero presents a vivid, open-ended and hence far more chaotic vision of politics during his lifetime. The vagaries of textual transmission are therefore a key factor in the creation of the 'classic'

---

[3] See Sion-Jenkis 2000: 192–201 on ancient conceptualisations of the 'ages' of Rome; cf. Alonso-Nuñes 1982.

republic. Another important factor is the particular Roman construction of past and present and their sense of never-ending decline.

Before the 'Fall'

The longing for an idealised past was deeply ingrained in the mentality of the Romans, for whom the present invariably appeared inferior to the age of the ancestors. The example of the *maiores* offered an undisputed guide to conduct in the public and private sphere, as illustrated by canonical stories of their deeds and sayings.[4] The reverence for the *maiores* created an enduring sense of decline and loss which can be traced even at the height of expansion and military success, well before the conventional turning point of 133, which suggests it existed independently of actual social and political changes.[5] Thus the Elder Cato, Polybius, and later Poseidonius and Calpurnius Piso all operated with this meta-narrative, each setting the starting-point for the decline at different moments according to their particular literary and ideological aims.[6] By far the most important contribution, of course, remains that of Livy, who is to a great extent responsible for the tripartite narrative framework we operate within today. However, what is perhaps most striking about Livy's surviving books on this period is how little attention is paid to domestic politics. The main emphasis consistently lies on military affairs and foreign engagements, while events at home, generally, are treated cursorily.

At regular intervals, however, certain domestic episodes are given prominence, but they appear to be carefully selected to fit a particular narrative pattern. Among the longest and most detailed we find the dispute over the repeal of the *lex Oppia* in 195 (34.1–8), the trials of the Scipiones in 187 (38.54–60), the suppression of the Bacchanalia in 186 (39.8–19), Cato's censorship in 184 (39.40–4), the story of Ligustinus set in 171 (42.32.6–35.2) and finally the dispute over Paullus' triumph in 167 (45.35–9). Some of these events seem to have been singled out less for their historical importance than for the particular exemplary qualities they carried. As such they may be interpreted as part of a 'counter-narrative' of incipient moral

---

[4] See Mouritsen 2014 with lit.

[5] On the idealised picture of the middle republic, see also Bleckmann 2002: 226, who stresses the importance of the decadence model, even among pre-Gracchan writers.

[6] Cato: Gel. *NA* 6.3.14 (Cornell F87); Polyb. 2.21.8; Poseidonius: Diod. Sic. 37.3; Piso: Plin. *Nat.* 34.14; 17.244 (Cornell F36, 40). This model was naturally reinforced in the later historiographical tradition when the Gracchi became widely associated with the 'crisis', e.g. Dion. Hal. *Ant. Rom.* 2.11.3. Cf. Bringmann 1977: 32; Lintott 1994: 6–10.

decline running underneath the main story of external success and expansion. They anticipated what was to come in the second part of Livy's work, which was entirely dedicated to the last century of the republic, and should at least in part be understood as an attempt to trace the roots of the contemporary problems the republic faced when Livy embarked on his monumental undertaking. These episodes are singled out as the early symptoms of a slow, almost imperceptible, process of moral decline caused by expansion, wealth, and foreign influence. In this way, Livy ingeniously managed to weave an alternative 'plot line' into the story of the 'middle' republic, one of old fashioned virtue gradually being eroded while Rome triumphed abroad.

Livy does not ignore domestic politics completely. But in order to present a picture of a political system that was essentially stable and undermined only by external influences which threatened ancestral mores, events that did not fit the concept were consistently downplayed. Sometimes he leaves out episodes mentioned in other sources, such as Culleo's interference in the registration of citizens by the censors, the sumptuary law of 182 and the dispute over the *lex annalis* proposed by the tribune M. Pinarius Rusca (pr. 181).[7] On other occasions Livy's account is surprisingly brief despite the dramatic potential of the events. For example, we are told that in 194 Q. Pleminius, who had been imprisoned for his crimes in Locri, planned to set fire to the city to enable his escape, but was denounced by accomplices and executed (34.44.7–8). It requires little imagination to picture how this event in a different narrative framework might have been expanded into a dramatic, almost Catilinarian tale of political upheaval and moral decline. However, in its second-century context the incident was reduced to a brief anecdote.

Livy's agenda and 'plot' structure is inseparable from our image of politics in the 'classic republic'. They determined his selection and presentation of political events, and since issues of considerable import and gravity were often reduced to short notices, we sometimes have to read between the lines to get a more accurate picture of the period. Doing so suggests that the seemingly stable era of aristocratic government may in fact have been as fraught with tension and rivalry as any other period. And, as one would expect in oligarchic systems, the primary source of friction appears to have been elite competition over status, honours, and distinctions. We find repeated references to the senate and those acting on its

---

[7] Plu. *Flam.* 18.1; Macr. 3.17.2–3; Cic. *De orat.* 2.261.

behalf trying to contain the problem of increased electioneering and private spending through stricter regulation.[8] In 180 the *cursus honorum* was formalised by the *lex Villia annalis*, while electoral campaigning was discouraged during the early second century through a variety of initiatives aimed at curbing *ambitus* and munificence. In addition to these structurally conditioned sources of conflict the elite frequently quarrelled over specific issues, often associated with individual members of the senate and their demands for triumphs, commands and military levies. Clashes over triumphs feature prominently in Livy's books on this period, probably because they represented a domestic corollary to the foreign engagements that remained Livy's primary focus in this part of his narrative.[9] Elections and candidatures also caused frequent disputes as members of the elite tried to bend the rules.[10]

Magistrates often conducted bitter feuds while in office, sometimes with their own colleagues.[11] For example, in 169 a tribunician proposal on public contracts was opposed by the censors, triggering an unruly meeting that was called to order by the censors themselves, in turn provoking the aggrieved tribunes to confiscate the property of one censor and charge the other with treason (43.16). On some occasions tribunes caused tension by ignoring senatorial opposition, as happened in 188 when *suffragium* was extended to the Volsci, while on others disputes got out of hand and tribunes resorted to *prehensio*, arrests of office holders, as in 151 and 138.[12] The impression is that of a fairly regular stream of political conflicts, which despite the lapidary accounts clearly seem to have caused considerable

[8] Livy reports strong competition at the elections in 193 (35.10.1) and again in 192 (35.24.4). In 190 he likewise noted electoral competition (37.47.6), which reoccurred at the censorial election the same year (37.57.9). In 185 the hard fought elections caused disturbances (39.32.5–12), followed by the stormy election which saw Cato becoming censor (39.40–1). In 181 (40.19.11) an *ambitus* law was passed. In 182 (40.44.12) Sempronius Gracchus reportedly spent heavily during his aedileship, and Livy also notes the disgrace associated with repeated failure at elections (40.37.6). In 174 (41.28.4) we again hear of strong competition, with games being held, while in 169 increased display by aediles is mentioned (44.18.8).

[9] Contested triumphs are recorded in 200 (31.20); 200 (31.49.8–11); 199 (32.7.4); 197 (33.22.1–23.4); 193 (35.8); 191 (36.40.10); 184 (39.38.4–10); 173 (42.9); 167 (45.35–39), cf. discussions in Pittinger 2008 and Lundgreen 2009b: 178–253. Controversial commands: 190 (37.51.1–6) and 178 (41.6.2–3). Debates over recruitment: 191 (36.3.4–5); 169 (43.14.2–5). 172 saw the trial of Popillius for his unjustified attack on the Ligurians (42.22), and in 174 Fulvius Flaccus looted a temple in Bruttium but was forced by the senate to retreat (42.3). Other examples of foreign policy causing disruption in Rome: 169 (45.21); 196 (33.25.4–7), cf. Plu. *Flam.* 2.

[10] 199 saw Flamininus' controversial candidature for the consulship (32.7.8–12). Similar electoral disputes occurred in 189 (37.57.9–58.2) and 184 (39.39).

[11] In 196 (33.42.2–4) a dispute broke out between quaestors and priests over unpaid taxes. Cf. 179 (40.45.7–46.16); 178 (41.7.4–10); 172 (42.10.9–15; 42.21).

[12] Liv. 38.36.7–9; *Per.* 48; 55; cf. Cic. *Leg.* 3.20.

controversy. Most likely this was not a new development emerging only in the wake of the Second Punic War: in the third century a number of similar instances had already been recorded, as Bleckmann showed in his deconstruction of the 'classic republic'.[13]

The Livian image of a united elite presiding over a smoothly running system of aristocratic power-sharing is likely to be too idealised. Even the partial and rudimentary record we have hints at continuous, often serious, conflict. We should therefore accept the possibility that our picture of the 'middle' republic as a period of broad elite consensus and stable senatorial control – over the *res publica* as well as its own members – may be a myth born out of hindsight. There are real implications for the question of periodisation, suggesting as it does a greater degree of continuity between the 'middle' and the 'late' periods; it becomes more difficult to maintain the notion of an abrupt change of direction in 133, when the aristocracy supposedly faced a sudden collapse of political cohesion.

The idea of a prolonged, almost permanent, state of crisis lasting a hundred years is, of course, meaningless, as Flower has reminded us.[14] Nevertheless, later ancient writers are unanimous in identifying the dramatic events of 133 as a turning point in the history of the republic; the question is what precisely they inaugurated. Modern scholars usually focus on two long-term consequences of Ti. Gracchus' tribunate. On the one hand, the unprecedented outbreak of political violence supposedly set an example so powerful that it would eventually lead to the armed overthrow of the old political order. On the other hand, the year is also identified with the birth of a new kind of radical politics which reflected deep and irreconcilable ideological differences within the elite. Thus, out of Gracchus' tribunate are supposed to have emerged two different types of politicians, the so-called 'populares' and 'optimates', defined by personal commitment to distinct causes and/or class interests, the pursuit of which contributed greatly to the disunity and dysfunction of the late republic.[15] The centrality of the two concepts to current interpretations of late republican politics justifies a more detailed discussion of their origins and evidential basis.

---

[13] Bleckmann 2002: 228. They include Flaminius' land bill in 232, the disputes over Appius Caecus' refusal to accept a plebeian consular candidate (Cic. *Brut.* 55) and over the *provincia* distribution in 264, as well as the votes against naval campaigns in 252 and 247. In 264 the declaration of war was passed in the assembly while the senate was split, Polyb. 1.10.3–11.3.

[14] Flower 2010. Cf. Walter 2014a: 96, and Rilinger 1982.

[15] Cf. e.g. Nippel 1988: 55: '... seit den Gracchen bildete sich das neue Muster der popularen Politik heraus ...'.

Inventing the 'Populares' and 'Optimates'

The binary model of 'populares' and 'optimates' has for generations shaped interpretations of the late republic, widely seen as a battleground between competing ideologies and contrasting visions of Roman society. The categories are supposed to have come into existence in 133, although attempts to identify 'forerunners' of the Gracchi in the previous decades have also been made, presumably to make the transformation of Roman politics associated with that year seem less abrupt.[16] Despite the ubiquity of the 'populares'/'optimates'-model there is surprisingly little agreement among scholars as to the actual meaning of these concepts, their practical significance and political implications.[17]

The great nineteenth-century historian Theodor Mommsen presented them as straightforward political blocks and invested them with ideological identities that made them directly comparable to those of his own time. The 'left-right' framework he adopted can be traced back to the late eighteenth century, but Mommsen updated it by accommodating the newly introduced parliamentary parties of contemporary Europe into his model of republican politics.[18] While the anachronistic features of his 'parties' have been widely recognised, Mommsen's modernising approach to republican politics remains a powerful presence in current scholarship. Some modifications have taken place, with historians now envisaging looser and more transient groupings, or in the case of the 'populares' an ideological 'tradition' or, most recently, a 'family of ideas'.[19] The fact that the discussion about their nature and definition continues unabated may in itself hint at their fundamental elusiveness.

The so-called optimates have been fairly unanimously identified as the 'establishment party', representatives of the aristocracy who defended its interests (material as well as political) and generally behaved as the Roman equivalent of modern fiscal conservatives by opposing wealth redistribution and promoting a 'small state'. In order to enforce those policies, the 'optimates' emphasised the supremacy of the *senatus auctoritas* over the 'power of the people', and among their most prominent members we find politicians such as Scipio Nasica, Sulla and his followers, Catulus, Lucullus, Hortensius, and Cato. In many instances 'optimates' are defined, somewhat mechanically, as those who opposed the 'populares', although

---

[16] Taylor 1962 invented the concept of the 'forerunners' of the Gracchi.
[17] See the overview in Robb 2010.
[18] Mommsen 1854–5 passim, e.g. 1.290–322, 825–33. Cf. Strasburger 1939: 775–7.   [19] Arena 2012.

that merely shifts the focus onto the 'populares', who turn out to be even more difficult to pin down.

As the opponents of the 'optimates', 'populares' are typically described as 'progressive' and 'democratic' politicians whose 'left-wing' leanings led them to champion the cause of the people, standing up for the interests of the common man against the senate and its 'optimate' leaders. On closer inspection these definitions raise more questions than they answer; for how does one in practice identify individual politicians, laws and actions as 'popularis'? The canonical list of 'populares', including the Gracchi, Saturninus, Sulpicius, and Clodius, is well known and much-repeated but also strikingly short. Many other politicians have been placed in the same category but as soon as we move beyond the 'classic' examples we run into seemingly insurmountable difficulties of definition.

The definition of 'populares' as those who strove to improve the lives of the masses may seem a fairly straightforward way of measuring their political profile. However, even some of the classic 'populares', such as Sulpicius, hardly fit that description, since none of his recorded policies had much to do with the betterment of the *populus* and in fact appear to have been distinctly unpopular.[20] Attempts to define specific policies as either 'popularis' or 'optimate' face similar difficulties. A standard example of 'popular' legislation would, for example, be measures offering material support for the populace, above all in the form of free or subsidised food, as well as land for the poor. It could be argued, however, that such measures were not per se incompatible with traditional senatorial policy, given the extensive colonisation the senate had overseen in the past, and the grain provision which members of the elite occasionally organised on a private basis. Moreover, policies focused on the *commoda populi* were not the sole preserve of so-called populares. In 91 the younger Drusus passed both agrarian and grain laws with the support of most of the senate and its leaders, while in 78 Lepidus' *lex frumentaria* was apparently passed 'nullo resistente', 'without opposition', and in 62 Cato, the ultimate 'optimate', promoted a grain law with the senate's full approval.[21] And, viewed purely in terms of scale, Sulla, another 'arch-optimate', becomes the greatest 'popularis' of all, since he probably confiscated and redistributed more

---

[20] On Sulpicius' tribunate, see Powell 1990.

[21] Lepidus: Gran. Lic. 36.35 Crin. Cato: Plu. *Caes.* 8.4; *Cat. Mi.* 26.1; *Mor.* 818D. The *lex Terentia Cassia* (73) was also passed while the 'Sullan regime' was still in place. Later it was praised even by the supposedly 'optimate' Cicero, *Ver.* 2.5.52. For a list of senatorial initiatives, see Ungern-Sternberg 1991: 39–41. Individually, Roman aristocrats also provided material support for the plebs, e.g. Crassus, who distributed privately funded grain in 70, Plu. *Crass.* 12.2 cf. Garnsey 1988: 210–11.

land in Italy than any other Roman politician. On the other hand, Caesar, supposedly at the opposite end of the spectrum, substantially reduced the number of grain recipients in Rome during his dictatorship (Suet. *Iul.* 41.3).

Measures defending the people's political rights and independence have also been perceived as typically 'popularis', the primary example being the *leges tabellariae* of the later second century, which introduced written ballots in assemblies and courts. While they might seem clear-cut cases of legislation empowering the *populus* – and indeed were opposed by many senators – their political significance is in fact difficult to pin down. As Lundgreen noted, secret ballots are not inherently more 'democratic' than public voting. Furthermore, the reforms appear to have had no discernible impact on voting patterns, suggesting they did not 'liberate' citizens from elite control.[22] After the reforms proposals were no more likely to be rejected or adopted than before, nor did the profile of those elected to public office show any change. Unsurprisingly, therefore, no attempt was ever made to reverse the ballot laws, whose most puzzling feature remains the hostile senatorial reaction they provoked.

Often 'populares' and their laws are identified purely by association or – in accordance with the binary model – through their opponents. That is, for example, the case with enfranchisement laws which have been classified as 'popularis' despite the fact that they were distinctly unpopular. Extending citizenship to foreigners held little appeal for the Roman populace and neither did the regular attempts to exploit the many freedmen in Rome by granting them greater voting power. Nevertheless, these measures have been labelled as 'popular' because of the controversy they caused and the objections they faced from senators concerned about political stability.[23] Likewise, some initiatives targeting senators are classified as 'popularis', e.g. C. Cornelius' attempt to curb senators' exploitative loans to foreign envoys, while other laws regulating elite behaviour such as *ambitus* and *luxuria* are never given that label. Sumptuary laws, which one would expect to fall into this category, are surprisingly not associated with 'popularis' politics, and were indeed implemented by both Sulla and

---

[22] Cic. *Leg.* 3.39, cf. Plu. *Mar.* 4.2–4. Interestingly, Cicero appears to have objected to the *lex Maria* narrowing the voting *pontes* more than he did to the *leges tabellariae*. See Gruen 1991: 257–61; Jehne 1993; Yakobson 1995; Marshall 1997; Ritter 1998; Vishnia 2008; Lundgreen 2009a.

[23] There are also notable inconsistencies, e.g. the younger Drusus who may have proposed extensions of citizenship, probably to the Latins, with the support of the senate, cf. Mouritsen 1998. No strong objections are recorded to Pompeius Strabo's – albeit poorly documented – grant of Latin status to the Transpadane Gauls.

Caesar, supposedly polar opposites. On the other hand, the long-running dispute over jury composition is often placed in that context, although it does not fit a simple 'people versus elite' dichotomy. C. Gracchus' reform of the *repetundae* court did not 'democratise' it, but merely handed control to non-senatorial members of the elite. And when L. Cotta finally, after several changes back and forth, restored majority control to non-senators in 70, it appears to have been implemented in broad agreement with the senate.

In each case there were, of course, specific factors influencing the decisions, but examples like these nevertheless illustrate the difficulties involved in attaching political labels to certain types of legislation. The more closely one looks at the categories the more they seem to dissolve. It was precisely this problem that led Christian Meier, the author of the most comprehensive study of 'populares', to suggest a radical reinterpretation which stripped the concept of its ideological content.[24] Abandoning Mommsen's left-right scheme, he applied a purely functional approach which concentrated on observable patterns of behaviour. From that perspective the so-called populares appeared as 'dissident' politicians (usually tribunes) who used the assemblies against the will of the senatorial majority. Behaving like a 'popularis' simply meant employing a specific strategy, the *ratio popularis*, in order to pursue specific policies and generally get ahead in Roman politics; as such it did not per se reflect a particular ideology or commitment. The 'optimates', on the other hand, were simply those who rejected this method and obeyed the collective authority of the senate. In this interpretation they become the 'mainstream' senators, who caused no trouble and attracted little attention. This part of Meier's analysis followed in the footsteps of Hermann Strasburger, who in 1939 had argued that the term 'optimates' simply denoted the senate and particularly its inner circle of dominant nobles, making them a social category rather than an ideologically defined 'party'.

After the ground-breaking work of Meier and Strasburger, historians began to downplay the ideological aspect, while some even questioned the relevance of these categories altogether. Erich Gruen could, for example, criticise the work of Burckhardt for its adoption of 'a simplistic and rather old-fashioned dichotomy between optimates and populares as if they were identifiable groups that divided the political landscape between them'.[25] And following this approach the terms were typically used as convenient

---

[24] Meier 1965. Cf. Ferrary 1997; Roddaz 2005: 98; Ungern-Sternberg 2014: 95.
[25] Gruen, 1990: 179–81, on Burckhardt 1988, cf. Gruen 1991: 253.

shorthand for the senatorial majority and those who broke the consensus, without any implication of sharp ideological divides (as I have in the past also done myself).

In recent decades, however, the pendulum has swung back towards ideological readings of Roman politics. In accordance with this paradigm 'populares' and 'optimates' are once again described in modernising idioms as 'progressives' and 'conservatives', often with implied value judgements. Proponents of the revisionist school have pointed to situations which seem to go beyond a mere 'strategy' and indicate a higher level of commitment.[26] In response to the problems involved in identifying a consistent 'popularis' programme (which originally inspired Meier's model), they have shifted the focus away from the policies themselves and onto the underlying motivation. Since policy itself offers no viable guide to identifying 'populares', a new criterion has been introduced, which is the strength and sincerity of the motives behind them. This has now become the real test of a true 'popularis', and final proof of selfless altruism is provided by the personal sacrifices they made, some even laying down their lives for the 'popular cause'. The revival of Mommsen's ideological model, albeit without the formal 'party' structures, coincides with the rise in 'democratic' interpretations of Roman politics, which it logically complements.[27] Thus it could be argued that if the people really held power in Rome it would be a natural expectation to find their interests promoted by their democratically elected champions. The link between democracy and 'populares' remains tenuous, however, not least because candidates apparently never ran on specific policies or associated themselves with particular ideologies during their campaign.[28]

Attempting to distinguish the two types by their degree of ideological purity is likely to lead us into a methodological cul-de-sac. Personal motivation is, at any time, a dubious criterion for classifying politicians, but in Rome the inner-most thoughts of the protagonists are, with the possible exception of Cicero, little more than speculation. And even if our evidence had been fuller, their 'true' feelings would probably still escape us,

---

[26] Cf. Perelli 1982; Doblhofer 1990; Mackie 1992; Wiseman 1994; 2009; 2010; Eder 1996; Zecchini 1997: 37–50; Santangelo 2008; Tan 2008; Tiersch 2009: 55; Arena 2011; 2012; Duplá 2011; Beness and Hillard 2012; Atkins 2013: 10. Cf. the survey in Robb 2010: 15–33.

[27] As indeed stressed by Millar 1986: 4, the 'father of Roman democracy'.

[28] *Pace* Yakobson 1999. Yakobson 2010 recently suggested that the very existence of 'populares' lent Rome a democratic aspect and ensured popular influence no matter how they were chosen. The argument appears to turn the definition of democracy upside down, allowing the label to be applied to any 'moderate' oligarchy which occasionally extends socio-economic benefits to wider sections of the population.

personal motivation by its very nature being changeable as well as mixed. Certainly, we cannot deduce initial intentions from final outcomes; the Gracchi evidently did not anticipate a violent end at the hands of their opponents when they embarked on their tribunates. This is not to deny the existence of altruism or commitment to particular causes among the Roman elite (who were complex human beings like any others), but neither should we expect unrealistic levels of moral and political clarity – or overestimate our ability to separate layers of conscious and unconscious motivation.

The ideological approach offers only a very partial explanation of the categories under discussion. It does not, for example, account for the many supposed 'populares' who espoused policies only tenuously linked to the *populus*, Sulpicius again being a case in point. In those instances the model seems to fall back on Meier's 'functional' definition of a 'popularis' as somebody who – for whatever reason – challenged the senatorial majority. The problem is that numerous politicians at some point defied the senate – and hence would have to be classified as 'populares' – but did so for reasons that seem unrelated to the lives of the masses.

It follows that faced with a choice between the two current models, Meier's interpretation, being the more consistent, would have to be preferred. Nevertheless, Meier's approach raises questions of its own; for the binary division implied in the concepts of 'populares'/'optimates' sits uneasily with Meier's general understanding of Roman politics, which he presents as an ever-shifting pattern of fluid associations and changing allegiances, all focused on the issues of the day – rather than fixed ideological positions. It was precisely to overcome this tension that Meier reduced the 'populares' to their lowest common denominator, which was the lack of senatorial backing. But that begs the question why the Romans created a category for such a diverse group of politicians, many of whom had little in common apart from their strategy, and indeed gave them a name that associated them with the universally acknowledged source of political legitimacy, the *populus*.[29] If 'populares' simply were those who employed a particular method to further their policies and careers, why did that make them members of a specific category defined in sharp contrast to those who did not? Conversely, if the 'optimates' were identified as those who adhered to senatorial authority, the category becomes devoid of any

---

[29] It should also be noted that in Meier's model Cicero's definition of the two terms in the *Pro Sestio*, 96–101, which forms the basis for all modern discussions, has been transformed almost beyond any recognition.

political content, since the majority would always be 'optimates' whatever policy they happened to agree on. In other words, if we follow Meier's approach to its logical conclusion, the two concepts become virtually meaningless, as illustrated by the famous vote in December 50 when the senate rejected the hard-line 'optimate' opponents of Caesar and endorsed Curio's compromise option by 370 to 22. On that occasion the leading 'optimates' did not have the rest of the senate behind them, effectively turning men like Cato into 'populares'.[30]

We are confronted with a seemingly insoluble conundrum: a political terminology that appears to defy both ideological and practical explanations. The inability to reach even the vaguest consensus about the meaning of these categories suggests we revisit the primary evidence and ask whether Roman politicians really were divided into two categories known as 'populares' and 'optimates'. As noted earlier, 'optimates' has long been recognised as a straightforward descriptor for the leaders of the senate.[31] As a standard term for the ruling class it was widely used, often in parallel with 'boni', which denoted the propertied classes in general and therefore overlapped with 'optimates'. Its generic nature is illustrated by the fact that it could be employed about foreign aristocracies, as Cicero did when he referred to the 'optimates' of Asian towns in the *Pro Flacco*.[32] If we accept this definition of 'optimates' as a term denoting the senatorial elite, the so-called populares – qua senators – themselves become 'optimates', precluding any meaningful distinction. This problem is strikingly highlighted in Cicero's speech on the response of the *haruspices*, which had contained a warning 'not to let death and danger be wrought for the fathers and leaders through discord and dissent among the optimates … '.[33] Cicero accused Clodius of fomenting this 'optimatium discordiam', and since it would make no sense to blame a politician for causing a split among his adversaries, the implication is that Clodius himself formed part of that group. If 'optimates' was a category to which all politicians naturally

---

[30] Plu. *Caes.* 30.3; *Pomp.* 58.5; *Ant.* 5.4; App. *BC* 2.30, cf. Timmer 2009 393–4. Cato's right-hand man, M. Favonius, also suffered defeats at his attempt at the aedileship and praetorship, suggesting that despite his impeccable 'optimate' credentials he was not particularly popular with the propertied classes who decided these elections, *Fam.* 8.9.5 (SB 82) (Caelius), cf. Ryan 1994; Pina Polo 2012: 82, who notes that he may have suffered 'up to four *repulsae* in his political career'.

[31] Cic. *Rep.* 1.55; *Leg.* 3.17, use 'optimates' synonymously with aristocrats, the latter contrasting them with *multitudo*. Already the Elder Cato had used 'optimates' for 'aristocrats', Serv. *A.* 4.682, and in Plautus *Men.* 571–4, we find its cognate 'optumi' carrying the same meaning.

[32] *Flac.* 54, 58, 63. Cf. Robb 2010: 187.

[33] *Har.* 40: 'ne per optimatium discordiam dissensionemque patribus principibusque caedes periculaque creentur … '. (53, Cicero argues sophistically that Clodius is not affected since he is no *princeps*). Cf. Robb 2010: 89.

belonged, then 'popularis' cannot for obvious reasons have been defined as its opposite.[34] Our sources, above all Cicero, often refer to the political views of the 'optimates', e.g. in the context of the disputes between the senate and Clodius, Caesar and Pompey. But that does not make them comparable to a 'party' or carriers of a particular oligarchic ideology or programme, although there was a natural expectation that members of the senate and the ruling class would adhere to a basic code of conduct and uphold the existing social order. Cicero could therefore play on the double meaning of 'optimates', noting that the *principes* may carry the name but not the substance, and on another occasion wonder whether there are any of them left, since the 'optimates' no longer behave like 'optimates'.[35]

'Popularis' is a far more complex term than 'optimas', as Robb recently demonstrated in her important study of Roman political terminology.[36] Her comprehensive analysis of all the ancient attestations revealed some interesting features. She observed, for example, that 'populares' and 'optimates', contrary to common perception, are contrasted or juxtaposed only very rarely, and that some contemporary authors did not use them at all, most strikingly Sallust (see further below). Crucially, Robb showed that 'popularis' covered a much wider range of meanings and usages than is often appreciated. Etymologically derived from *populus*, it covered any kind of association with the people and could as such be positive, negative or entirely neutral. 'Popularis' could be used pejoratively in the sense of 'populist', or 'pandering to the lowest instincts of the people'. It also covered the modern 'popular' as in 'well liked' (or seeking popularity). Even more positive was the usage of 'popularis' as 'friend of the people', and 'acting in the people's interest' (or at least pretending to do so). Entirely neutral was the sense of 'countryman' or 'member of a group or association'. Finally, it could denote any type of activity linked to the people, including meetings or speeches delivered before crowds.

It follows that describing someone simply as 'popularis' would not have been immediately intelligible, which explains why it often appears with additional phrases indicating the particular sense in which it is used. Although its multivalency would have made it rather unsuitable as a political label, that did not apparently limit its popularity in political discourse. Indeed, all sides of political arguments might claim to be true

---

[34] Similarly, in *Ac.* 2.72 (*Luc.*) Cicero notes that 'seditiosi cives' and 'populares' try to appear like 'boni' by invoking respectable predecessors, cf. 2.13, a comment that, however tendentious, makes no sense if 'populares' were defined in opposition to 'boni/optimates'.

[35] *Rep.* 1.51; *Att.* 2.5.1 (SB 25): 'quid enim nostri optimates, si qui reliqui sunt, loquentur?'

[36] Robb 2010.

'populares' (in the positive sense), while dismissing their opponents as the wrong kind of 'populares', i.e. 'populists' and false friends of the *populus*. For example, in the agrarian speeches to the senate and at a *contio* Cicero asks rhetorically who is the real 'popularis': Cicero himself, who works for peace and harmony, or Rullus, who endangers these values.[37] Likewise in the Philippics, Cicero attacks Fufius Calenus, declaring that 'Previously we could not deter you from being *popularis*, yet now we cannot persuade you to be *popularis*', deftly using the term in two different ways, first as 'populist' and then as 'supporter of the people's interest'.[38]

Examples such as these are often dismissed as instances of 'slippery' political language.[39] The twisting of words and concepts is, of course, integral to any political discourse; one could, for example, envisage a contemporary situation where an opponent claimed that a Liberal Party is in fact not liberal, playing on the ambiguity of the name. However, such a strategy is feasible only if there is a party called the 'Liberals' and an established set of values associated with 'liberal'. But in the case of 'popularis' the existence of a particular type of politician named 'Populares' is itself open to dispute. The suggestion that Cicero in these passages is subverting a 'standard' meaning of 'popularis' is therefore circular, since it assumes the presence of a well-defined category of 'Popular' politicians with recognised characteristics. The inherent ambiguity of the term is, in other words, explained away by reference to the 'two-party-model' itself.

We are in fact dealing with a multiplicity of meanings, none of which was more 'real' than the others. Thus the various different meanings of 'popularis' in the political discourse can all be explained within the semantic range identified by Robb, without taking recourse to 'parties', 'traditions', 'ideologies' or any other unifying traits commonly associated with this putative category. In the entire ancient record only one text lends itself directly to a binary understanding of Roman politics: Cicero's famous excursus in the *Pro Sestio*. It is to this particular discussion that the entire theory ultimately can be traced. In 56 Cicero defended his protégé Sestius against a charge of *vis*, political violence, committed during the campaign for Cicero's recall from exile. As part of his defence Cicero launches into a highly unusual digression about Roman politics, ostensibly triggered by

---

[37] *Agr.* 1.23, 2.6–10, 17, 102.

[38] *Phil.* 8.19: 'antea deterrere te, ne popularis esses, non poteramus; exorare nunc, ut sis popularis, non possumus', cf. Robb 2010: 76–7. Cf. e.g. *Rab. perd.* 11–15. *Att.* 2.20.4 (SB 40), 'populare nunc nihil tam est quam odium popularium', again playing on the double meaning of 'popularis': 'populist' and 'popular'. Cf. *Att.* 1.19.4 (SB 19).

[39] E.g. Atkins 2000: 479.

the prosecutor's query about the identity of the 'natio optimatium', the 'tribe of optimates', to which Cicero apparently had referred in an earlier intervention. Taking his cue from this question, Cicero famously declares that there had always been two types of politician, 'optimates' and 'populares', the former defined as everybody who is neither 'criminal nor vicious in disposition, nor frantic, nor hampered by troubles in their households', while the latter are those who wished everything they did and said to be agreeable to the masses'.[40] As definitions of political groupings, strategies or traditions these descriptions make little sense, and as importantly they are not matched by Cicero's own usage elsewhere. In the rest of his extensive corpus 'optimates' carry the standard meaning of senatorial elite, with no apparent attempt ever to widen its social application.

The categories presented in the *Pro Sestio* are therefore unique to this speech. They should be understood in the context of the wider political purpose of the excursus, which was to identify Cicero himself with the *res publica*, the senate and all good Romans, and correspondingly to isolate his opponent Clodius, not just from his natural political hinterland in the *nobilitas* but also from other politicians who had previously pursued their policies directly through the assemblies; their example – however regrettable in Cicero's view – might still seem to provide a precedent – and hence legitimisation – for Clodius' actions. In Cicero's 'model' Clodius is therefore not included among the 'populares', because he, unlike his predecessors, was not actually popular; the popular backing he claimed was little more than hired crowds and strong-arm men, while the 'real' people despised him.

The *Pro Sestio* was a daring attempt to turn the tables on Clodius, reversing his opponent's natural superiority as a scion of one of Rome's noblest families and presenting Cicero, the new man from Arpinum who had only recently returned from ignominious exile, as the true representative of the Roman establishment. To that end he redefined one of the conventional terms used for the senatorial elite, 'optimates', and turned it into an almost all-embracing name for upstanding and respectable citizens. This expanded category of 'optimates' was then contrasted with those who pandered to the masses through populist measures. This new bisection of the political class did not include Clodius, whose failure even to gain the approval of the mob made him an outcast. Ironically, therefore, the

---

[40] *Sest.* 97: 'Omnes optimates sunt, qui neque nocentes sunt nec natura improbi nec furiosi nec malis domesticis impediti', the 'malis domesticis' clearly referring to financial problems. Populares, *Sest.* 96: 'Qui ea quae faciebant quaeque dicebant multitudini iucunda volebant esse'.

foundational text for the modern 'party' model explicitly excludes one of the most famous 'populares' from its own definition.[41]

The picture Cicero presents should be appreciated for what it is, namely a brilliant rhetorical 'conjuring trick' that responded to a very particular challenge facing the orator in 56. As far as we know, he never repeated it, although the distinction between the real and the false *populus* was useful for dismissing opponents who claimed popular support. Elsewhere he simply used 'optimates' for the (leading) senators, while 'popularis' appears regularly in all its senses, both positive and negative. Modern attempts to identify examples of 'Sestian' usage in other parts of Cicero's work are generally problematic since they presuppose – rather than demonstrate – the existence of the 'parties'; without this 'template' for Roman politics, other interpretations become possible, indeed compelling.[42]

Cicero's bold rhetorical self-reinvention in the *Pro Sestio* has presented historians with a deceptively simple model which at first sight seems to provide a key to unlocking the secrets of Roman politics. But the terminology Cicero uses turns out to be unique and unlike anything else found in the ancient sources. It could, of course, be argued that removing the term 'popularis' from our vocabulary does not affect the actual practice of politics; or in other words, there might still be a 'popular' side to Roman politics even if it was not called that. However, all attempts to describe such a 'democratic/progressive' strand of politics ultimately rely on the term 'popularis' to give it structure and definition. We are therefore not dealing with an observable phenomenon for which the *Pro Sestio* happens to offer a convenient label. Rather, it is the other way round; Cicero's use of 'popularis' in that particular speech has reified what would otherwise have remained discrete, difficult to classify events and individuals and turned them into manifestations of a single political movement.

Meier's classic study of 'populares' was – somewhat ironically – hamstrung by its basic premise. As an encyclopaedia article on the lemma 'popularis' its very point of departure was the reality of the concept as well as its relevance for the study of the Roman republic. This created a tension since Meier discovered that it had virtually no identifiable features. His meticulous analysis of the individuals described as 'popularis', their background and apparent intentions, left him with a category of

[41] Robb 2010: 65–8, 165–6. As we saw, it is also at variance with the near-contemporary speech concerning the *haruspices*, which presented Clodius as an – albeit wayward – 'optimas'.

[42] For example, *Comm. pet.* 5, with its rare juxtaposition of 'popularis' and 'optimates', does not in itself indicate a 'two-party' model and freed of this supposition can be interpreted very differently, cf. below pp. 134–35.

politicians who, apart from their willingness to defy the senate, had no clear or unifying characteristics. On that basis he concluded that we were dealing with a *ratio popularis*, that is, a method by which politicians relied entirely on the assemblies. However, after Robb's work it is now clear that while there indeed existed a 'popularis ratio', there were no 'populares', since those who employed the strategy did so for such a wide range of purposes that the Romans did not perceive them as members of a specific category to which a single label could be attached. This is also the impression conveyed Sallust, the other contemporary source on late republican politics.

Sallust: Politics without 'Optimates' and 'Populares'

According to Ronald Syme, 'Sallust is also in part to blame for the prevalence of another doctrine, namely the belief that Rome had a regular two-party system, Optimates and Populares'.[43] The suggestion that Sallust somehow was responsible for this model (from which Syme distanced himself) is surprising, since he uses an entirely different terminology and presents a picture of Roman politics that is not easily reconciled to a binary, 'Sestian' model. Indeed, through the writings of Sallust one enters a political world distinctly different from that encountered in many modern textbooks.

Sallust never uses the term 'optimates', while 'popularis' occurs in two different meanings in the *Bellum Catilinae* and the *Bellum Iugurthinum*, neither of them coinciding with Cicero's 'Sestian' definition. In the former, 'popularis' is employed in the sense of 'participant' in the conspiracy and in the latter as 'countryman'/'subject (of a ruler)'.[44] The labels, otherwise considered standard political coinages, are in other words absent from the works of a contemporary observer who had personal experience of Roman politics and its public discourse. His rejection of the term 'optimates', a common label for the most influential senators, is probably deliberate and may be explained by the implicit claim to superiority and entitlement it conveyed. His aversion to such language is evident from his stated objection to 'bonus' as a standard epithet for any person of wealth.[45] Rather than buying into the elite's self-definition as 'optimates' he consistently prefers the social descriptor 'nobilis'. The absence of 'popularis',

[43] Syme 1964: 17.
[44] *Cat.* 22.1; 24.1; 52.14; *Jug.* 7.1; 35.9; 48.1; 58.4; 70.2; 74.1; 111.2. Cf. Robb 2010: 114–15.
[45] *Hist.* 1.12Maur.

on the other hand, cannot be similarly explained, i.e. as a reflection of Sallust's political standpoint; for while 'optimates' are replaced by the roughly equivalent 'nobiles', the opponents of the nobles do not appear as a distinct category in Sallust's political universe, neither in the guise of 'populares' nor under any other name.[46]

The political divisions outlined by Sallust are entirely different from those presented in Cicero's *Pro Sestio*. According to Sallust, society was split into two 'partes', one being the *populus*, the other the *nobilitas*.[47] We are, in other words, dealing with a subsection of the senate pitted against the rest of society.[48] Since the *nobiles* were defined not by a specific ideology but by ancestry and *honores* (and by implication power, prestige and resources), we are far removed from the 'conservative' senatorial party of modern textbooks. This particular part of the elite, whose most prominent members Sallust denounced as 'pauci' (the few, i.e. the oligarchs) was itself riven by internal divisions, described as *factiones* (terminologically distinguished from *partes, Jug.* 41.1). According to Sallust, the *factiones* were largely driven by selfishness and greed, albeit to varying degrees. Thus, some nobles preferred true glory (*vera gloria*) to unjust power (*iniusta potentia*), which naturally caused internal friction that occasionally escalated into open conflict. As prime examples of these rare upstanding *nobiles* Sallust mentions the Gracchi, whose attempt to vindicate the *libertas* of the plebs and expose the crimes of the *pauci* he extolled (*Jug.* 41.10; 42.1).

Sallust's attack on the greed and arrogance of the nobles has, in accordance with the binary model, led to his own classification as a 'popularis' and follower of Caesar, supposedly also a champion of the 'people's cause'. But as Syme demonstrated long ago, Sallust's position is far more complex; for while his hatred of the nobles is evident, his sympathies are more elusive. Despite honourable exceptions such as the Gracchi, opponents of the nobles, whatever their professed aims, are portrayed as driven by the same base and selfish motives. All politicians, according to Sallust, used specious pretexts to justify their actions. The tribunes who took office after 70 are, for example, condemned as young men, ferocious because of their age and temper, who attacked the senate and excited the plebs with *largitio*

---

[46] On the absence of 'populares'/'optimates' in Sallust see Strasburger 1939: 773. Paananen 1972: 41–2 rightly saw Sallust's reluctance to use 'optimates' as politically motivated, but his explanation of the absent 'populares' is less convincing. On the one hand, he notes that the term is too ambiguous to be useful as a political label, while, on the other hand, he readily accepts Cicero's 'Sestian' model, without asking how Cicero – and others – could use it if it was too vague for Sallust.

[47] *Jug.* 41.5, 'Ita omnia in duas partis abstracta sunt, . . . ', cf. 'populi partium', 43.1.

[48] Syme 1964: 171 noted the over-simplification of this dichotomy, the nobility being neither united nor representing the whole senatorial class.

and promises.[49] The tribunes supporting Marius' consular candidature are even described as 'seditiosi', while Lepidus' high-minded rhetoric is undercut by references to his own profiteering during the Sullan proscriptions.[50] Sallust's picture of the common people is hardly more flattering; although oppressed, they are presented as lethargic and impassive, even denounced as a criminal mob prone to *seditio* and *discordia*.[51]

Sallust's portraits of the protagonists of the recent past hardly fit the 'populares'/'optimates' model either. The depiction of Sulla is surprisingly nuanced and almost positive in the *Bellum Iugurthinum* (95–6), while that of Marius is more equivocal than one might have expected. Similarly, both Cato and Caesar are presented as great men and their famous debate in 63 as a clash of personalities rather than ideologies.[52] In fact, the political arguments Sallust ascribes to his characters as well as his own comments on their actions rarely match a simple split between 'populares and 'optimates'. In Sallust's works *libertas populi Romani* and *senatus auctoritas* are never presented as alternative sources of power and legitimacy nor do they mark distinct ideological creeds. Instead they appear as part of a shared understanding of the *res publica* embraced by political leaders and *populus* alike. For example, the tribune Memmius, supposedly a 'popularis', complains that 'the senate's authority has been prostituted to a ruthless enemy'.[53] And Macer's speech implies that his 'optimate' opponents also claimed to defend *libertas*, while in the *Histories* Sallust mentions influential men who are 'attempting to win absolute rule masquerading as champions of the senate or of the people'.[54] The point is made even clearer when he comments on the use of pretexts 'honestis nominibus'; some maintained they were defending 'populi iura' others 'senatus auctoritas', but under this pretence of caring for public welfare – 'bonum publicum simulantes' – they all worked for self-advancement (*Cat.* 38.3). The implication is that Sallust regarded *senatus auctoritas* as a positive concept behind which

---

[49] *Cat.* 38.1: 'homines adulescentes, summam potestatem nacti, quibus aetas animusque ferox erat, coepere senatum criminando plebem exagitare, dein largiundo atque pollicitando magis incendere'.

[50] *Jug.* 73.5; *Hist.* 1.55.18Maur. As Syme 1964: 169 observed: 'Sallust betrays – or rather avows – strong feelings against the nobilitas. Their enemies (it will be pertinently observed) do not always come off very well'.

[51] *Jug.* 41.3: on the rise of 'lascivia atque superbia' among the people after fall of Carthage; 41.5: people beginning to abuse their *libertas* and robbing, pillaging and plundering; 86.3: the poor considering anything honourable for which they receive pay; 66.2: the *volgus* is fickle, as is usually the case, prone to *seditio* and *discordia* and eager for *novae res*.

[52] As Syme 1964 ch. 8 noted, it is Caesar who in fact comes out worse of the two.

[53] *Jug.* 31.25: 'Hosti acerrumo prodita senatus auctoritas'.

[54] *Hist.* 3.48.22Maur: ' … vindices uti se ferunt libertatis'; *Hist.* 1.12Maur: 'sub honesto patrum aut plebis nomine dominationes adfectabant'.

politicians could hide less honourable motives. Defending the senate's standing and influence was to Sallust as creditable as protecting the people's interests. While there were clearly differences of emphasis, the two ideals are presented as in principle complementary and universally accepted by all politicians (see further below pp. 159–64).

Sallust, in sum, presents a society split between a powerful elite and an oppressed *populus*, whose interests some nobles claimed to champion – for a variety of motives but usually to their own advancement. All invoked similar lofty ideals and values, but most were in reality guided by self-interest. The dissenting nobles and their factions carried no particular labels, for the simple reason that they lacked the common characteristics which would have enabled such a categorisation. However, while ideological demarcations seem absent, socio-economic distinctions were important. Thus, 'new men' occupy a prominent position in Sallust's vision of Roman politics and are frequently presented as the real 'opposition' to the nobles.

Despite his broad-brush approach and obvious moralising, Sallust's image of Roman politics remains entirely consistent and firmly rooted in the social realities of the late republic. It dissolves the conventional dichotomies into a fluid picture of factional strife, conducted in a blurry ideological grey-zone of common values – and equally tainted motives. While not denying the existence of conflicts in which participants employed different tactics and rhetorical strategies, Sallust takes us beyond simple notions of 'conservative' and 'liberal' wings of the Roman elite.

Politics without 'Parties'

If we follow Sallust's example and abandon the notion of 'popularis' as a particular political category, the politicians in question lose their identity as part of a distinct ideological tradition, let alone 'party', and become, quite simply, office holders who at certain moments in their career used their powers without the backing of their peers.[55] Liberated from the ideological divisions implied by the 'populares'/'optimates' distinction, Meier's model offers a clear and persuasive interpretation of political conflict in the late republic. It also allows us to look afresh at some of the key figures and periods of the late republic, without the constraints of the binary model.

[55] Robb 2010: 162–4.

Amy Russell recently showed that it is impossible to make sense of tribunician activities during the period 100–91 by using the categories of 'populares' and 'optimates'.[56] But nowhere do the shortcomings of the conventional labelling become more apparent than in the case of the so-called 'triumvirs', typically classified as 'populares' – although Cicero explicitly noted that while the senate had lost power it had gone to three 'homines immoderatos' rather than the *populus* (*Att.* 2.9.2 (SB 29)). Pompey is, for example, often described as a Sullan 'optimas', who turned 'popularis'. Paradoxically, he would become the leader, at least militarily, of the 'optimates' towards the end of his life. Still, this supposed movement between opposite camps helps little to explain his place in Roman politics; essentially, he was a *nobilis* who exploited military opportunities with such ruthless determination (and success) that it alienated him from large sections of the aristocracy.[57] A particular 'popularis' programme is, on the other hand, difficult to trace.[58] His command against the pirates, administration of the *annona*, provision of lavish games and public buildings may have secured him widespread popularity, but did, of course, also entrench his dominant position in Rome.[59] The modern notion of Pompey as a 'popularis' therefore seems rooted in the senate's hostility rather than in any discernible political principle or programme.

While Pompey may have courted popularity on a grand scale, no conventional 'popularis' traits can be associated with his ally in 60, Licinius Crassus, who most certainly was no 'friend of the people'; indeed, his profiteering from Sulla's proscriptions and later exploitation of the urban plebs became notorious.[60] Apart from their early rise under Sulla's tutelage, only rivalry and mutual dislike seem to have bound him to Pompey. He may occasionally have clashed with prominent sections of the senate, but only in support of other parts of the elite, not least the wealthy *publicani*.

---

[56] Russell 2013.

[57] The 'party' model also breaks down when confronted with the well-known story about the crowd allegedly responding to Catulus' concerns about investing so much power in one man that if something happened to Pompey they would prefer Catulus as commander instead. The implication is that 'the people' would happily replace its favourite 'popularis' with an inveterate 'optimate' and supposed enemy of their interests, Cic. *Man.* 59; Vell. 2.32.1–2; Val. Max. 8.15.9; Plu. *Pomp.* 25.5.

[58] Vervaet 2009: 424 spoke of Pompey's programme in 70 as a 'platform of popularis reform', but see below pp. 146–47.

[59] He did organise land distributions, but mostly for his own veterans, in 70 (*lex Plotia*) (see Smith 1957; Gabba 1976) and (unsuccessfully) in 60 (*lex Flavia*). According to Cicero, *Att.* 1.9.4 (SB 19), the latter would also help remove 'sentina urbis' and repopulate Italy, which might imply that urban poor were among the beneficiaries.

[60] Although he did organise private grain distributions during his consulship, Plu. *Crass.* 12.2.

Finally, their associate and – initially – junior partner Caesar has almost universally been identified as one of the standard bearers of the 'popularis' cause.[61] But while he undoubtedly antagonised fellow aristocrats on numerous occasions, it is difficult to point to any concrete measures he passed in support of the masses. Although controversial, his actions by and large remained within the range of normal factional politics, including the public display of his Marian connections through *laudationes* and public statues as well as his call for restoration of the sons of exiles. Such anti-Sullan gestures may, just like his exceptionally lavish games, have brought him fame and popularity. Caesar's pursuit of popular favour was noted by all ancient commentators, suggesting he may have been unusual in continuing this strategy well after the early career stages when most politicians abandoned it.[62] But it was essentially a style, involving gestures, spectacle and generosity, as well as a public show of defiance towards the nobility.[63] Whether it had much impact on the lives of the poor is a different matter.[64]

Caesar's status as a 'popularis' is closely linked to his Marian/Cinnan connections and much-advertised opposition to the Sullan regime (although that was far from consistent since he married Pompeia, Sulla's grand-daughter, after the death in 67 of his first wife Cornelia, the daughter of Cinna).[65] The labelling of politicians 'by association' puts the focus on the turbulent period in the 80s when 'conservatives' and 'democrats' supposedly clashed for the first time in open military conflict, causing a deep and lasting rift through the ruling class. Historians tend to explain the civil war of the 80s in terms of the familiar two-party model, while also retaining elements of conventional 'factionalism', turning 'populares' into 'Marians' and 'optimates' into 'Sullans'.[66] Nowhere in the ancient sources is the conflict actually described as one between 'populares' and 'optimates', and when looked at more closely it quickly

---

[61] Gruen 2009: 24 represents an exception.

[62] Cicero, *Phil.* 2.116, notes that Caesar had by 'muneribus, monumentis, congiariis, epulis multi-tudinem imperitam delenierat', making no reference to any particular political actions. Cic. *Prov.* 38, implies that it was a career move usually brought on by insecurity or rejection.

[63] Gruen 2009: 25–6, argues that Labienus' restoration of election of priests, which Caesar supported, was no radical measure, nor did he benefit himself since the *pontifex maximus* was already elected.

[64] Caesar's first agrarian law provided for the veterans and was initially not considered particularly radical (see below). Cicero found the amount of Campanian land designated for redistribution relatively modest, providing for just 5000, which meant that the triumvirs were bound to lose support of 'reliqua omnis multitudo', *Att.* 2.36.1 (SB 36). As dictator he would later reduce the grain dole and dissolve the *collegia*, Suet. *Iul.* 41.3; 42.3.

[65] For a summary, see Badian 2009.

[66] Marshall 1984. For an excellent overview of the period, see Linke 2005. Strasburger 1939: 786 remains fundamental.

begins to dissolve into a complex mix of conventional power struggles, personal vendettas and factional strife, with an added element of elite class conflict, all heightened by the exceptional militarisation of Italy in the wake of the Social War.

The transfer of the Mithridatic command from the consul Sulla to his old rival Marius provided the trigger. This step was in itself entirely un-ideological (there was a long history of disputes over provincial commands) – even if the 'usurping' general in question was highly 'popular' in a conventional sense.[67] The tribune Sulpicius who facilitated the move cannot be easily classified. While he certainly was a thorn in the flesh of many senators, none of his policies appears to have been particularly aimed at the 'People'.[68] The sources associate him with attempts to redistribute the recently incorporated Italians among all the voting tribes. But there is no reason why granting political influence to barely defeated enemies, against whom Rome had recently fought a bloody war, would have endeared him to the 'populus Romanus'.[69] The 'popularis' status of Sulpicius has therefore been restored by redefining citizenship bills as 'progressive' rather than 'popular' – which obviously reflects a very modern left–right perspective – and by stressing the senatorial opposition most of them faced.

His ally Marius, another 'popularis' according to the conventional taxonomy, obviously enjoyed broad popularity for his military exploits and was hailed as the saviour of Rome. His multiple consulships also testify to his appeal among the well-off voters who controlled the *comitia centuriata*. Politically, however, it is difficult to pinpoint any overtly 'ideological' measures, apart from the controversial narrowing of the voting 'bridges', carried early in his career as tribune in 119.[70] Later he took radical steps to provide for his landless veterans in collaboration with Saturninus, but similar settlements were, of course, organised by Sulla without the attribution of 'popularis' motives. Again, therefore, his political label ultimately comes down to senatorial hostility towards the new man and his personal enmity with Sulla.

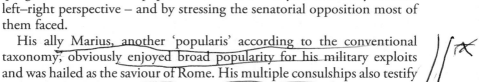

[67] Examples include e.g. Liv. 22.25–26 (cf. Plu. *Fab. Max.* 8; Polyb. 3.103.3–8) (217); 27.20.11–21.4 (cf. Plu. *Marc.* 27) (209); 41.6.2–3 (178).

[68] According to Plutarch, *Mar.* 35.2, Sulpicius fell out with the senate so severely that he set up his own 'counter-senate', composed of 600 *equites*. He also imposed a limit on senators' debt, Plu. *Sull.* 8.2, cf. Evans 2007.

[69] That also applies to Sulpicius' proposal to redistribute former slaves, which held no conceivable popular appeal.

[70] Plu. *Mar.* 4.2–4, who also notes that Marius blocked a proposed grain distribution during his tribunate.

Cinna, his supposed successor as champion of the 'popularis' cause, is never described as 'popularis' and the label largely derives from the description of his opponents as 'optimates'.[71] Apart from the unresolved question of tribal registration of the Italians, which probably held little popular appeal, the most pressing political issue during his so-called *dominatio* was the need for debt reform after the Social War. The financial situation in Rome was dire and further damaged by Mithridates' attack on Asia, which caused great loss of public revenue. While debt reform was usually a toxic political issue, fiercely resisted by the propertied classes, the monetary law passed by Valerius Flaccus in 86 seems to have enjoyed broad elite support.[72] In addition to the *equites*, substantial sections of the senate also appear to have backed Cinna, which according to most definitions would rule him out as a 'popularis'.[73]

It is difficult to identify any clear ideological demarcations in the conflict, which Cicero later presented as a wholly personal dispute between Marius and Sulla.[74] In this struggle the stance taken by most senators was probably dictated by purely tactical and opportunistic considerations. From the first outbreak of violence in 88 down to Sulla's final victory in 81 it is impossible to point to any consistent political fault lines between the combatants. Paradoxically, therefore, it only becomes a clash between 'optimates' and 'populares' when the war is over; for it is Sulla's actions as dictator that have defined the preceding conflict – and indeed the concept of 'optimates' as a whole.

Sulla's reforms have come to embody 'conservative' values and hard-line 'class' politics in the late republic, although several of his measures are difficult to fit into that model. They include the sumptuary laws and the new rules regulating provincial commands, which would seem to reflect traditional oligarchic concerns about maintaining elite discipline and control. Sulla's new system of courts, the *quaestiones*, on the other hand, was probably a response to practical demands, in the same way as his doubling of the number of quaestors from ten to twenty and the creation of two additional praetors. It was long assumed that Sulla abolished the grain dole, which was undoubtedly regarded with suspicion by the elite. However,

---

[71] Cf. Strasburger 1939: 786, who noted that neither were Carbo, Fimbria or Sertorius.

[72] According to Sallust, it was carried 'volentibus omnibus bonis', *Cat.* 33.1–2; cf. Lovano 2002: 72.

[73] Many senators co-operated with Cinna, including leading nobles like Philippus, cos. 91; L. Flaccus, cos. 100; Perperna, cos. 92; Scaevola, cos. 95; in addition to men like Verres and Hortensius. Only later did they join Sulla who therefore can hardly be regarded as 'the leader of the senate'. Badian 1962b; Frier 1971; Lovano 2002: 59–60.

[74] E.g. *Har.* 54, his references to Marius and Sulla are remarkably even-handed and imply they were not split by anything other than *dissensio*, as was also the case with Cinna and Octavius.

Santangelo has convincingly shown that the evidence is less than compelling.[75] While several measures were passed, their precise impact is a matter of conjecture. Moreover, senatorial misgivings about the dole should not be confused with modern 'fiscal conservatism', since economic redistribution through taxation played no part.[76] In addition to confirming the citizenship and tribal allocation of the Italians, Sulla also introduced lavish games (a common means of gaining popularity) and, most importantly, distributed land to his veterans on an unprecedented scale. Although not 'altruistic' in nature, these measures nevertheless demonstrate the complexity of political labelling, since under different circumstances they could easily have been described as 'progressive'.

Among Sulla's most controversial acts was his transfer of the courts from equestrian to senatorial control, which in turn necessitated a major expansion of the senate and the addition of 300 new members.[77] The judicial reform had already been proposed in 91, indirectly triggering the Social War (cf. Cic. *Off.* 2.75; *Brut.* 115), and stripping the *equites* of their judicial role undoubtedly entrenched the position of the senate. However, it did not represent 'class politics' in any conventional sense, since it merely shifted power between different sections of the elite. Sulla's resentment towards the *equites*, amply demonstrated by the proscriptions which mostly targeted this order, also defies conventional ideological explanations.[78]

Although Sulla's victory is often described as the triumph of the senate over the *populus*, the most obvious victims of his reign were other members of the elite. In fact, the conflict can be seen as one between an inner circle of old aristocratic families and those outside it, particularly the *equites*. Thus contemporary sources consistently present the Sullan regime as domination by the *nobiles* rather than by the senate.[79] For example, in his speech for Roscius of Ameria Cicero repeatedly tells the jurors (and his readers)

---

[75] Santangelo 2014: 10–12. Sall. *Hist.* 1.55.11Maur; cf. Garnsey 1988: 209–11.

[76] Cf. Jehne 2014a: 68, who noted that since the rich were not taxed, it was not a question of economic redistribution or 'the poor living off the rich'. C. Gracchus' subsidies came not from wealthy Romans but from the provincials, cf. Ungern-Sternberg 1991: 32.

[77] Bonnefond-Coudry 1989: 718–20. See also Santangelo 2006.

[78] In *Clu.* 151 Cicero describes Sulla as 'homo a populi causa remotissimus', but the passage is a good example of the pitfalls involved in taking statements out of context. The discussion deals with the composition of jury panels and therefore has little to do with the 'popular cause' in any conventional sense. Indeed, Cicero in the same breath mentions Sulla's 'odio, quod habuit in equestrem ordinem', a stance demonstrated by his persecution of *equites* during the proscriptions. Cf. Hinard 1985: 116–35; Diehl 1988: 29–31, 109–11, 175–6. *Pace* Badian 1962a: 232.

[79] Badian 1962b 61: ' . . . Sulla's victory, as all agree, was that of the *nobilitas*'; cf. Steel 2014, who questions whether Sulla actually strengthened the senate.

that the elder Roscius, whose name posthumously had been put on the proscription lists, always had been a strong supporter of the *nobilitas* and celebrated its victory.[80] Cicero further declares that he himself also supported 'causam nobilitatis' and denied that his defence of the younger Roscius implied any criticism of this group.[81] Indeed, Cicero supported the victors because, as he put it, *humilitas* was contending with *dignitas* over prestige and distinction (136). And by *humilitas* he does not refer to 'ordinary' people, for as he later explains, the nobles could not endure 'equestrem splendorem' and therefore recaptured the *res publica* by arms (140–1).

The *Pro Roscio Amerino* was delivered at a sensitive moment when the former dictator was still alive, but ten years later Cicero presented precisely the same analysis of the civil war. In his prosecution of Verres he accused him of having joined Sulla, not because he wished to defend the cause of the *nobilitas* or restore its honour and *dignitas*, but for purely opportunistic reasons and personal enrichment.[82] For Sallust too, the *nobiles* were the winners of the civil war, thus presenting a picture of the conflict very similar to that of Cicero, our earliest surviving source.[83] Crucially, the Sullan faction was defined not according to ideological, political or institutional criteria but in purely social terms as the most prominent part of the aristocracy. It was therefore not the victory of the senate (and certainly not over 'the people'), but of a section within it that had by armed force established a position of unprecedented strength.

The distinct position occupied by the *nobiles* in Roman politics deserves closer attention and may help explain some episodes of the late republic that have been interpreted as ideological clashes, but could be seen as reactions against a class which generated widespread resentment among other sections of the elite. A prime example of that discourse comes from 65, when Cicero defended C. Cornelius, the tribune of 67, against a charge of *maiestas*; his speeches are preserved in fragments along with Asconius'

---

[80] *Rosc. Am.* 16, Roscius senior had always been 'nobilitatis fautor', especially during 'hoc tumultu proximo, cum omnium nobilium dignitas et salus in discrimen veniret'. He had defended 'eam partem causamque', and exulted in 'victoria nobilitatis'; being a 'hominis studiosissimi nobilitatis', 21.

[81] *Rosc. Am.* 135–8, 140–2, 149.

[82] *Ver.* 2.1.35: Verres betrayed his commander Carbo but not 'cupiditate defendendae nobilitatis aut studio partium'; cf. 37, where Cicero claims Verres did not become a Sullanus to restore 'honos et dignitas nobilitati'.

[83] Sall. *Hist.* 3.48.3Maur, cf. 'paucorum dominationem', 6, and 'imaginibus suis', 18. Valerius Maximus 9.2.1, probably drawing on Livy, states that Sulla 'laudably defended the authority of the nobility', 'egregie namque auctoritate nobilitatis defensa . . .'.

commentary. Cornelius is usually classified as a 'popularis', while Cicero allegedly delivered 'the most popularis speech of his career' in his defence.[84] Once again, the picture may be considerably more complex. There is little doubt that Cornelius had incurred the displeasure of leading senators partly through his policies and partly because of the methods he used. Among his proposals were measures to curb *ambitus* and stop exploitative loans being imposed on provincial envoys. He also tried to force the praetor to obey his own decree and limit the senate's ability to grant legal dispensations, *privilegia*. None of these measures posed any serious threat to senatorial interests, nor did they undermine the senate's *auctoritas*, as Cicero is keen to emphasise (1 fr. 33). It even appears that many senators supported them.[85] Despite the controversy surrounding Cornelius, we are therefore not dealing with a simple 'people versus senate' conflict. The target of his proposals was the *nobiles*, who dominated the senate, but, as the outcome of the case demonstrates, enjoyed little support among the rest of the elite.[86] We have to remember that Cicero's rhetorical attack on the 'pauci', which might easily be mistaken for conventional populism, was aimed squarely at a jury composed entirely of members of the elite. It was to their views and prejudices that Cicero tailored his two speeches and the strategy clearly worked, since Cornelius, as Asconius (81C) informs us, was resoundingly acquitted by a large majority.

Cicero's own personal circumstances should also be taken into account, since he had recently held the praetorship and now was aiming for the consulate. From an electoral perspective his defence represents a two-pronged approach. On the one hand, it appealed to the powerful *equites*, lower-ranking senators and the propertied men of the first class, naturally resentful of the overbearing *nobiles*, whose influence, though important, may not have been decisive in consular elections. On the other hand, the case also offered an opportunity to woo Pompey, then the dominant figure in Roman politics, whom Cornelius had recently served as quaestor. In his

---

[84] Griffin 1973: 212.

[85] Asc. *Corn.* 61C, says that except for the 'familiares principum civitatis' many of the senatorial jurors were well-disposed towards Cornelius.

[86] *Corn.* 2 fr. 11. Cicero warned about the oligarchs' 'miserrimum crudelissimumque dominatum', 2 fr 12. Cf. Ward 1970: 555: 'He made it clear that his only adversaries in this case were the oligarchic optimates, the *pauci*, those unregenerated "few" who would not relinquish the smallest prerogative to the other orders of the state'. In 70 Cicero could even claim in front of a senatorial jury that *totus ordo* was oppressed by 'paucorum improbitate et audacia', *Ver.* 1.36. 'Pauci' is a standard term for a senatorial clique, while *improbitas* and *audacia* typically are associated with opponents of the senate. Here, however, they are applied to the very core of that order, illustrating the internal divisions within the ruling class, even at the highest levels. It also underscores the fluid nature of the political terminology which could be employed by all sides of any argument.

defence of Cornelius, Cicero positioned himself as a supporter of the people's 'sovereignty' and as a vocal critic of the *principes*. Since Cornelius received the support of the propertied classes and most of the senators, Cicero's line must have been entirely acceptable to this class – which makes it ironic that his defence could later be described as a 'popularis' act. The social differentiation within the elite itself must be borne in mind when looking at cases like these and indeed at Roman politics in general. The senate was not identical with the elite, and its dominant families were often defied by other affluent sections of society, most obviously when bills were passed and higher magistrates elected against their express wishes, e.g. Marius or before him Scipio Aemilianus, Flaminius, and Varro.[87] Instances such as these suggest that the notion of an all-powerful nobility controlling public life is most likely a myth. Within the elite itself complex divisions and tensions existed, which means that political struggles cannot be reduced to a simple template of 'senate versus people'.

Cicero is often assumed to have gone through an early 'popularis' phase, before becoming a respectable stalwart of the 'optimates'. The theory is partly inferred from some of his forensic oratory, since his defence of Roscius may have provoked Sulla – despite Cicero's own insistence on his support for the regime – and he clashed again with members of the Sullan establishment in his prosecution of Verres. But these actions were by all accounts challenges to parts of the nobility rather than 'the senate'. The main evidence for Cicero's 'popularis' phase has therefore been derived from a celebrated passage of the *Commentariolum petitionis* (4–5), which incidentally also contains one of the very few combinations of 'popularis' and 'optimas' in Latin literature.

The author of the booklet, Cicero's brother Quintus, writes that Cicero had always agreed with the 'optimates' and had never been in the least 'popularis'; in fact he had only spoken 'populariter' in order to attract the support of Pompey. The context makes clear that the 'optimates' are in fact the *nobiles*, whom Quintus mentions in the previous sentence.[88] Again, therefore, we are faced with a social group not a politically defined category. 'Popularis', on the other hand, must here refer to a certain populist style and manner aimed at winning popularity – and frowned

---

[87] Varro: Liv. 22.33.9–35.4; Flaminius: Pfeilschifter 2005: 52–65; Aemilianus: Astin 1967: 61–9. Vishnia 1998 notes the power of 'non-senatorial elites' in the *comitia*. Interestingly, in 123 Fannius defeated Opimius to the consulship with C. Gracchus' active support, implying that the timocratic assembly backed the preferred candidate of a 'popularis', Plu. *CG* 8.2, 11.2.

[88] Robb 2010: 144.

upon by the nobility. Quintus later expands on this point by noting that Cicero gained support from 'urbanam illam multitudinem' by 'praising Pompey, accepting the case of Manilius, defending Cornelius'.[89] The key element here seems to be Pompey's well-documented popularity, which would have provided a strong incentive for Cicero to take Manilius' case and possibly also for his defence of Cornelius. Presumably, it was also the Pompeian connection that generated the wide interest which Quintus implies the case attracted.[90] Cicero had already tried to gain the great man's support the previous year, when he intervened on Pompey's behalf in the debate over the *lex Manilia*; which also offered an excellent opportunity to court the favour of influential *equites* concerned about their Asian investments. It pitted him against parts of the nobility, intent on thwarting Pompey's ambitions, but since the senate was deeply split on the issue, Cicero's step was neither very radical nor particularly risky. As Cornelius' case suggests, the *nobiles* could be defied almost with impunity.[91]

Cicero's actions in this period therefore fit easily into a conventional picture of a new man manoeuvring strategically between powerful men, factions, and groupings. There are, however, aspects of his speech for Cornelius, its style and arguments, that might be interpreted as 'populist' attempts to appeal to a wider audience. Thus, key passages appear to have dealt with the tribunate and its place in the Roman constitution, one of the most controversial and heated topics of the late republic. Cicero delivered a vigorous defence of the powers of the tribunate, which according to the traditional 'party' model would place him firmly in the 'popularis' camp.[92] It also takes us directly back to Sulla, the archetypal 'optimas'; for while most of his actions are difficult to place on a conventional 'left–right' scale, he did implement one major constitutional change that would seem to fit the modern 'popularis–optimas' model, which was his neutralisation of the tribunate as an active political force. Sulla deprived the tribunes of independent initiative and even made their office a career dead-end, retaining only their *ius auxilii* (Cic. *Leg.* 3.22) and perhaps also their right of *intercessio*.[93] This particular reform has more than anything come to define his regime as 'optimate' in the modern tradition and there can be

---

[89] *Comm. pet.* 51: 'Pompeio ornando, Manili causa recipienda, Cornelio defendendo'.
[90] From a practical perspective we may wonder how many non-elite Romans would have attended the case and listened to the complex legal arguments.
[91] The case evidently riled the nobles, as Vatinius later reminded him, Cic. *Vat.* 5.
[92] Cic. *Corn.* 1 frr. 48–9, 52; 2 fr. 3 =Asc. *Corn.* 76, 78–9C. Ward 1970: 555.
[93] App. *BC* 1.100, Hantos 1988: 74–9. The fate of the veto is unclear, ibid. 130–47. Cf. Keaveney 2005: 140–1.

little doubt about its controversial nature. To understand its background and significance as well as its eventual repeal we may briefly reconsider the place of the tribunate in Roman politics.

Sulla and the Tribunate

While the origins of this office are largely lost in time and later mythologising, its exceptional status seems indisputable. Created during the so-called Struggle of the Orders in order to defend the plebeian population against patrician 'state' coercion, it also provided an institutional platform from which prominent plebeians could challenge the political ascendancy of the patrician elite. As leaders of the plebs and excluded from official power the tribunes had no clearly defined remit apart from the general promotion of plebeian interests. After the plebeio-patrician compromise in the fourth century, which gradually extended full equality and access to state offices to the plebeians, the tribunate effectively became redundant, rooted as it was in an institutionalised segregation that no longer existed.[94] With plebeians holding supreme executive power it made little sense to maintain a specifically plebeian office whose task it was to protect other plebeians from these very same magistrates. Surprisingly, however, the tribunate was retained and gradually integrated into the 'normal' state apparatus, albeit playing a very different role in the political process.

The tribunes' new function was based on their customary right to convene the plebs and propose resolutions binding for this group. With the *lex Hortensia* of 287, plebiscites gained the status of law, paradoxically allowing a section of the population to legislate for the whole community. It also turned the erstwhile 'defenders of the plebs' into the main legislators of the republic. In the following centuries the tribunes became chiefly responsible for the drafting and passing of new statutes and bills.[95] In doing so they met a practical need caused by the regular absence of the consuls from the city along with the growing complexity of Roman society, which required increased regulation.[96] The transformation of the tribunes into legislators, while retaining their traditional negative powers of *auxilium* and *intercessio*, suggests a high degree of conformity and integration into the new plebeio-patrician elite, to whom they can no longer have been

---

[94] Cf. Bleicken 1981: 94, who noted that after the settlement it no longer had any 'politisches Ziel'.

[95] For an attempt at quantifying tribunician legislation, see Williamson 2005: 3–61, esp. 16–19. Cornell 1995: 344: 'Plebiscites become the normal method of legislation, proposed by the tribunes on behalf of the Senate'.

[96] Pina Polo 2011: 99–121 on consuls as legislators.

perceived as a threat. Presumably, they were expected to wield their extensive powers (made even greater by the largely affirmative role of the assemblies) in accordance with the broad interests of their peers (who now included the patricians). And this is indeed the impression conveyed by the historical record of the middle republic, which shows tribunes deferring to the opinion of the senate or even acting on its behalf.[97]

An example of the latter comes from 172 when the consuls (Liv. 42.10.9–15) tested the senate's patience by refusing to leave for their provinces, prompting the tribunes to intervene on its behalf (42.21). Similarly, when the praetor M'. Iuventius Thalna was about to propose war on Rhodes in 167 without consulting the senate, two tribunes intervened and blocked the initiative (Liv. 45.21). In 191 colonists in the *coloniae maritimae* complained about the draft and approached the tribunes, who simply referred their case to the senate (36.3.4–5). In 171 two of the tribunes played a similarly compliant role when the *primipilarii*, famously led by Ligustinus, appealed to them (Liv. 42.32.6–35.2) by referring the matter back to the consuls, while the other tribunes agreed to investigate. Likewise in 199 two tribunes blocked Flamininus' premature run for the consulship on grounds of legality, only relenting when the senate allowed his election to go ahead.[98]

On many occasions tribunes also performed a vital 'policing' role within the ruling class, enforcing internal discipline and holding former magistrates to account, particularly those who used their powers without consulting the senate. That was, for example, the case in 173–172 with the dispute between the senate and M. Popillius Laenas over his treatment of the Ligurian Statielli (Liv. 42.7.3–10.15). The consul simply refused to obey the senate, and only through the intervention of two tribunes could an inquiry be set up. A similar illustration of the co-operation that generally existed between senate and tribunes comes from 170, when C. Lucretius Gallus was prosecuted by tribunes after he had been rebuked by the senate. Likewise in 189 tribunes charged the censorial candidate M'. Acilius Glabrio for having misappropriated booty.[99]

---

[97] Cf. Bleicken 1955: 55–63; 2003: 95–8, describing the tribunes as a mere tool of the senate. Likewise Hölkeskamp 1990: 448; Nippel 1995: 10. *Contra* Badian 1990b: 458–62; 1996.

[98] Plu. *Flam.* 2.1–2; Liv. 32.7.8–12. Pfeilschifter 2005: 52–67.

[99] Liv. 43.7.5–8.10; 37.57.9–15. In 184 Q. Fulvius Flaccus controversially ran for praetor while already aedile; the tribunes intervened but were split on the issue, Liv. 39.39. More instances are listed in Forsythe 1988: 114, who plausibly argues that the first *repetundae* law, the *lex Calpurnia de repetundis* from 149, also enjoyed senatorial support. The law allowed restitution of lost funds, but no further punishment, while keeping the juries wholly senatorial. It was promulgated following the failed measure against Ser. Sulpicius Galba for his mistreatment of the Lusitani, a bill backed by the senate.

Instances such as these suggest that the tribunes had become fully integrated into the governmental structures of the republic. However, the legislative – and regulatory – functions of the tribunes also placed them at the heart of any political dispute, which often hinged directly on the position they took.[100] A case in point is the row in 189, when the praetor was deprived of his province by the *pontifex maximus* because of religious duties, which triggered an appeal to the tribunes and the *populus* (Liv. 37.51.1–6). Likewise in 184 a fierce argument broke out over levies for the Spanish wars; both sides had supportive tribunes, causing political deadlock (Liv. 39.38.8–10). In 196 a dispute between two urban quaestors and all the priests over unpaid taxes naturally led to appeals to the tribunes. On this occasion, however, the tribunes, unusually, refused to intervene on behalf of the priests, who therefore had to pay the sums demanded of them (Liv. 33.42.2–4).

Examples of 'radical' tribunes confronting the senate over important matters of policy are rarely attested. Among the classic instances from the third century are Flaminius' distribution of land in the *ager Gallicus* in 232 against senatorial opposition and the *lex Claudia* from 218, which restricted the commercial involvement of senators (and their sons).[101] They do not, however, fit a simple 'elite versus (popular) tribune' scenario, since Flaminius went on to become praetor and twice consul, evidently with the support of the better-off who dominated the *comitia centuriata*. Moreover, we are told that Flaminius' support for the *lex Claudia* made him so popular that it secured him a second consulship, implying a far more complex political situation and internal divisions within the elite. In the second century such clashes between tribunes and senate remained equally rare. Exceptions include Q. Terentius Culleo's controversial law from 189 on the census registration of citizens, which was opposed by the senate.[102] The following year C. Valerius Tappo proposed that the Volsci be granted *suffragium* but four tribunes opposed the measure because it lacked *auctoritas senatus*. Normally, that would have settled the matter but Livy tells us that when it had been established that the decision lay with the *populus*, the tribunes relented and the bill went ahead to ratification in the assembly (Liv. 38.36.7–9). The passage is remarkable, as it appears to introduce a radically new constitutional principle – the suspension of

---

[100] Badian 1990b: 460–2 interpreted them as remnants of their traditional 'oppositional' character, but more likely it was a direct consequence of the particular role they had been given.

[101] Liv. 21.63.3–5. Clemente 1983; Vishnia 1996: 34–48; Bringmann 2003. The measure was probably less radical than often thought and may be seen as part of the elite's ongoing self-regulation.

[102] Plu. *Flam.* 18.1. See Mouritsen 2011a: 264.

tribunician collegiality and their right to block each other's proposals. The implications would have been far-reaching, effectively removing one of the main regulatory mechanisms from the political system. More likely, therefore, Livy's passing comment simply describes the negotiated solution that was reached when the opposing tribunes backed down under the rhetorical pretence of deferring to the People's 'sovereignty'.[103]

It is, of course, impossible to generalise about an institution as complex as the Roman tribunate. Still, there seems to be little grounds for perceiving the office as inherently radical or 'oppositional', in the sense that it was expected to act as an institutional counter-weight to the senate or the consuls. Its historical and ideological bond to the plebs, of course, remained, but as the political meaning of 'plebs' changed fundamentally, so did the implications of this connection. When plebeians assumed supreme magisterial power, it no longer made any sense to define the tribunes as 'defenders of the plebs' – whom were they supposed to protect plebeians against? Tribunes evidently derived their powers from the plebs – and formally relied on its particular protection – but that did not set them apart since all office holders claimed popular mandates. It is therefore not surprising that we look in vain for any consistent political profile. Tribunes frequently disagreed amongst themselves over policy issues, reflecting the absence of any definite ideological character associated with their office.[104] At the same time, tribunes repeatedly found themselves at the centre of political controversy. Still, that was due to their pivotal role in the political process, which meant that virtually every issue, personal as well as policy-related, ended up on their – metaphorical – desk.[105] Looking at the forms their involvement took reveals no clear or consistent pattern or direction. The overriding impression is of ad hoc interventions responding to the particular circumstances of each case.

Nevertheless, their extensive powers – to propose new statutes, block proposals, halt public business, intercede on behalf of citizens and regulate the behaviour of members of the elite – made it imperative that effective

---

[103] Badian 1972: 700 envisaged a real constitutional shift in 188, which in turn led him to interpret Octavius' veto in 133 as a serious breach of convention, 706–11; cf. Brunt 1988: 22. The argument rests on the assumption that the assembly acted as an actual decision-making body, which seems doubtful given the almost complete absence of rejections. Removing the right to veto plebiscites would therefore in effect have amounted to giving each tribune the power to make law.

[104] The tribunes had no monopoly on 'popular' causes. For example, when dispute arose in 169 over the levy, it was the praetors who pleaded the case of the people in the senate against the consuls, Liv. 43.14.2–4.

[105] Cf. Bleicken 1981: 98, who noted that the 'Form und Gegenstand ihrer ... Aktivität' were 'praktisch unbegrenzt'.

controls were in place to ensure that tribunes exercised them responsibly, i.e. in accordance with the broad interests of the elite. The most fundamental tool was the simple principle of collegiality, which required consensus on contentious issues – and as Cicero noted, one could almost always find a dissenting tribune to block unwanted bills (*Leg.* 3.24). This method was not fool proof, however, and some controversial measures did manage to get onto the statute book. Unacceptable laws could subsequently be annulled by the senate on procedural or religious grounds, while troublesome tribunes might be punished afterwards by the censors.[106] These measures were applied only when the usual regulatory methods had failed; the primary means of reconciling the powers of the tribunes to the system of aristocratic government was through negotiation, persuasion and the application of informal pressure by senior senators, partly in private but also at *contiones* and at the final debates before votes were cast. Ultimately, one could argue that tribunician compliance with the principles of the *res publica* was rooted in social conditioning, education and the particular ethos inculcated in young nobles from an early age.[107]

The aristocratic culture of co-operation went hand in hand with an equally strong competitive spirit. The fact that many tribunes also hoped for further advancement must have encouraged conformity. Thus, after the formalisation of the *cursus honorum* it became customary for tribunes to hold the office early in their career, normally between the quaestorship and the aedileship (although it seems to have been possible to go straight to the tribunate without the quaestorship, probably to expand the entry points to the senate.)[108] When the tribunes' entitlement to a place in the senate was regulated later in the second century it marked the final step in their integration.[109]

While the tribunes had become functional parts of the everyday working of the republic, their potentially disruptive powers remained intact. Reading between the lines of Livy's 'middle republic' one senses a political system performing a precarious balancing act, which invariably involved the tribunes. The system functioned most effectively when the

---

[106] On means of blocking bills see De Libero 1992. In 169 a tribune who had attacked the censors was removed from his *tribus* and made *aerarius* (44.16.8), while in 131 a censor refused to enrol a tribune in the senate after a dispute, Liv. *Per.* 59; Plin. *Nat.* 7.143. M. Duronius (tr. by 97) was expelled from the senate after he had repealed a sumptuary law, Val. Max. 2.9.5.

[107] On the education and social conditioning of the elite see Scholz 2011.

[108] The tribunes were not themselves covered by the *lex annalis*, Astin 1958. For examples of tribunes who had not held quaestorship, Hantos 1988: 20 n.3, cf. Wiseman 1971: 99.

[109] Formalised by the *lex Atinia*, Gel. *NA* 14.8.2. Develin 1978a; Vishnia 1989; Badian 1996: 202–8; Tatum 2010.

ruling class was able to maintain a degree of unity which could then be brought to bear on 'dissident' tribunes who threatened to rock the boat. In those situations the *senatus auctoritas* carried tremendous weight and often sufficed to bring them back into line, explaining why the system did not collapse under the weight of its internal contradictions. However, real problems arose when the senate was split or at loggerheads with powerful groups outside of it, above all the *equites*; then the tribunes were far more difficult to rein in.

The tribunate in many respects retained its institutional separation long after it had become an integral part of the Roman political system. The incorporation of the historically 'oppositional' tribunate into the plebeio-patrician state was an extended process which in some sense never reached full completion. The tribunate always stood apart from the rest of the institutional framework and maintained much of its original autonomy.[110] It was formally still the office reserved for a subsection of the citizen body, albeit one that now made up the large majority. The tribunes continued to feature separately in official despatches, alongside the consuls and the senate, and it seems that as late as 201 a law existed (probably passed 232–209), banning anyone with a living father who had held curule office from standing for plebeian offices. The rule counteracted concentration of power by limiting the career options of young nobles and opening them up for *novi homines*, but it might also reflect an enduring perception of the tribunate as somehow distinct from the magistracies.[111] It was the tribunate's anomalous status that allowed Polybius to identify the office as a uniquely 'democratic' element within his 'mixed constitution'. His was, of course, a highly formalistic analysis of the Roman republic and it is precisely the tribunate's formal distinctiveness that allowed this classification. It could therefore be argued that it was the tribunes, i.e. the persons holding the office, who became 'normalised', not the office itself; while tribunes on an individual level were fully part of the ruling class, they occupied an office that still carried traces of its original separateness. It was this feature that enabled the tribunate to be reinvented in the later republic.

These observations become relevant when we turn to the later second century and the dramatic events that prompted Sulla's reform of the tribunate. In the second half of the second century there are signs of

---

[110] Badian 1996: 208 on the tribunes never 'entirely shedding their original function as magistrates of a separate plebs'. Cf. Bleicken 1981: 93, commenting on the 'Besonderheit' and 'Ausnahmecharakter' of the tribunes, as illustrated by their *sacrosanctitas*.

[111] Cf. the case of C. Servilius, whose father, presumed fallen, turned out to be alive, thereby rendering his son's election as tribune in 201 illegal, Liv. 27.21.10.

increased tension within the elite, tension which inevitably put greater pressure on the tribunes. It expressed itself in various cases of rule breaking, such as *prehensio* by tribunes in 151 and 138, when consuls were dragged off to prison.[112] Although attempts to define these instances as presaging the later upheavals of the Gracchi are somewhat teleological, the tendency towards greater friction and willingness to enter into open confrontation is difficult to dispute. The events of 133 illustrate both the problematic aspects of the tribunate and the factors which had neutralised them in the past. It saw a complete breakdown of the political process, the demotion of a tribunician colleague, an unprecedented attempt at re-election, a refusal to budge on crucial issues of landholding, foreign policy and public finances, with a catastrophic violent outcome. As such, the year 133 exposed structural weaknesses in the system, which had always been present but up until that point largely contained.

The fundamental problem facing the republic was, put simply, that legislation was far too easy to implement, since the assemblies provided only routine validation and there were few constitutional means by which a determined tribune could be stopped.[113] Usually, it was done by the application of collective pressure or through tribunician intervention, neither method being certain of success. Therefore, confronted with a critical situation like the one in 133, the elite had no formal authority to make errant members comply. For that reason contested issues might at any time 'spill over' into the assemblies, placing these in a new role as the final arbiters on measures on which the ruling class had been unable to reach a negotiated agreement.[114] The issue became most urgent when the elite's views were not clear-cut and rival groupings leaned on the tribunes. The fact that the aristocratic republic was predicated on cooperation and general willingness to compromise naturally shifts the focus from the tribunes onto the senate, whose role it was to provide leadership and mediation when the ruling class was split. We may therefore briefly

---

[112] Liv. *Per.* 48; 55; cf. Cic. *Leg.* 3.20. In 109 the tribunes threatened to imprison a censor, Plu. *Mor.* 276F. L. Scipio was also threatened with prison by tribunes, Gel. *NA* 6.19; Liv. 38.60. Later examples, David 1993: 223 n.18, including Plu. *Mar.* 4.2–3.

[113] The ease of legislation is illustrated by attempts to pre-empt abrogation by inserting clauses against repeal, cf. e.g. Santalucia 2012; Lundgreen 2014a: 123 on Clodius' law exiling Cicero, which included elaborate provisions that prohibited even the discussion of his recall, Cic. *Red. sen.* 8; *Att.* 3.23.2 (SB 68), cf. *Att.* 3.13.1 (SB 59); 3.15.6 (SB 60), *Dom.* 68–70, and against obstruction of the implementation of the law, Bleicken 1975b: 450 n.247. Promoters of controversial laws might also insist that oaths be sworn by senators to uphold the law, cf. App. *BC* 1.29; Plu. *Mar.* 29.1–2; *Att.* 2.18.2 (SB 38); App. *BC* 2.12; Plu. *Cat. Mi.* 32.3; Cass. Dio 38.7.1–2.

[114] Bleicken 1975b: 445–52 argued that *intercessio*, traditionally the most important intra-organ control, weakened after 133 as vetoes were ignored or interceding tribunes driven away by force.

consider how the collective body of the elite fulfilled this vital function as well as the implications this had for the development of the 'disruptive' tribunate.

From a modern perspective, the senate appears as a constitutional para-dox, since it formally held very limited powers but de facto acted as a 'governing body'. This paradox is more apparent than real, however, especially when we think beyond conventional constitutional logic. Roman institutions were defined as much by custom and *mos* as through normative rules and allocated powers and jurisdictions. Thus, in the same way as the extensive powers of the *populus* were heavily circumscribed by practice and conventions, so the senate's effective authority extended far beyond its formal powers. This was in fact the secret of its strength. As Hölkeskamp noted: ' . . . the power of the Senate was really based on the fact that it did not have any formally defined or precisely circumscribed responsibilities and was therefore not restricted to a specific set of concrete political topics or areas of "competence". It was the very lack of positively defined "rights" that was the real reason for its immense authority.'[115]

In this context, it is important to reiterate that the senate was not a parliament, for despite acting as a deliberative body its primary purpose was to focus opinion and formulate a strategy behind which the ruling elite could unite. Debates were therefore only partly about weighing up and testing arguments; they were as much about reaching agreement and 'streamlining' opinion by identifying majority views and marginalising dissent. This is evident from the highly structured format of senatorial debates, where a strict speaking order was applied in accordance with rank and seniority.[116] The taking of votes was therefore the exception rather than the norm, usually happening when the outcome was already clear and unequivocal. *Discessio*, in other words, served as a means of demonstrating unity, and was designed to paper over rather than expose divisions among the senators.[117]

The formation of senatorial policy thus relied on a high degree of consensus, and as long as that existed the senate's lack of clear definition and formal authority was indeed a strength. However, when the elite were split, the senate became paralysed and powerless. It has been argued that the crisis of 133 reflected precisely the absence of senatorial leadership, since the senate provided no mediation between the warring tribunes.[118] This was the moment the system failed dramatically and the open, indeed

---

[115] Hölkeskamp 2010: 26.   [116] Cf. Ryan 1998, with Flaig 2004.   [117] Timmer 2009: 395.
[118] Eder 1996: 447.

violent, clash between a tribune and his peers set in motion an ideological reinvention of the tribunate, which was possible because only the tribunes, not the tribunate, had been 'normalised'. 'Defence of the people' could now be used to justify defiance of one's peers in the senate, giving the traditional bond between tribunes and plebs a new political meaning. As David has argued, the transgressions of some tribunes in the late republic, including the breaking of rules for *intercessio*, the arrest of senior magistrates (*prehensio*) or the issuing of threats against them, and the demotion of other tribunes, were probably validated by the retrospective invention of early republican precedents.[119] In this process, the 'radical tribunate' of the early republic may have been conceived, mirroring the 'radical' tribunate of the late republic, which it served to legitimise. This was possible because the archaic features, mentioned above, still set it apart from other public offices, and what made this reinvention so much more dangerous for the aristocratic republic was the way in which the stories pitted the tribunate against the senate rather than the patriciate, thereby creating the basis for an entirely new polarity between senate and tribunate. As such the historical redefinition of the tribunate may have provided further impetus to a succession of tribunes in the last century of the republic, who openly challenged the senate.

The failure of traditional means of managing the tribunate left the senate and its leaders with a seemingly insoluble problem: a central element of the ancestral constitution was no longer subject to collective control and threatened at any point to upset the established socio-political order.[120] It is against this background that Sulla's reform of the tribunate may be viewed; for while the dramatic events of 88 provided the immediate trigger, the problem went much deeper. From a constitutional perspective it could be argued that by removing the tribunes' ability single-handedly to propose (and effectively make) laws and enforcing the principle of collective government, Sulla merely rectified a structural flaw in the system; or put differently, he aligned theory and practice in the Roman constitution by giving the senate formal powers that matched its de facto governing position.

But the move was also utterly revolutionary and unprecedented, reflecting the extreme situation after the first civil war when normality had been suspended and the dictator settled personal and political scores with

---

[119] David 1993, who draws attention to episodes such as Liv. 2.41; 2.44.1–6; 2.54; 2.56.
[120] Badian 2009: 11 observed that 'the tribunes . . . had *de facto* power superior to that of the magistrates (even the consuls) . . . '.

impunity. Under regular circumstances, neutralising the tribunate would have been unthinkable, however troublesome some tribunes may have appeared. And without the personal slight Sulla had experienced at the hands of Sulpicius, even he might not have taken the radical step of overturning centuries of constitutional practice. It may therefore not have been long after Sulla's death that the first calls for a return to political normality were raised. Already in 78 the consul Lepidus seems to have embraced the issue of tribunician restoration, although the evidence is conflicting.[121] Later in the 70s several tribunes campaigned for their rein-statement, including Sicinius and Macer. The first step in the dismantling of the Sullan reform came in 75, removing the ban on tribunes holding higher offices. It was passed by a staunch member of the nobility, Aurelius Cotta, and five years later two other pillars of the Sullan nobility, Pompey and Crassus, fully reinstated the tribunes' legislative powers.[122]

The debate over the tribunate is presented in our sources as a straightforward conflict between *populus* and senate, the latter having neutralised the powers of the people by eliminating the champions of their cause. This picture is bound to be oversimplified; as always when our sources refer to 'the people' we have no real idea whom they are talking about. In some respects the position of the senate was indeed strengthened, above all in relation to the courts and the *equites*. Still, contemporaries such as Cicero and Sallust describe it unambiguously as the triumph of the *nobiles* rather than the senate, and the reform must have entrenched the power of this inner circle even further. While the tribunate itself possessed no definite particular character, it did give Roman politics a dynamic aspect, which made it very difficult for any single faction or group of families to control it. The senate, far from being a single unified body – let alone a forum for open debate – was highly structured and hierarchically organised, with the formation of senatorial policy in the hands of powerful, consular families of long-standing prominence. The tribunate provided a potential counterweight to the entrenched power of the leading families which filled the ranks of consuls and *consulares* and generally held sway in the senate.[123] After the Sullan reform that was no longer the case, and with

---

[121] Recently questioned by Burton 2014: 409, who described it as: 'a conflict between two beneficiaries of the Sullan system who despised each other'. *Pace* Arena 2011; Santangelo 2014.

[122] The same year Sulla's judicial changes were also rolled back and the censorship reintroduced, paving the way for full enfranchisement of the Italian former allies.

[123] Sulla's changes to the senate's internal structure would also have affected the debates, since the first speaker was no longer an 'independent' *princeps senatus*, but a consular appointed at the beginning of each year directly by the consul, who was therefore able to set not just the agenda but also to rely on a supportive opening *sententia*.

the curbs on the tribunate the political system lost its most active and unpredictable element. The Sullan reforms seriously limited the opportunities for ambitious politicians to make their mark, advance their careers or promote particular issues without noble consent. Indeed, Cicero could accuse the senators of subjecting the *civitas* to 'regiam istam vestram dominationem', 'that monarchical tyranny of yours', in the courts and in the whole *res publica*, a tyranny that was broken only when the tribunes were given back to the *populus* (*Ver.* 2.5.175).

The restoration of the tribunate may therefore not have been the 'democratic' backlash against 'reactionary' conservatives often assumed. It was supported, indeed implemented, by leading nobles, probably under pressure from other parts of the elite, who must have felt the domination of the Sullan faction stifling and oppressive. The extent of popular engagement may have been overestimated, although there is no reason to doubt it was welcomed by wide sections of the population.[124] Few probably benefitted personally from the tribunes' right to intervene on behalf of citizens – a right so symbolically powerful that even Sulla did not challenge it.[125] Still, their historical role as 'guardians of the plebs' carried a strong ideological charge, which may have played a part in the eventual repeal of the Sullan reform. In a sense it simply marked a return to the ancestral constitution of which the tribunate was an integral element. As such it also responded to an innate traditionalism that could be found across Roman society. Even Cicero accepted that the tribunate had an important, not least symbolic, role to play as the embodiment of the ideal *res publica* as a polity founded on – and inseparable from – the *populus*. This was a fairly consistent stance that can be traced across his career, from the Verrines, where he emphasises the tribunes' role as protector of *libertas*, alongside the magistrates, the courts, the senate and the *populus* itself, to his defence of the tribunate in the speeches for Cornelius.[126] In the Philippics, Cicero complains that good tribunes are no longer able to defend the state against violence and

---

[124] Some sources refer to 'the people' rejoicing in the restoration of the tribunes' power, others to a more lukewarm reception. And as always it is not clear who constituted the crowds in question. In *Ver.* 1.44–45, Cicero argues that the *populus* wanted the tribunate restored, but because of the scandalous law courts, which even Catulus appreciated when he endorsed Pompey's bill. Cicero further indicates that while Pompey's restoration of the tribunate was greeted with 'strepitus et grata contionis admurmuratio', a huge clamour arose when the court reform was mentioned. Still, it remains an open question whether 'the man in the street' would have been much affected by Sulla's jury reform.

[125] Cicero, *Ver.* 2.5.163, referred to 'graviter desiderata et aliquando reddita plebi Romanae tribunicia potestas', but did so in the context of Verres' abuse of Roman citizens, implying the issue was personal protection not legislation.

[126] *Ver.* 2.5.143, cf. 163; Cic. *Corn.* 1 frr. 48–9 =Asc. *Corn.* 76C.

accuses Antony of having abolished *intercessio* (*Phil.* 1.25; 2.6). Even in the *De legibus* the tribunate is accorded a central role in his ideal constitution, which they regulate by blocking bad laws (3.11, cf. 3.23–5).

The ban on higher offices after the tribunate would not have endeared Sulla to the aspiring young aristocrats, for whom it represented an entry point to the senate or, more likely, a stepping stone on the career ladder that would take them above the 'humble' quaestorian class. There is no evidence for senatorial opposition to its repeal, and it is telling that Cotta, according to Cicero, incurred the displeasure of the *nobiles* – rather than the senators – for passing this measure.[127] Eventually, the complete restoration of the tribunate's powers became almost inevitable and towards the end of the 70s there was little resistance left, with even Catulus supporting the repeal.[128] At that point the Sullan reform was most likely considered a step too far, and one which carried painful associations of tyranny and civil war.

The dismantling of Sulla's tribunician laws returned Roman politics to the situation before his intervention, with the structural problems that had prompted it in the first place still unresolved. The tribunate presented an insuperable conundrum, being both disruptive and indispensable. Cicero could, on the one hand, accept the office as an essential part of the constitution and, on the other hand, rail against 'vis tribunicia' that in practice was beyond control. But that, we might note, was a quality of the office, not the office holders who included politicians ranging from Cato to Clodius. If Sulla's reform was not a 'conservative' measure against a particular type of 'popular' politics as much as a radical restructuring of the constitution, the archetypal 'optimate' vanishes along with the category the dictator has come to personify. We are again reminded that while political conflict obviously was rife, it cannot be reduced to a simple binary scheme. That raises the question about how disputes were conceptualised and played out, or in other words: 'What was Roman politics about?'

Content and 'Style' in Late Republican Politics

In the vast array of studies on late republican politics appearing in the last generation one particular argument seems to have gained almost universal traction, which is the notion that Roman politics was more than a zero-

---

[127] Cic. *Corn.* 1 fr. 52 cf. Asc. *Corn.* 66.24–67.2C: the bill was supposedly 'invita nobilitate', but met with 'magno populi studio' (although the meaning of *populus* as always remains unclear).
[128] Cf. Gruen 1974: 28; *contra* Santangelo 2014: 5–10.

sum 'power game' but dealt with 'real' issues that mattered to the politicians who espoused them as well as to the population at large. This consensus has emerged as a reaction to what is often decried as the 'cynical' approach that – rightly or wrongly – has become associated with the works of Ronald Syme and others of his generation. The new paradigm may reflect the changing sensibilities of western scholars, not dissimilar to the reintroduction of 'popular power' into Roman politics. Among the first historians taking issue with the notion of politics as little more than a cover for personal ambition and elite rivalry was Moses Finley, who declared that: 'What I cannot believe is that the electoral contests and military operations were a game for honour and booty, for titles and triumphs, and nothing else.'[129] Finley's attempt to counter the somewhat reductionist 'game' model of Roman politics was welcome and overdue, but in recent years the balance has tipped entirely in the other direction, to the extent that many historians now identify ideological fault lines as *the* defining features of Roman politics.

Political opinion in Rome was frequently split and across a wide range of issues, but when we look at the stance taken on individual measures it is difficult to trace any consistent or clear-cut 'party lines'. Christian Meier therefore suggested that senators tended to position themselves flexibly according to the nature of the issue, a characteristic for which he coined the term 'Gegenstandsabhängigkeit', 'dependency on the matter at hand'.[130] The fluidity intrinsic to the formation of elite opinion is unsurprising since the basic distribution of power and resources hardly ever entered the discussion; the content of Roman politics remained remarkably limited by modern standards, a result partly of the narrow scope of the 'state' and partly of the general consensus that prevailed on most fundamental issues.[131] The debate about the tribunate in the wake of Sulla's reform was unparalleled in its constitutional implications and reflected the exceptional circumstances of the period. By contrast, new measures were by and large fairly modest in terms of their consequences, responding to current issues rather than shifting the balance of power and resources

---

[129] Finley 1983: 98–9. Criticism of the 'power model' continues. Recently, Santangelo 2014: 22 insisted that politics in the 70s was not 'a reshuffle of alliances and loyalties within the senatorial nobility' but about issues, which seems to introduce an unnecessary dichotomy since one does not exclude the other.

[130] 1980: XXXII-XLIII; cf. 1984: 188, noting that in their political stance 'Sie wechselten von Fall zu Fall'.

[131] Hölkeskamp 2010: 39–40; Meier 1965: 595 noted that the 'populares' never questioned the fundamentals. Ferrary 1997: 229 was struck by the contrast between the policies and aims of the 'populares' and their far more radical methods.

between major political constituencies. Even the most daring step in that direction, C. Gracchus' reform of the *repetundae* court, merely reallocated influence from one section of the elite to another. And Clodius, the *enfant terrible* of the late republic, never attempted to undermine senatorial government as such.[132] Interestingly, some measures with potentially far-reaching consequences were proposed to tackle short-term problems. For example, the entirely 'respectable' Ser. Sulpicius suggested changing the voting order in the assemblies, merely to curb electoral bribery.[133] The distribution of economic resources, above all land, was – for obvious reasons – a source of ongoing debate, but even here the divisions may have been far less clear-cut than often assumed. Cicero, for example, supported parts of the *lex Flavia agraria* in 60, provided private interests were protected. The senate, however, rejected it, suspecting more powers for Pompey, while in 59 the senate was about to support Caesar's bill when Cato forcefully intervened, suggesting no senatorial objections in principle.[134] Similarly, Cicero's campaign against Rullus in 63 implies that the bill initially had been well received, perhaps even by his own peers in the senate.[135]

The large majority of senatorial sessions dealt with the issues of the day, many relating to foreign policy, which, of course, frequently gained a personal aspect. Confronted with these questions most senators adopted a stance influenced by a wide range of – not easily separable – motives, including political connections and expediency as well as the nature of the issue itself and the circumstances surrounding it – and indeed personal inclinations and principles. None of these are necessarily mutually exclusive, and trying to identify one as the decisive factor is likely to distort our understanding of the process. There was also a fundamental difference between modern politicians and Roman senators, who participated in government as members of their class and holders of public *honores*. 'Doing politics' was a function of their social status, not an expression of

---

[132] Cf. the important discussions in Fezzi 1999; 2008.

[133] *Mur.* 46–7. The passage is corrupt but Cicero appears to imply Sulpicius' proposed 'confusionem suffragiorum' would lead to 'aequationem gratiae, dignitatis, suffragiorum', 'equal distribution of influence, status and voting power'. Nicolet 1959: 153 therefore suspected Sulpicius of 'popularis' tendencies, but there is no evidence for that; the measure was clearly an attempt to address electoral bribery, cf. Adamietz 1989: 184–5.

[134] Cic. *Att.* 1.19.4 (SB 19); Cass. Dio 38.1–3.

[135] On other occasions the senate appears to have been genuinely concerned about public revenue, cf. e.g. *Att.* 2.36.1 (SB 36), and *Tusc.* 3.48, accusing C. Gracchus of emptying the *aerarium* with his *largitiones*, *pace* Ungern-Sternberg 1991. In 100 the quaestor Caepio opposed Saturninus' grain law, declaring that the treasury could not cover the expense, *Rhet. Her.* 1.21, cf. 2.17, where Caepio, on trial for *maiestas*, argued that he had saved the *civitas* from damage by preserving the *aerarium*.

commitment to specific causes; the absence of programmes during electoral campaigns illustrates their 'apolitical' character. Therefore, it would
probably be a mistake to expect the average senator to have entertained
strong personal views, distinct from those of his peers. A certain 'herd
instinct' is perhaps likely among the majority, allowing those with deeper
convictions and powers of persuasion rich opportunities for influencing
the outcome of debates. An obvious example is the Younger Cato, who,
despite his relatively modest rank in the senatorial hierarchy, on several
occasions shaped the majority view through the strength of his
personality.[136] As noted earlier, in 59 the senators had been inclined to
support Caesar's agrarian law until Cato spoke up against it, in the same
way as they apparently had favoured a more lenient approach to the
Catilinarians beforehand. There was, it would seem, a considerable degree
of open-endedness, perhaps even unpredictability, to the process of senatorial policy formation. Certainly, there is little trace of any unified 'conservative' block of 'optimates'. For example, when the senate debated the
crucial allocation of provinces in 56, the leading critics of the triumvirs
presented no united front, each pushing for a different solution. Similarly,
during the debate on the restoration of King Ptolemy of Egypt in
January 56, Bibulus and Hortensius, supposedly close political allies, presented alternative proposals and showed no sign of co-ordination.[137]

　　The role of the senate was partly practical, partly symbolic, and its
deliberations served to express the position of the *senatus* as a single
body. Its approval carried the status of *auctoritas*, a complex and multi-
layered concept that went well beyond any simple constitutional classification of powers. Its primary function was to embody the collective will of
the 'elders'. The ideal outcome of the proceedings was a unanimous
response which demonstrated the unity of the elite. The procedures were
therefore carefully designed to elicit such a response, with highly formalised debates and strict hierarchies and speaking order. The overriding aim
was to paper over disagreements rather than to expose them. Votes were
therefore usually taken when the outcome was clear and unambiguous; the
notion of *senatus auctoritas* carried by a narrow majority was almost
a contradiction in terms.[138] One might go as far as saying that reaching

---

[136] Cicero also notes that Cethegus, through his senatorial oratory, achieved an influence equal to that
of consulars, *Brut.* 178.

[137] Cic. *Fam.* 1.2. (SB 13), summarised the debate in a letter to Lentulus Spinther, mentioning separate
proposals by Bibulus, Hortensius and Volcacius Tullus (on behalf of Pompey).

[138] Timmer 2009.

agreement was more important than the content of this consensus, because oligarchic governments rely on internal unity for their survival.

It is against this backdrop that we may revisit the question of the 'dissident' tribunes, who played such a pivotal role in late republican politics. Traditionally, their powers were contained by a more or less formalised requirement that they be used only with the consent of the senate, although there were notable instances where that was ignored. During the late republic this situation occurred with increasing frequency, probably reflecting growing competition within the elite – rather than the rise of any 'popular party'. The tribunes in question were roundly condemned, but interestingly the censure was expressed in moral rather than political terms; basically they were denounced as 'bad people'. The standard term of political abuse was 'improbus', bad, which might be supplemented with a host of adjectives of a similar nature, e.g. 'audax', reckless, 'sceleratus', wicked, 'malus', bad, 'perditus', bankrupt, 'temerarius', impetuous, 'levis', fickle, 'impius', sacrilegious, 'furiosus', mad, 'desperatus', desperate.[139] The clear message conveyed by these terms of abuse is one of personal depravity, unpredictability and transgression. The terminology thus reflects the basic principles underlying the aristocratic republic, which required the individual to submit to the collective. Viewed from that perspective, the lack of conformity displayed by 'troublemakers' became signs of selfish ambition that endangered the very foundations of the existing political order.

There is no indication that they were ever conceived of as a particular type of politician, let alone labelled according to the policies they pursued. The political vocabulary is remarkable in its almost complete omission of any reference to the content of the actions that were condemned. For that reason it could be applied also to politicians conventionally categorised as 'optimates', such as Verres and Drusus the younger.[140] If their methods turned violent or caused civil disturbances, they would be described as *seditiosi*, irrespective of their aims and policies.[141] It illustrates a peculiarly Roman form of discourse which operated with types of actions rather than

---

[139] Helleguarc'h 1972: 526–34.

[140] In *Ver.* 1.36 Cicero attacks the nobility with the phrase 'paucorum improbitate et audacia' and Verres as 'homo improbus'; *Div. Caec.* 26, adding that he wishes to extinguish 'omnis improbitas'. Likewise, the younger Drusus, the champion of the senate, was denounced for his *temeritas* by his opponents, Cic. *Orat.* 213–14. Antony had apparently also used the phrase 'perditissimorum consiliorum auctorem' about his opponents, *Phil.* 3.19. Elsewhere, Cicero implies that opponents had called his own side 'malos cives' and 'homines improbos', i.e. the standard terms of political abuse, *Fam.* 6.6.10 (SB 234).

[141] Robb 2010: 150–65.

policies and categorised politicians according to their character and degree of conformity.

The term 'popularis', which has come to dominate modern studies, was occasionally included among the labels used to censure opponents. Still, far from being the most common, it was in fact employed relatively sparingly in that sense.[142] For a number of reasons, already discussed, it was not particularly well suited as a political signifier. It covered a surprisingly wide semantic spectrum, ranging from the highly laudatory, over neutral, to deeply pejorative. So unless the meaning was obvious from the context, a speaker would on every occasion have to specify how the word was used. This ambiguity set it apart from the usual political terms, which were all entirely unmistakable in their intent. Moreover, it associated the target with the *populus*, an indisputably positive concept in Roman politics, making it a somewhat double-edged sword in political invective; opponents might try to turn it into a form of praise by embracing its positive aspect. The interesting question is therefore why Cicero decided to use this particular term as basis for his digression in the *Pro Sestio*.

The 'foundational' text for the 'optimates'/'populares'-model is quite unusual in its choice of terminology and in its description of political categories. Cicero's principal objective in this speech was to undermine Clodius' claims to legitimacy and isolate him in every possible sense: from his peers and predecessors as well as from the *populus*. Clodius becomes not just a social outcast but also a political failure. Cicero therefore redefines the common term for the senate and its leaders, the 'optimates', to include a much wider section of the propertied classes, while contrasting them with 'populists', who for selfish reasons opposed this broad church of right-minded citizens. Normally, the latter would have been described in conventional derogatory terms such as *improbi* or *audaces*, but in this instance Cicero settled for 'populares'. He probably did so because he wished to focus on two related meanings of the word, that of 'popular' and of 'populist'; for whereas Clodius' predecessors, including the Gracchi, had achieved genuine popularity through their populism, Clodius had not even managed that, since the people despised him and only hirelings applauded. In Cicero's unique construction, Clodius was therefore not actually 'popularis' in the same sense as the Gracchi, whom he had tried but failed to emulate. He became separated not just from 'respectable' people, but also

---

[142] For examples of its use alongside other conventional terms, see Cic. *Clu.* 94: 'acerbus, criminosus, popularis homo et turbulentus', cf. 113: 'Quinctiana iniqua, falsa, turbulenta, popularia, seditiosa iudicia fuerunt'.

from the *populus*, the fundamental source of legitimacy in the Roman republic.

Cicero's choice of words is carefully tailored to the specific point he is trying to make. If he had stuck to usual terms such as *improbus* and *audax*, his entire argument would have collapsed since the Gracchi, Saturninus, and Clodius would all have merged into a single unambiguous category of 'bad people', from which the latter could not be differentiated as being any worse. The key objective of Cicero's strategy was precisely the isolation of Clodius, and by presenting Clodius as a 'failed populist' Cicero deprived him of the historical precedents that were vital to any politician venturing down a controversial path. As Cicero notes on several occasions, dissident tribunes tended to invoke notable predecessors to absolve themselves of the charge of novelty. Sometimes the models fall well outside the modern stereotype of the 'popularis', including Cicero's hero Scipio Aemilianus, while elsewhere, such as the *Pro Sestio*, they are the classic examples of the Gracchi and Saturninus.[143] What they all held in common was personal popularity, and it was Clodius' popular following that forced Cicero to extend his attack into a general disquisition about the nature of popularity, an excursus which despite its tendentious and self-serving nature casts a revealing light on a highly sensitive issue in Roman politics.

Popularity in the Late Republic

Cicero found himself up against one of the most effective popular leaders of the Roman republic: Clodius enjoyed wide support among the urban plebs and was able to call on their support at short notice, allowing him to dominate the political stage even when he held no public office. Faced with his opponent's popular following, Cicero had to deconstruct the entire concept of popularity. He did so first by separating the 'real people' from the crowds rallying to Clodius' cause. Cicero here draws on the common rhetorical distinction between the universally revered *populus* and the base manifestations of this concept, the *multitudo* or *vulgus*, which allows him to deny Clodius' supporters, however numerous, the status of 'the people'. In order to undermine Clodius' position further Cicero notes the elusiveness of 'popular opinion' and hence popularity. He famously identifies three fora where the views of the people were expressed: *contiones*, electoral *comitia*, and the theatre and other public entertainment venues (*Sest.* 106–27). However, when he notes that populists confuse the reaction of

---

[143] *Ac.* 2.13; 2.72; 2.75 (*Luc.*), cf. Robb 2010: esp. 65–8, 165–6.

a contional crowd with the sentiments of the entire *populus*, he is in effect observing that the *populus* as such has no meaningful way of expressing consent, which takes him dangerously close to questioning the very basis for the *res publica*; for while the comment may relate to the *contio* it is applicable to all claims of popular support, which invariably involved only a tiny minority of the population.

The fundamental problem was that while popularity in the broadest sense of general approval remained a source of immense prestige in Rome – precisely because of the ideological construction of the *res publica* – it was also inherently contestable. Claims to popularity were met with counter claims denouncing the apparent popularity of opponents as false, skewed or obtained by dishonourable means, by pandering to the people's lowest instincts, irresponsibly catering to their material needs or simply buying their support. These arguments were feasible because of the difficulty involved in measuring popularity in Rome, a society without effective general elections, polls or mass media.[144] 'Public opinion' was therefore destined to remain a source of dispute in a society which attached such importance to popular legitimacy but had no effective means of gauging it and, in a constitutional context, had to rely on a purely formalised notion of consent.

It was as part of this attack on Clodius that Cicero created a new political category, which he labelled 'populares' and defined in opposition to the much-expanded 'optimates'. They were identified as politicians who, driven by desire for popularity, commit irresponsible acts during their time in office. In some cases their activities did indeed make them popular, but more often they did not. The latter therefore belong to the paradoxical category of unpopular populist, of which Clodius is singled out as the prime example. The counter-intuitive description of Clodius as unpopular required that the very concept of popularity be redefined, which in itself tells us something about the sensitive nature of popularity in Roman politics.

Popularity was in principle a positive concept, *gratia* earned through honourable services and favours, and its attractions were considered self-evident and timeless. As Cicero's own example shows, the benefits were often intangible; after his consulship he would never have to face another public 'popularity test', but that did little to reduce his famous appetite

---

[144] Hence the elite's concern about the reactions of audiences at shows and in the theatre, cf. e.g. *Att.* 4.15.6 (SB 90); 2.19.3 (SB 39); *Fam.* 8.2.1 (SB 78).

for personal acclaim.[145] Rather than a practical means to an end the pursuit of popularity was an essential and accepted part of the Roman elite's one-upmanship. On the other hand, unseemly popularity-seeking of the kind Clodius and others were accused of raised suspicions of 'populism', routinely condemned as a character flaw and a potential source of civic disruption.[146] However, despite the moralising discourse against 'populists' it appears to have been a fairly common pattern of behaviour, which is probably best understood in structural terms as a function of the Roman career ladder. As importantly, it was not necessarily linked to – or indicative of – any particular type of politics, apart from the appeal to sections of the population outside the narrow circles of the nobility. Indeed, it might not even go beyond the adoption of a certain political style and personal demeanour. Intriguingly, one could apparently be a 'populist' without doing very much apart from acting like one.

Cicero illustrates this point in an interesting passage of the *Pro Sestio*, where he elaborates on the concept of 'false popularity'. Cicero looks at five tribunes from 59 and considers their later careers. Three of them were respectable pillars of the establishment, of whom two, despite achieving nothing in their tribunate, had already reached the praetorship by 56, while the other one clearly was destined to do so. The two 'populists', on the other hand, had more mixed careers; one (Alfius Flavus) was unsuccessful in his attempt at the praetorship (*Schol. Bob.* 135, 151St.), while the other, even more disreputable (Vatinius), failed miserably when he sought the aedileship. Cicero recognises that the 'moderate populist', whom Cicero describes as 'vir et bonus et innocens', had not actually disgraced himself politically or passed any harmful bills. He had simply misjudged what the 'real' people wished and in his pursuit of popularity taken the wrong course (and supported Caesar). The passage underscores the point that in Cicero's view 'populism' did not necessarily have any political content, but could express itself simply in a particular posture or style aimed at attracting popular attention and approval, in this case alignment with a prominent popular figure.

---

[145] Cicero revelled in signs of approval and popularity, suffering whenever hit by *invidia*. In 60 he had been tempted to join the 'triumvirs' by the prospect of 'peace with the mob', which he otherwise despised, *Att.* 2.3.4 (SB 23). And in 57 he enjoyed the applause of the 'infima plebs', *Att.* 4.1.5 (SB 73); cf. 2.6.2 (SB 26); *Q. fr.* 2.15.2.

[146] Cicero could, for example, in passing mention Pompey's 'popularis levitas' – 'populist frivolity', *Att.* 2.1.6 (SB 21).

In making this point Cicero inadvertently collapses the political model
he has just constructed, since it suggests that the sharp distinction between
'populists' and 'respectable' citizens which formed the core of his attack on
Clodius in reality was far more blurred. Indeed, the artificial nature of these
categories becomes even more apparent when we consider the careers of
those who went down what Cicero would have called the 'populist' route.
Cicero implies they were naturally shunned by upstanding 'optimates' and
suffered for their political choices, a picture which has contributed greatly
to the modern 'party-model' with its emphasis on ideological commitment
and personal sacrifice. However, a quick look at the roll-call of tribunes
usually classified as 'populares' shows that the large majority succeeded to
the praetorship, in many cases without any apparent difficulties. For
example, both the rejected tribunes from 59 actually went on to hold the
praetorship, including Cicero's bête noire Vatinius in 55 (and later the
consulship in 47).

In a similar vein we find controversial tribunes in the third century
such as C. Flaminius and Terentius Varro, who both challenged the
senate but went on to become consuls, the former twice.[147] In the
early second century Q. Terentius Culleo, tr. 189, passed a disputed
bill but became praetor in 187, while L. Valerius Tappo, tr. 195, who
clashed with Cato over the repeal of *lex Oppia* held the praetorship in
192.[148] Of the tribunes who supposedly 'democratised' voting in the
later second century, the majority enjoyed distinguished later careers,
including Cassius Longinus Ravilla (tr. 137, cos. 127, cens. 125),
C. Papirius Carbo (tr. 131, cos. 120), C. Coelius Caldus (tr. 107,
pr. 100/99, cos. 94), and Cn. Domitius Ahenobarbus (tr. 104, cos. 96,
cens. 92).[149] Only A. Gabinius, tr. 139, apparently reached no higher
office. Even the tribune of 131 Labeo Macerio, who had tried to hurl the
censor Metellus from the Tarpeian Rock, advanced to the praetorship in
122/121.[150] The tribune P. Decius, who prosecuted Opimius in 120 for his
violent suppression of C. Gracchus, reached the praetorship in 115.[151]
As tribune in 103 Norbanus had prosecuted Servilius Caepio, causing

---

[147] Flaminius was clearly less politically isolated than the biased sources imply, Vishnia 1996: 25–34;
Meissner 2000.
[148] Culleo: Plu. *Flam.* 18.1, failed attempt at consulship in 185.
[149] Cassius introduced secret ballot at trials, Carbo in legislative assemblies (and controversially tried to
legalise iteration of the tribunate), Coelius in trials for *perduellio*, while Domitius transferred
election of priests to the assembly.
[150] Liv. *Per.* 59; Plin. *Nat.* 7.143. For his praetorship, Stumpf 1985; Eilers 1996; Brennan 2000: 547.
[151] Cic. *De orat.* 2.132, 134–135, *Part.* 104, 106, *Brut.* 108; Liv. *Per.* 61; Auct. *De vir. ill.* 72.6.

disturbances and antagonising most of the senate, but nevertheless went on to become quaestor in 101, praetor 91/89, and consul in 83.[152] C. Marius caused considerable controversy as tribune in 119 and stumbled in his attempt at the aedileship. Still, he managed to scrape through to the praetorship in 116 – and, of course, went on to hold seven consulships thereafter.[153] C. Memmius, tr. 111, tormented the nobility over its management of the Juguthine War and was described by Sallust as 'vir acer et infestus potentiae nobilitatis' (*Jug.* 27.1), but held the praetorship in 104, and was consular candidate in 100 when he was killed by Glaucia.[154] Several high-profile tribunes in the 70s were also elected to the praetorship, despite the controversy they caused in office, among them L. Quinctius (tr. 74, pr. 67), C. Licinius Macer (tr. 73, pr. 68), and M. Lollius Palicanus (tr. 71, pr. 69).[155] Pompey's man Gabinius (tr. 67) progressed to the praetorship in 61 and the consulship in 58. In 61 the tribune Q. Fufius Calenus had assisted Clodius in the Bona Dea trial, incurring the wrath of many nobles, but still became praetor in 59 (and consul in 47).[156]

There were, of course, some who fared less well, such as the tribune of 66, Manilius, who was prosecuted for *maiestas*, and Cn. Sicinius, tr. 76, about whom the sources hint at a violent end. Others again simply disappear from the record after their tribunate, including Claudius, tr. 218, C. Valerius Tappo, tr. 188, and C. Licinius Crassus, tr. 145. In their case absence of evidence is not proof of failure. Finally, the tribune of 67, C. Cornelius, also vanishes despite his elite support and connections to Pompey, which makes one suspect an early death.

What becomes clear is that going down what used to be called the 'popularis' route, supposedly a momentous step by which members of the elite seceded from their peer group in order to serve the interests of the people, in reality involved little risk. Only a few suffered grave consequences, which had obviously not been anticipated when they embarked

---

[152] Dismissed as 'homo improbus' by Cicero, *De orat.* 2.203, he was later prosecuted for violence but acquitted.

[153] Marius failed twice in his attempt at the aedileship, implying that however much he may have antagonised the senate during his tribunate, it did not translate into general popularity, Cic. *Planc.* 51. Paradoxically the 'popularis' Marius was therefore more successful in the 'aristocratic' *comitia centuriata* than in the 'democratic' *comitia tributa*.

[154] This trajectory defies any conventional classification, since he clearly opposed the *nobiles*, but remained popular with the rest of the elite, before being killed by another politician who according to traditional taxonomy was a 'popularis'.

[155] Quinctius was *homo novus* and almost 50 when tribune. Macer was prosecuted in 66 and committed suicide. Palicanus failed at his consulship bid.

[156] Other examples from this period include Pompey's man L. Flavius, tr. 60, pr. 58, and Clodius' ally C. Cato, tr. 56, pr. 55? (cf. *MRR* 3.169).

on their activities. The notion of irreparable damage seems rooted in the 'party' model of Roman politics, which somewhat anachronistically implies it meant 'crossing the floor' and joining the opposite side. Populism – for that is how opponents regarded their actions – seems to have been considered a fairly 'innocent' transgression in most cases. Despite Cicero's insistence to the contrary, it appears that for the most part it did their careers little harm. The entire category of 'populists' might therefore be seen as yet another result of Cicero's strategy to isolate Clodius, which required clear demarcations to be drawn where none existed.

'Populism' typically described specific actions or forms of behaviour at certain moments, not a distinct category of politicians. It was probably an accusation many faced at some point during their career. Cicero himself was certainly accused of populism over his defence of Cornelius (cf. *Vat.* 5), and most likely also when he took on the case against Verres. As we saw, neither hurt his career, and the public (including the propertied classes without whose support one could not reach the highest offices) therefore seems to have given aspiring politicians considerable leeway to make a name for themselves. Thus 'populism' was particularly linked to early careers when younger men needed to raise their profile in order to stand out from the competition. Tribunes had just one year to make their mark and leave a lasting impression on the public that would decide their fate when the time came for the next round of elections. Name recognition was essential in Roman politics and the tribunate, with its extensive powers and prerogatives, served as a perfect vehicle for achieving that. It was also highly competitive, with ten equally ambitious younger men striving for public attention.[157] The tribunate was not the only option, however (and patricians were, of course, excluded), and one could decide to hold the aedileship instead as a means of attracting positive attention. An alternative – or parallel – route to fame was offered by the courts, where controversial prosecutions provided an effective way to public renown.[158]

The 'political public' appears to have appreciated the needs of aspiring politicians at the early stages of their career; indeed it showed remarkable indulgence, even when they went beyond what was normally tolerated. Despite Cicero's vilification, Clodius clearly enjoyed widespread support, also among the elite, many of whom even acquiesced to the exiling of

---

[157] Cf. Russell 2013.
[158] E.g. Cic. *Div. Caec.* 70; *Cael.* 73; cf. *Brut.* 159; *De orat.* 3.74; *Off.* 2.47; Plu. *Luc.* 1.1–2. David 1983; 1992; Jehne 2000c: 179–83; McCall 2002: 118–23; Tatum 2013.

Cicero.[159] And he not only reached the aedileship in 56 without any problems but was also well on course for the praetorship when he was killed in 52.[160] Again we look in vain for any sharp division between so-called populists and 'optimates'; in reality, the strategy was probably relatively common and broadly accepted as a phase which many politicians went through during their career.

This does not mean that popularity was no cause for concern, and Cicero's *Pro Sestio* is a rare attempt to grapple with the problem of the popular – but disruptive – politician who was able to claim superior legitimacy, authority, and prestige because of his *gratia* and widespread support. To counter these claims Cicero effectively resorted to sophistry. On the one hand, he distinguished between the right and the wrong kind of popularity, the former achieved by honourable means and for the right ends, the latter irresponsibly and for purely selfish reasons. On the other hand, he divided the *populus* into the real and the false people, thereby drawing attention to the basic problem in Rome, namely that popular legitimacy essentially was notional since the 'will of the *populus*' remained fundamentally elusive. Both sets of distinctions are, of course, rhetorical and transparently self-serving. But while they hardly qualify as an analysis of Roman politics, they do draw our attention to the language of politics and the oblique and complex ways in which it relates to 'practice'.

Discourse and Ideology

In recent years the language, rhetorical strategies and arguments presented by political agents during the late republic have become the object of renewed scrutiny, resulting in some highly sophisticated and important studies. This has also added further weight to the notion of 'troublesome' tribunes constituting a distinct 'popular' movement in the late republic. In surviving speeches delivered at *contiones*, in the senate and even in the courts, scholars have identified the outline of two sharply contrasting political ideals, one championing the interests of the people and the other emphasising the primacy of the senate. The former, mostly espoused by tribunes, powerfully asserted the rights of the *populus* and fought for its

---

[159] Cicero privately complained that the elite had abandoned him, e.g. *Fam.* 1.9.10, 13 (SB 20), and later felt compelled to deny it in public, *Dom.* 95; *Red. pop.* 13. Fezzi 1999: 321 noted the striking passivity of the senate in 58.

[160] Cicero takes Clodius' election for granted, even raising the spectre of a future consulship; it was just a question of which year it would happen, *Mil.* 24, 88–90; cf. Tatum 1999: 234.

libertas against senatorial oppression, while the latter insisted on the senate's prerogatives and right to guide public policy.

The two discourses might at first seem to suggest a political world divided by almost irreconcilable differences in values and ideology. But before looking more closely at the debate itself we may note that it adds yet another paradox to Roman politics; for the discourse generally appears to be far more radical in tone and argumentation than the actual issues under discussion. Thus, no matter how emphatically the people's interests and 'sovereignty' may have been asserted, the republic never saw any concrete attempts to change the nature of Roman society or shift the balance of power. There is, in short, a peculiar incongruence between the 'popular' rhetoric and the far more modest initiatives it was used to promote.[161]

The question we have to ask is therefore whether all is really as it seems. Was the political stage dominated by two fixed ideological positions or are we in fact dealing with a set of rhetorical strategies defined by the constitutional structure of the Roman state? The *res publica* rested on the twin pillars of *senatus populusque Romanus*, which ideally acted in unison, the *populus* remaining 'sovereign' while accepting the leadership of its elected magistrates who followed the advice of their peers in the senate. However, since tribunes and magistrates were not bound by the advice of the senate but could act on their own, disputes were almost inevitable and in that case the *populus* always prevailed. The implication was that either side of a conflict had to articulate their case in very specific terms dictated by the formal distribution of powers in the *res publica*. Or put differently, the constitutional framework in which politicians operated automatically turned policy disagreements into rhetorical contests between *populus* and aristocracy.

Tribunes who failed to get the backing of their peers, or decided to ignore them altogether, were bound to invoke the powers invested in them by the plebs. In tactical terms that meant they could justify their course of action only by insisting that popular *libertas* trumped all objections from the senate. Their opponents, for their part, had no other option than to stress the senate's traditional leading role and condemn the breach of the *mos maiorum* which the tribunes' actions represented. It follows that all political arguments were conducted according to a particular formula which pitted the people's *libertas* against the senate's authority. Political agents on either side of a dispute had little choice but to frame the discourse in those particular terms. The impression of two oppositional ideologies

[161] Cf. Ferrary 1997.

may therefore be the product of a specific rhetorical 'game', whose rules and conventions became so standardised that they could even become the object of parody.[162]

A closer look at the argumentation also suggests that the underlying ideological tenets were considerably more unified than often realised; for while *libertas populi Romani* and *senatus auctoritas* may have been invoked by opposing sides of political disputes, neither of these concepts were questioned in principle by their adversaries. It is, for example, extremely rare for a tribune or any other politician at loggerheads with the senate to attack the institution itself or question its authority. Not only were they themselves members of that body, but its *auctoritas* also appears to have been recognised as a fundamental part of the Roman constitution, unchallenged even by its fiercest critics. In Sallust's *Bellum Iugurthinum* the tribune Memmius, who waged a relentless campaign against leading nobles, presented himself as a defender of the *senatus auctoritas*. Conversely, Clodius could, as we saw, be blamed in public for splitting the 'optimates' (i.e. senators), with the clear implication that not only was he part of that class but also that the charge would damage him. When Labienus prosecuted Rabirius in a trial that is often seen as a direct attack on the *senatus consultum ultimum*, he was accused of slandering the senate, which again suggests that even 'dissidents' would never admit to targeting the senate as such.[163] To avoid that charge they typically denounced parts of the senate, usually the leading *nobiles*, accusing them of unduly dominating their peers.[164] Their opponents, they insisted, were therefore not the senate but a small clique which prevented it from exercising its free judgement. To further tarnish their motives these 'pauci' were often described as driven by personal animus and self-interest rather than political principle. Cicero's *Pro Cornelio*, as we saw, offers a revealing glimpse into the argumentative strategy employed in these situations, showing how

---

[162] Val. Max. 2.9.5, suggesting it had become a kind of rhetorical default setting shaping almost all public debates involving tribunes, cf. Russell 2013. Sallust also lets Catiline deliver a caricature of a populist speech to his followers, in which he pits *libertas* against the power of 'paucorum potentium' and complains that the indebted aristocrats had been reduced to 'volgus', *Cat.* 20.6–7. The commonplace nature of these arguments is illustrated also by Antonius' defence of Norbanus, Cic. *De orat.* 2.124, 167, 198–200; cf. *Part.* 104–5. Even in a trivial *ambitus* trial Cicero could invoke the people's prerogatives, *Planc.* 11.

[163] Cic. *Rab. perd.* 21. Interestingly, Clodius accused Cicero of having produced a false *senatus consultum* in 63, *Dom.* 50: 'M. Tullius falsum senatus consultum rettulerit', implying he would have accepted its force had it been genuine. Caesar also accepted the use of the SCU as justified, apart from the one instance where it was aimed at himself, *Civ.* 1.7.

[164] For example, in his speech for Norbanus, Antonius noted that the Roman people had gained freedom and security against the opposition of the *nobiles* – not the senate, Cic. *De orat.* 2.199.

a speaker would defend the senate while criticising the 'oligarchs'. Cicero had already used it to good effect in the *Divinatio in Caecilium* and the Verrines, and later it would form a central plank of Caesar's self-justification in the *Bellum civile*, which argued that rather than fighting the senate he was in fact restoring its autonomy. Sallust even has Catiline, in his famous last address, encourage his men to fight for *libertas*, while claiming his opponents merely sought to uphold 'potentia paucorum' (*Cat.* 58.11).

Also on the other side of the argument the position was considerably more nuanced than the traditional 'party-model' allows. While casting doubt on the motives, wisdom, and popularity of their opponents, the proponent of the senatorial majority view never seems to have tried to undermine tribunes by questioning the supremacy of the *populus* or the powers invested in their officials.[165] Instead they justified their position by arguing that it was precisely the people's best interest that informed the senatorial view. What might appear to be a confrontation between two opposite political principles thus turns out be a rhetorical contest in which both sides claimed to be the true defenders and exponents of a shared set of ideals.

Morstein-Marx aptly described the striking political uniformity of the Roman republic as an 'ideological monotony'. He coined this phrase to define the oratory presented at public meetings and therefore suggested we might be dealing with a specific 'contional ideology', shaped by the need of speakers to appeal to popular audiences.[166] However, when we look more broadly at political rhetoric there seems to be little difference in tone or content between speeches delivered in courts, at *contiones*, or to the senate.[167] Cicero could, for example, warn a popular assembly that the trial of Rabirius was an attack on *auctoritas senatus* and *consensio bonorum* (*Rab. perd.* 2–4). Conversely, when Cicero insists that he is the true *popularis*, i.e. 'defender of the people', he does so both at *contiones* and in the senate.[168] Also, speeches addressed to senators are focused

---

[165] In *Leg.* 1.43–44, Cicero notes that the fact that something has been passed by the *multitudo* does not in itself make it right. However, this radical statement (which has been somewhat modified by the use of *multitudo* instead of *populus*) belongs to a distinct theoretical discourse and is to my knowledge without parallel.

[166] Morstein-Marx 2004: 239–40.

[167] A particular focus of interest has been Cicero's treatment of the Gracchi, supposedly more positive at *contiones* than in other fora, e.g. *Agr.* 2.10, 31; *Rab. perd.* 12–15; cf. Beranger 1972; Robinson 1994; Van der Blom 2010: 103–7. The contrast has been overstated, however. Cicero is, for example, surprisingly sympathetic towards the Gracchi in the *De haruspicum responso*, 41, delivered to the senate, and in the *De domo sua*, 24, C. Gracchus is described as 'maxime popularis' in the positive sense of supporter of the people's interests; cf. Robb 2010: 79.

[168] *Agr.* 1.23; *Phil.* 8.19.

overwhelmingly on the freedom and interests of the *populus Romanus*. Thus in Cicero's speech to the *pontifices* on his house he invokes the *populus Romanus* no fewer than eighty-six times. One passage is particularly instructive since he first recalls earlier peaceful times resting on the people's *libertas* and the senate's guidance, before comparing them to the age of Clodius, which was marked by the crushing of the people's *libertas* and the extinction of the senate's *auctoritas*.[169] Such instances are far from isolated, similar points being made in e.g. Cicero's thirteenth Philippic, which repeatedly pairs *senatus auctoritas* and *libertas populi Romani*.[170] Even in private correspondence, the two central ideals of Roman public life are presented as equal and inseparable, as happened in Cicero's letter to Plancus in 43 (*Fam.* 10.6.2 (SB 370)). Examples such as these have often been dismissed as aristocrats stealing the clothes of their 'popularis' opponents for political gain, but not only does the argument presuppose the existence of fixed ideological identities, it also overlooks the widespread use of this type of language across the political spectrum, even among the senatorial leaders themselves.[171]

All participants in public life appear to have subscribed to a unified vision of the *res publica*, in which the senate's *auctoritas* and the people's *libertas* were not defined in opposition to each other.[172] They were complementary and inseparable precisely because the elite saw itself as the protectors of the public interest. While it is easy to doubt the sincerity of such claims, we cannot exclude the possibility that Roman senators may have believed their own rhetoric and seen themselves as true defenders of the common good – which just happened to coincide with those of their own class.[173] Even Nasica's notorious outburst at a *contio*: 'Be silent, citizens, if you please. I understand better than you what is for the public good', is for all its aristocratic haughtiness ultimately phrased as an expression of concern for the people's interest.[174]

---

[169] *Dom.* 130, 'Tempus illud erat tranquillum et in libertate populi et gubernatione positum senatus. Tuum porro tempus libertate populi Romani oppressa, senatus auctoritate deleta'.

[170] *Phil.* 13.33, 47, cf. 5.53.

[171] E.g. Spielvogel 1993: 39. Nippel 1995: 5 also suggested the orator 'Antonius, though notorious as a defender of the Senate's authority, in this particular instance was clearly adopting a line of argument typical of the *populares*, ... '.

[172] On the almost universal appeals to *libertas*, see e.g. Mouritsen 2001: 9–13. Cf. Wirszubski 1950 and Arena 2012.

[173] See Jehne 2013c on the role of the senate as protector of the common good.

[174] Val. Max. 3.7.3: 'Tacete, quaeso, Quirites', ... 'plus ego enim quam vos quid rei publicae expediat intellego'.

There were important political implications of this shared ideological platform, for as long as the elite consistently spoke the language of inclusion and popular freedom, it remained almost impossible to formulate a genuinely democratic alternative to the oligarchic regime. It followed that the political system as such never became subject to debate, at least not in the public sphere, which was dominated entirely by the issues of the day. The closest we come to a discussion about the fundamentals is Cicero's *De legibus*, where his brother Quintus expresses what may be the most sustained case for oligarchic reform that has reached us. He is, however, countered by the character of Cicero himself who wishes to retain the constitution largely intact, despite its apparent weaknesses.[175] Whether similar theoretical exercises were produced from a 'democratic' perspective is unclear, but there is no trace of them in the surviving record. To our knowledge no Roman politician ever proposed legislation that would significantly shift the balance of power enshrined in the ancestral constitution; the political system was therefore destined to remain unchanged despite its many paradoxes and contradictions. But within this framework rhetorical strategies evolved which could be used to justify open conflict rather than compromise, a development that would have serious consequences for the Roman republic and take us to the much-debated 'fall' which marked the end of collective government.

The End of the Republic

Since the renaissance historians and political theorists have argued about the nature and causes of the process by which the aristocratic government of Rome came to a dramatic end during the first century BCE.[176] One of the intriguing aspects of the 'fall of the republic' is its relatively limited impact and scope. It did not mark the collapse of Roman society or civilisation and the Roman state did not disintegrate but continued to thrive for centuries afterwards. Neither did the 'fall' affect Rome's overseas empire, which survived intact and was even expanded despite the upheaval. No province cast off Roman rule, nor did the empire split into multiple kingdoms or polities, as had happened to the Macedonian empire after the death of Alexander. The social order also remained largely untouched by the turmoil, with the basic hierarchies carrying on into the imperial era – although the remnants of the old aristocracy assumed a new role as court

---

[175] On the nature of the *De legibus*, see Girardet 1983; Dyck 2004: 15–20.
[176] Recent narratives include Steel 2013 and Alston 2015.

nobility. The changes were thus largely confined to the political sphere; for however traumatic the experience of civil war, it was essentially the transition from one type of government to another.

The 'fall of the republic' also happened remarkably fast. Just a few decades after Cicero in the 50s had provided vivid eyewitness accounts of a creaking but still functioning republic, there was little left of the old power structure; civil war had brought an end to centuries of aristocratic power sharing and left a single ruler in its place. While the eclipse of the republican elite was abrupt and irreversible, the roots of its decline have traditionally been traced back almost a hundred years, to 133, when the tumultuous events of Ti. Gracchus' tribunate supposedly marked the beginning of the 'late Republic'. As already noted, sharp periodisations of this kind invariably raise methodological issues, and in this case it seems clear that the changes ushered in by the Gracchi were less radical than often assumed; there is, for example, little evidence that they introduced a new kind of ideologically based politics that split the elite down the middle. The year 133 does, however, still represent an important milestone in the history of the republic.

Ti. Gracchus' tribunate saw the gathering of a perfect political storm in which a number of sensitive issues came together to highly combustible effect. Political conflict, sometimes divisive and acrimonious, was, of course, nothing new – despite Livy's attempt to present the 'middle republic' as a consensual age largely devoid of domestic strife. Still, solutions had usually been found through a combination of informal negotiation and peer pressure (and a certain willingness to defer to superiors). In 133 a number of factors prevented that from happening. Traditional factional politics played a part, as powerful senators lined up behind the tribune in a challenge to rival sections of the elite. On a more personal level Ti. Gracchus himself, already resentful towards parts of the senate after the Numantine affair, seems to have been unusually strongly committed to the reform, as indicated by the demotion of Octavius and the attempt at re-election.[177] Most crucially, however, the economic importance of the agrarian issue itself entrenched elite opposition to an unprecedented degree. Gracchus' proposed redistribution of public land, *ager publicus*, threatened vital interests of the Roman ruling class, including senators, *equites* and *boni* in general, whose power and status depended directly on the security of their landed estates.[178] By targeting their holdings of *ager*

---

[177] On the impact of Numantia, Cic. *Brut.* 103; *Har.* 43; Plu. *TG* 5–7.
[178] On Roman *ager publicus* Rathbone 2003 is essential; cf. Roselaar 2010.

publicus, which may have allowed long-term *possessio* but not Quiritary ownership, Gracchus' reform exposed the precarious nature of parts of the elite's economic basis.[179] At the same time, Gracchus' plan responded to an actual demand for land among the Roman poor, which at least during the initial stages ensured Gracchus unparalleled popular support and boosted his position to a level where it gave rise to accusations of seeking *dominatio*. As a result of these personal, political, and economic factors, compromise on either side became impossible, causing senators to intervene directly and physically remove the threat posed by the tribune. In doing so, they inadvertently exposed a fundamental weakness of the aristocratic republic, which relied on consensus but, as their actions showed, had few legal means of enforcing compliance.

A basic paradox of Roman politics was that real power came to reside in the one body that formally held very little. The system therefore worked on the premise that the bodies which held the power did not exercise it. That applied to the *populus* in particular but also to magistrates and tribunes, who were restrained by their brief tenure, collegiality, and peer pressure, and in the case of the lower magistracies also by their hopes for future preferment. A central thesis of this study is therefore the direct reversal of Polybius' thesis that the secret of Rome's success lay in her political system. Rome seems to have triumphed despite her constitution, because she had found a modus vivendi which neutralised the weaknesses inherent in her political make-up, above all its lack of a clear and workable division of powers.[180] The secret of the republic's success should therefore be sought outside her constitution, in social, ideological, and geo-political features. Of course, the checks and balances described by Polybius were not just a figment of his imagination. But his theoretical framework led him to identify these interdependencies as part of the political system, whereas in fact they were external to these institutions. The system worked because of strong social cohesion underpinned by a powerful ideological framework often summed up in the concept of *mos maiorum*, the traditions and norms passed down from the ancestors.[181] When observance of this unwritten code of conduct began to weaken, the flaws in the constitution became all too apparent.

---

[179] On property ownership, see Garnsey 2007: 177–95.

[180] Cf. Eder 1996: 440 noted the structural flaws in Rome's political system, which 'may have been destroyed from within'. Lundgreen 2009b: 272–3 rightly stresses the importance of 'negative powers' in stabilising the political process, powers that became less and less effective during the late republic, cf. Bleicken 1975b: 445–52.

[181] See Linke and Stemmler 2000; Walter 2004; Mouritsen 2014.

As explored in previous chapters, a major consequence was that the assemblies acquired a new role, becoming instruments of government, controlled by annual office holders rather than by the elite collectively. This development in turn paved the way for unlimited influence accruing in the hands of individuals. Examples range from Sulla's dictatorship, via the commands of Pompey, to the provincial tenure of Caesar, his later powers as consul and dictator, and finally culminating in the *lex Titia* which formalised the 'Second Triumvirate'. These measures were incompatible with the aristocratic principles of power sharing but in formal terms perfectly legal. Thus there was nothing to prevent the *res publica* from voting itself out of existence through an entirely legitimate process. Indeed, there were no limits to the assembly's powers or the scope of its decisions – as long as correct procedure was followed; the highly formalised concept of legitimacy investigated in the opening pages turn out to have far-reaching consequences.[182]

Characteristic of the late republic is less the widening of ideological divides often envisaged, as much as the exponential rise in 'rule-breaking' among members of the elite. Although the Roman republic functioned only as long as the ruling class adhered to a basic code of conduct, we find from the time of the Gracchi a growing disregard for traditional norms and conventions. The principle of collective government was increasingly honoured in the breach, as illustrated by the new role of the tribunes as independent legislators with direct access to the assemblies. The introduction of violence as a political tool marked a natural corollary to this trend. Despite deep-rooted social and religious taboos against political violence, its use soon became institutionalised by the ruling class itself; in 121 the senate issued the first so-called *senatus consultum ultimum* in order to lend the killing of C. Gracchus and his followers a veneer of legality. It took the form of a 'decree of last resort', exhorting citizens to take up arms in defence of the *res publica*.[183] The decree lacked formal legitimacy but would

---

[182] Cf. Lundgreen 2014a: 130–4. Straumann 2011 argued that the Roman political system operated with a set of 'hierarchical' rules that in effect subjected comitial legislation to certain basic constitutional principles. As evidence for such overriding rules he refers to Cic. *Caec.* 95–96 and *Leg.* 3.11, 44, but the argument about the sanctity of private property in the former is closely linked to the argument of the case, while the stipulations in the *De legibus* regarding *privilegia* and the role of the *comitia centuriata* seem to relate directly to Cicero's own personal experience of exile and restoration. In practice, there appears to have been virtually no attempt to regulate what kind of bills could be brought before the assembly.

[183] The literature is extensive, e.g. Ungern-Sternberg 1970; Nippel 1995: 60–9; Golden 2013: 104–49. Giovannini 2012: 181 recently defined it as a 'call to arms ordering Roman citizens to fight against other Roman citizens and to kill them if necessary'.

nevertheless be employed repeatedly over the following decades whenever the senate faced a serious challenge to its position. Although originally an attempt to demonstrate the authority of the senate, the 'normalisation' of force highlighted the basic weakness at the heart of government, which was no longer able to assert itself in the traditional manner. The senate's powerlessness was most vividly demonstrated in 52 when it saw no alternative but to invite Pompey to assume full control of the state in order to restore order in Rome after the death of Clodius, a far-reaching step that would lead directly to civil war.

The weakening of elite cohesion went beyond politics and also affected the military sphere, once the bedrock of aristocratic rule. As Wolfgang Blösel has recently shown, in the late republic extended military service was no longer the norm among the elite, leaving many nobles with little experience in the field. Provincial administration, closely connected to military commands, saw a similar development, since it was increasingly avoided by members of the elite reluctant to leave the capital for longer periods. Not only did this development affect the traditional identity of the ruling class, it also led to disparities in outlook, values, and, above all, competences. Thus, the result was a shortage of qualified commanders, which in turn led to extended tenures for those capable, paving the way for the 'great men' of exceptional military clout, who with their excessive prestige and resources were able to take on the republic itself.

Together these factors suggest something quite remarkable happening during this period, namely a ruling elite that appears to lose its collective sense of purpose and instinct of survival, becoming seemingly oblivious to the fundamentals on which its ascendancy depended. It remains a striking fact that the 'fall of the republic' was not caused by any threat external to the elite; what we are observing is a class that had reached a point where it was no longer capable of upholding its own rule. The question is how we explain such a phenomenon. A common approach has focused on increased competitive pressures on the elite, partly driven by the growth of empire, which raised the stakes and weakened traditional restraints. While undoubtedly true, the question is whether such a general explanation tells the whole story; after all, the Roman elite had always been competitive, often balancing precariously between consensus and disruptive individualism. So what were the specific factors that eventually pushed it over the edge?

Sallust famously insisted that the growth of empire had destroyed old-fashioned virtue by introducing greed, self-indulgence, *luxuria* and materialism. While obviously couched in conventional terms of personal moral failings, his analysis was also rooted in contemporary experience. The huge influx of wealth and resources from the provinces had inevitable consequences for the cohesion of the Roman elite. Not only were the proceeds of empire not evenly distributed among its members; it also led to a vast increase in the expenditures associated with the pursuit of *honores.* The direct cost of politics (e.g. bribery) grew enormously, as did the pressures to conform to the increasingly opulent lifestyle expected of those in the public eye. The result was a further polarisation of the elite, which saw greater disparities in wealth as well as a corresponding rise in personal indebtedness. The rapid fluctuations in the economic fortunes of individual politicians are well documented and the – seemingly ever-present – spectre of bankruptcy must have further contributed to the destabilisation of the elite.[184] It gave political competition a much sharper edge than had previously been the case; failure was no longer a simple matter of wounded pride but had potentially ruinous consequences for a politician's social status and economic standing. Viewed from this perspective the patterns of rule-breaking and disregard for established norms we can observe in the later republic become logical responses to a new economic reality. Catiline may be the classic example of an indebted aristocrat driven to desperate actions, but most likely he was simply an extreme manifestation of a wider structural problem, which affected large sections of the Roman elite. Indeed, their willingness to join military adventures may at least in part be explained by the financial incentives they offered; after all, civil war invariably involved redistribution of private property on a vast scale.[185]

Political violence – and its most extreme form of civil war – was a symptom of political instability as well as one of its causes, at the same time expressing and escalating underlying conflicts.[186] As it became more common, contradictions inherent in the political system were exposed, with cracks in the constitutional setup widening under the strain of elite competition. The distribution of powers meant the republic could function only if all involved played by a certain set of – mostly unwritten – rules,

---

[184] See for example Shatzman's detailed survey of Cicero's finances, 1975: 403–25.

[185] On debt and political instability, see the classic article by Frederiksen 1966. On Catiline, see Giovannini 1995.

[186] Walter 2014a described political violence as a mere epiphenomenon since it was relatively easily suppressed. Still, it must have affected the basic rules of political interaction. The impact was noticeable already in 121, when the force was no longer private but involved soldiers and received the backing of the *senatus consultum ultimum.* In 132 a tribunal had been set up, prosecuting some of Ti. Gracchus' followers, who were exiled and in some cases killed, Gruen 1968: 60–2; Badian 1972: 727. But in 121 the killing of C. Gracchus and Fulvius Flaccus was followed by a far more extensive purge of their followers, reportedly counted in their thousands.

which were increasingly flouted in the late republic, a process undoubtedly accelerated by the frequent experience that one could break the consensus without suffering long-term career damage.[187] Erich Gruen famously argued that the 'fall of the republic' was not the inevitable result of an 'autonomous' process of terminal decline but was caused by a single disastrous event, the outbreak of civil war in 49.[188] But while Caesar's crossing of the Rubicon may have been the immediate trigger for the 'fall', civil war becomes a reality only when a number of structural preconditions are in place, most obviously the complete breakdown of elite consensus. And since wars are not conducted by generals and their lieutenants alone, without a populace willing to join the warring factions and fill the ranks of their armies no civil conflict can ever reach the scale of the late republican wars.

The society that witnessed the aristocracy's dramatic collapse was a very different one from that which had seen its rise to power. In material terms, most ordinary Romans of the late republic, unlike their mid-republican ancestors, probably benefitted little from the expanding empire. The population appears to have been growing along with economic polarisation and general impoverishment.[189] At the same time, slave labour was imported on a vast scale to serve the needs of an increasingly distant elite. Indebtedness must have been common also among the poor, who would often have suffered displacement as a result. These developments had direct political repercussions, as demonstrated by Ti. Gracchus' attempt to address the problem. In addition there were crucial military implications. The traditional system of recruitment, which had drawn exclusively on the class of small landowners, was reformed and proletarians admitted to the legions. As Peter Brunt demonstrated, the process provided a fertile breeding ground for the rise of 'private armies' controlled by individual commanders rather than the senate; ultimately, it was the failure to keep military forces under effective public control that sealed the fate of the republic.[190]

---

[187] As Cicero, *Rep.* 1.31, suggests the fundamental transgression of the Gracchi was the division they caused, creating, as he said, two senates and nearly two peoples. The logical response of the ruling class was therefore to build a temple to Concordia.

[188] As summed up in his oft-cited maxim: 'Civil war caused the fall of the Republic – not vice versa', Gruen 1974: 504. The most important contributions to this debate have been Meier 1980 (with Winterling 2008), (English summary of his ideas in 1990); Deininger 1980; 1996; 1998; Rilinger 1982; Brunt 1988; Welwei 1996; Jehne 2009a; 2009b; Walter 2009. See also the detailed overview in Hölkeskamp 2009; cf. Morstein-Marx and Rosenstein 2010.

[189] See De Ligt 2012: 159–62, 167–71.

[190] The classic account of the military factors remains Brunt 1988: 240–80. The process arguably began already with the extension of military commands during the middle republic, which meant that

Needless to say, the particular course taken by these events was contingent on a variety of factors, several of which have already been mentioned. However, one element has received relatively little attention in this context and that is the contribution of the Italian revolt in 91, which may have played a more pivotal role than often appreciated.[191] The destabilising effect of the conflict lay not just in the vast expansion of the Roman citizen body which followed the allied defeat, but also in the fact that for the first time in over a hundred years it brought large-scale military campaigning back to Italian soil. The impact on Roman politics was profound as well as instantaneous. Already in 88, Sulla exploited the presence of standing armies in Italy to seize power and for a period suspend the republican government altogether.[192] The crucial transition from political violence to civil war was, in other words, due to a coincidence of exceptional, essentially unrelated factors; the fact that a major war against foreign enemies was being fought directly on Rome's doorstep offered unprecedented opportunities for generals to grab power. More specifically, it allowed the rivalry between Marius and Sulla to be taken to an entirely new level.[193] The former's extraordinary career and run of consulships had created deep divisions within the elite and vividly demonstrated the limits to the nobility's power. Sulla's aristocratic 'revolution' represented a direct response to this challenge, but it could never have happened without the allied uprising turning the geo-political landscape of Italy up-side-down.[194]

The Social War was not just instrumental in turning political conflict into civil war; there were also long-term demographic consequences, which further unsettled the republic. The allied revolt led to the wholesale incorporation of the Italians into the Roman state. The outcome was an exceptionally large, disparate and culturally heterogeneous population, which comprised foreign peoples who had recently attempted to overthrow Roman hegemony. Many of them suffered material losses and displacement as a result, and it seems a fair assumption that substantial sections of

political principles were broken to meet military needs, cf. Kloft 1977; Hölkeskamp 2011: 136–40, 147–51; Casavola 1988: 35–6; Blösel 2011.

[191] The main reason has been the long-dominant interpretation of the war as the final step towards national unification and the enfranchisement of the allies as a response to Italian demands for full incorporation into Rome. For a critical assessment of this tradition, see Mouritsen 1998.

[192] This may explain why Appian, our only continuous narrative for this period, takes such trouble to integrate the Social War, the all-important trigger for the Civil War, into his story of ever-increasing political violence, even trying to connect it back to the Gracchi, cf. Mouritsen 1998 ch. 1.

[193] Sulla was not alone in exploiting the exceptional military and political circumstances created by the Social War. Also Pompeius Strabo went 'rogue' after the war, and the unprecedented killing of Q. Pompeius Rufus by Roman soldiers in 88 further illustrates the suspension of normality.

[194] For the personal enmity between Marius and Sulla in the late 90s, see Stein-Hölkeskamp 2013.

this vastly increased citizen body probably felt little or no loyalty towards the *res publica Romana*, of which they had become part. The presence of recent opponents in the Roman armies during the first century must therefore be taken into account when trying to understand the events of the late republic, since they undoubtedly added another degree of volatility to an already unstable situation. Prior to the war Rome had in a sense been sitting on a ticking time bomb, being dependent on allied manpower but refusing their demands for an equal share of the empire. The aristocracy's failure to find a peaceful solution to what was at that time the most pressing and potentially dangerous issue facing Rome was to have far-reaching consequences for its own long-term survival. As Ronald Syme noted long ago, the ascent of the first emperor also marked the moment when the Italians finally came close to the levers of power and in effect replaced the old nobility.[195]

[195] Syme 1939 e.g. ch. 24.

Bibliographic Essay

The Roman republic, its politics and spectacular 'fall' have fascinated centuries of scholars and historians, going all the way back to renaissance Italy, where humanists such as Flavio Biondo and Machiavelli first subjected the republican constitution to serious study. Since then the amount of written works on the topic has grown exponentially and the sheer scale of the secondary literature means that this brief survey can merely skim the surface and mention a few major contributions, mostly from the last decades.

Useful introductions to Roman politics include Nicolet 1980, Beard and Crawford 1985, Patterson 1999, as well as the relevant chapters in Wiseman 1985b, Flower 2014, and Morstein-Marx and Rosenstein 2010. The fundamental syntheses of Roman politics and its workings remain Meier 1980 (1966), Gruen 1974, Finley 1983, Brunt 1988, and Pani 1997. Although very different in scope and approach, each of these works represents invaluable contributions to our understanding of the political process.

The Political System

The fundamental study of the Roman republican constitution remains Mommsen's monumental *Das Römische Staatsrecht*, which still provides an inexhaustible source of information and interpretations, now to be read in conjunction with the papers in Nippel and Seidensticker eds., 2005. A useful overview of the political institutions in English can be found in Lintott 1999, while a short summary can be found in Mouritsen 2015a. A number of important studies have appeared dedicated to individual institutions and offices. For the assemblies, Taylor 1966 and Staveley 1972 are still essential; for levels of participation in assemblies, see Mouritsen 2001. The consulship was recently discussed by Pina Polo 2011, who is also responsible for an important study of the *contio*, 1996. Brennan published an exhaustive study of the praetorship in Rome, while the workings of the senate have been the subject of detailed investigations by Bonnefond-Coudry 1989 and Ryan 1998. For the evolution of Rome's constitution the standard accounts are Cornell 1995 and the papers collected in Raaflaub 2005 (1986). Linke 1995 offers an original interpretation of Rome's early state formation drawing on anthropological approaches. On public law in republican Rome Bleicken 1975b is fundamental, as is the edition of statutes in Crawford 1996.

Leaders and Masses

Gelzer's classic work on republican politics and society from 1912 (and Seager's 1969 English edition) is still worth consulting on these issues. Nicolet 1980 represented an innovative way at looking at politics from the perspective of the citizen rather than the politicians. The volume edited by Wallace-Hadrill 1989 is still important on *clientela* in Rome. Through a series of articles culminating in the monograph *The Crowd in Rome in the Late Republic* Millar sparked a lively debate on the extent of popular influence on Roman politics. Critical responses include Jehne ed. 1995c and Hölkeskamp 2010 (2004). The interaction between politicians and the 'people', its scale and implications, have been the object of intense discussion in recent years, mostly focused on the *contiones*. Among the contributions have been Pina Polo 1996, Mouritsen 2001, Morstein-Marx 2004, Flaig 2003, and the collection of papers recently published by Steel and Van der Blom 2013.

While much Anglo-Saxon scholarship since Millar's intervention has evolved around the existence (or absence) of a Roman 'democracy', German scholarship has over the last two decades moved in a different direction, developing its own distinctive voice and approach to the Roman republic and particularly its 'political culture'. The result has been some stimulating and original new contributions to our understanding of the republic. For example, Hölkeskamp 2011 (1987) traced the formation of the *nobilitas* and its distinct value system, Flaig 2003 applied sociological models in the study on political performance and rituals, while Jehne in a series of articles has explored a wide variety of aspects of political practice and ideology in republican Rome. In a major study Walter 2004 considered the relationship between public memory, ideology and politics. The identity of the elite is also the subject of Flower's interesting discussion of ancestor masks, 1996. The *mos maiorum* is the subject of an important volume edited by Linke and Stemmler 2000.

The Practice of Politics

In a ground-breaking chapter Hopkins and Burton 1983 investigated the composition of the Roman elite and its degree of continuity and fluidity. Their results were refined in a study by Badian 1990c which concentrated on the consuls, reaching somewhat different but nevertheless compatible results. Most recently Beck 2005 revisited the issue in a major study.

Traditionally, an important strand of scholarship interpreted political practice according to the so-called *factio* theory, which assumed that family groups, reconstructed on the basis of marriages, adoptions and office holding, formed the basic building stones of Rome's political structure. The leading proponents of this approach were historians like Münzer and Scullard, but after the critiques of e.g. Meier 1980 (1966) and Brunt 1988 the approach has been largely abandoned. In its place the 'two-party-model' has emerged as the dominant framework used to interpret Roman politics, especially during the later republic. While central already to Mommsen's *Römische Geschichte*, it was most fully developed in Taylor's 1949 classic exploration of Roman 'party politics'. Despite fundamental criticism by e.g. Strasburger 1939, Meier 1965, and Gruen 1974, the binary model has now become part and parcel of the discussion, often closely associated with Millar's 'Roman democracy' paradigm, cf. e.g. Wiseman 2009. Most recently Robb's 2010 examination of political terminology has placed the issue on a new footing, and there may be signs that the 'ideological' trend may have peaked, cf. Russell 2013.

The end of the Roman republic has been much debated, and the classic contributions remain those of Syme 1939, Meier 1980 (1966), Gruen 1974, and Brunt 1988, who still define the main positions. Jehne's (2009b) exploration of Caesar's options represents an original addition to this discussion. Most recently Blösel 2011 has added another aspect to the debate, focusing on the 'demilitarisation' of the Roman ruling class which was to have far-reaching consequences for its survival.

Bibliography

Adamietz, J. 1989. *Marcus Tullius Cicero. Pro Murena*. Darmstadt.

Almond, G. A. and S. Verba 1963. *The Civic Culture*. Princeton.

Alonso-Nuñes, J. M. 1982. *The Ages of Rome*. Amsterdam.

Alston, R. 2002. 'The role of the military in the Roman revolution', *Aquila* 3: 7–41.

    2015. *Rome's Revolution. Death of the Republic and Birth of the Empire*. Oxford.

Amici, C. M. 2005. 'Evoluzione architettonica del Comizio a Roma', *RPAA* 77: 351–79.

Arena, V. 2011. 'The consulship of 78 BC. Catulus versus Lepidus: an optimates versus populares affair', in *Consuls and res publica. Holding High Office in the Roman Republic*, ed. H. Beck, A. Duplá, M. Jehne and F. Pina Polo. Cambridge: 299–318.

    2012. *Libertas and the Practice of Politics in the Late Roman Republic*. Cambridge.

Asmis, E. 2005. 'A new kind of Model. Cicero's Roman constitution in De republica', *AJPh* 126: 376–416.

Astin, A. E. 1958. *The Lex Annalis before Sulla. Coll. Latomus* 23. Brussels.

    1967. *Scipio Aemilianus*. Oxford.

Atkins, E. M. 2000. 'Cicero', in *The Cambridge History of Greek and Roman Political Thought*, ed. C. Rowe and M. Schofield. Cambridge: 477–516.

Atkins, J. W. 2013. *Cicero on Politics and the Limits of Reason*. Cambridge.

Badian, E. 1962a. 'From the Gracchi to Sulla (Forschungsbericht 1940–59)', *Historia* 11: 197–245.

    1962b. 'Waiting for Sulla', *JRS* 52: 47–61.

    1972. 'Tiberius Gracchus and the beginning of the Roman revolution', *ANRW* 1.1: 668–731.

    1990a. 'Diskussion: Sektion I Politik und Religion', in *Staat und Staatlichkeit in der frühen römischen Republik*, ed. W. Eder. Stuttgart: 84–9.

    1990b. 'Kommentar: Magistratur und Gesellschaft', in *Staat und Staatlichkeit in der frühen römischen Republik*, ed. W. Eder. Stuttgart: 458–75.

    1990c. 'The consuls 179–49 B.C.', *Chiron* 20: 371–413.

    1996. '*Tribuni plebis* and *res publica*', in *Imperium sine fine. T. Robert S. Broughton and the Roman Republic*, ed. J. Linderski. *Historia* Einzelschriften 105. Stuttgart: 187–213.

    2009. 'From the Iulii to Caesar', in *A Companion to Julius Caesar*, ed. M. Griffin. Oxford: 11–22.

Beard, M. and M. H. Crawford 1999. *Rome in the Late Republic.* 2nd edn. London. 1st edn. 1985.

Beard, M., J. North and S. Price 1998. *Religions of Rome.* Cambridge.

Beck, H. 2005. *Karriere und Hierarchie. Die römische Aristokratie und die Anfänge des cursus honorum in der mittleren Republik. Klio* Beiheft 10. Berlin.

Beck, H., A. Duplá, M. Jehne, and F. Pina Polo eds. 2011. *Consuls and res publica. Holding High Office in the Roman Republic.* Cambridge.

Beness, L. and T. Hillard 2012. 'Another voice against the "tyranny" of Scipio Aemilianus in 129 B.C.?', *Historia* 61: 270–81.

Béranger, J. 1972. 'Les jugements de Cicéron sur les Gracques', *ANRW* 1.1: 732–63.

Bergk, A. 2011. 'The development of the praetorship in the third century BC', in *Consuls and res publica. Holding High Office in the Roman Republic,* ed. H. Beck, A. Duplá, M. Jehne, and F. Pina Polo. Cambridge: 61–74.

Betts, E. 2011. 'Towards a multisensory experience of movement in the city of Rome', in *Rome, Ostia, Pompeii. Movement and Space,* ed. R. Laurence and D. J. Newsome. Oxford: 118–32.

Bleckmann, B. 2002. *Die römische Nobilität im Ersten Punischen Krieg. Untersuchungen zur aristokratischen Konkurrenz in der Republik. Klio* Beiheft 5. Berlin.

Bleicken, J. 1955. *Das Volkstribunat der klassischen Republik. Studien zu seiner Entwicklung zwischen 287 und 133 v. Chr. Zetemata* 13. Munich.

   1975a. *Die Verfassung der römischen Republik.* Paderborn.

   1975b. *Lex Publica. Gesetz und Recht in der römischen Republik.* Berlin – New York.

   1981. 'Das römische Volkstribunat. Versuch einer Analyse seiner politischen Funktion in republikanischer Zeit', *Chiron* 11: 87–108.

Blom, H. van der 2010. *Cicero's Role Models. The Political Strategy of a Newcomer.* Oxford.

Blösel, W. 1998. 'Die Anakyklosis – Theorie und die Verfassung im Spiegel des sechsten Buches des Polybius und Ciceros "De re publica", Buch II', *Hermes* 126: 31–57.

   2011. 'Die Demilitarisierung der römischen Nobilität von Sulla bis Caesar', in *Von der militia equestris zur militia urbana. Prominenzrollen und Karrierefelder im antiken Rom,* ed. W. Blösel and K.-J. Hölkeskamp. Stuttgart: 55–80.

Bonnefond-Coudry, M. 1989. *Le sénat de la république romaine de la guerre d'Hannibal à Auguste. Collection de l'École française de Rome.* 273. Paris – Rome.

Botsford, G. W. 1909. *The Roman Assemblies from their Origin to the End of the Republic.* New York.

Brennan, T. C. 2000. *The Praetorship in the Roman Republic.* 2 vols. Oxford.

   2014. 'Power and process under the Republican "constitution"', in *The Cambridge Companion to the Roman Republic,* ed. H. Flower. 2nd edn. Cambridge: 19–53. 1st edn. 2004.

Bringmann, K. 1977. 'Weltherrschaft und innere Krise Roms im Spiegel der Geschichtsschreibung des zweiten und ersten Jahrhunderts v. Chr.', *A&A:* 28–49.

2003. 'Zur Überlieferung und zum Entstehungsgrund der *lex Claudia de nave senatoris*', *Klio* 85: 312–21.

Brunt, P. A. 1971. *Italian Manpower 225 B.C. – A.D. 14.* Oxford.

1988. *The Fall of the Roman Republic and Related Essays.* Oxford.

Bruun, C. ed. 2000. *The Roman Middle Republic. Religion, Politics, and Historiography c. 400 – 133 B.C. Acta Instituti Romani Finlandiae* 23. Rome.

Burckhardt, L. A. 1988. *Politische Strategien der Optimaten in der späten römischen Republik. Historia* Einzelschriften 57. Stuttgart.

1990. 'The political elite of the Roman Republic: comments on recent discussion of the concepts *nobilitas* and *homo novus*', *Historia* 39: 77–99.

Burton, P. 2014. 'The revolt of Lepidus (cos. 78 BC) revisited', *Historia* 63: 404–21.

Casavola, F. P. 1988. 'Relazione introduttiva', in *Roma tra oligarchia e democrazia. Classi sociali e formazione del diritto in epoca medio-repubblicana.* Napoli: 23–37.

Cavaggioni, F. 2010. *Generali e sconfitta militare a Roma agli albori della repubblica (509–290 A.C.).* Padova.

Champion, C. B. 2004. *Cultural Politics in Polybius' Histories.* Berkeley.

Clemente, G. 1983. 'Il plebiscito Claudio e le classe dirigenti romane nell'età dell'imperialismo', *Ktema* 8: 253–9.

Cornell, T. J. 1991. 'Rome: the history of an anachronism', in *City States in Classical Antiquity and Medieval Italy*, ed. A. Molho, K. Raaflaub, and J. Emlen. Ann Arbor – Stuttgart: 53–69.

1995. *The Beginnings of Rome. Italy and Rome from the Bronze Age to the Punic Wars (c.1000–264 BC).* London – New York.

2000. 'The *lex Ovinia* and the emancipation of the Senate', in *The Roman Middle Republic. Religion, Politics, and Historiography c. 400–133 B.C.*, ed. C. Bruun. *Acta Instituti Romani Finlandiae* 23. Rome: 69–89.

Courrier, C. 2014. *La plèbe de Rome et sa culture (fin du IIe siècle av. J.-C. – fin du Ier siècle ap. J.-C.).* Rome.

Crawford, M. H. ed. 1996. *Roman Statutes. BICS* Suppl. 64. London.

David, J.-M. 1983. 'Sfida o vendetta, minaccia o ricatto: L'accusa pubblica nelle mani dei giovani Romani alla fine della Repubblica', in *La paura dei padri nella società antica e medievale*, ed. E. Pellizer and N. Zorzetti. Roma – Bari: 99–112.

1992. *Le patronat judiciaire au dernier siècle de la République romaine.* Rome.

1993. 'Conformisme et transgression: à propos du tribunat de la plèbe à la fin de la République romaine', *Klio* 75: 219–27.

Deininger, J. 1980. 'Explaining the change from Republic to Principate in Rome', *Comparative Civilizations Review* 4: 77–101.

1996. 'Der Wandel von der Republik zum Prinzipat in Rome: ein Ausnahmefall der antiken Verfassungsentwicklung?' in *Griechenland und Rom. Vergleichende Untersuchungen zu Entwicklungstendenzen und –höhepunkten der antiken Geschichte, Kunst und Literatur*, ed. E. G. Schmidt. Tbilisi – Erlangen – Jena: 81–94.

1998. 'Zur Kontroverse über die Lebensfähigkeit der Republik in Rom', in *Imperium Romanum. Studien zu Geschichte und Rezeption. Festschrift für Karl Christ zum 75. Geburtstag*, ed. P. Kneissl and V. Losemann. Stuttgart: 123–36.

De Libero, L. 1992. *Obstruktion. Politische Praktiken im Senat und in der Volksversammlung der ausgehenden römischen Republik.* Hermes Einzelschriften 59. Stuttgart.

Deniaux, E. 1993. *Clientèles et pouvoir à l'époque de Cicéron. Collection de l'École française de Rome.* 182. Paris – Rome.

De Sanctis, G. 1907. *Storia di Roma I-II. La conquista del primato in Italia.* Turin.

Develin, R. 1975. 'Comitia tributa plebis', *Athenaeum* 53: 302–77.

1977a. 'Comitia tributa again', *Athenaeum* 55: 425–6.

1977b. '*Lex curiata* and the competence of magistrates', *Mnemosyne* 30: 49–65.

1978a. 'The Atinian plebiscite, tribunes and the Senate', *CQ* 28: 141–4.

1978b. 'Scipio Aemilianus and the Consular elections of 148 B.C.', *Latomus* 37: 484–8.

1978c. 'The third century reform of the *comitia centuriata*', *Athenaeum* 56: 346–77.

1979. 'The voting position of the equites after the centuriate reform', *RhM* 122: 154–61.

1985. *The Practice of Politics at Rome 366–167 B.C. Coll. Latomus.* 188. Bruxelles.

Diehl, H. 1988. *Sulla und seine Zeit im Urteil Ciceros.* Hildesheim.

Doblhofer, G. 1990. *Die Popularen der Jahre 111–99 vor Christus: eine Studie zur Geschichte der späten römischen Republik.* Vienna.

Duplá, A. 2011. 'Consules populares', in *Consuls and res publica. Holding High Office in the Roman Republic*, ed. H. Beck, A. Duplá, M. Jehne, and F. Pina Polo. Cambridge: 279–98.

Dyck, A. R. 2004. *A Commentary on Cicero, De Legibus.* Ann Arbor.

Eder, W. 1990a. 'Der Bürger und sein Staat – Der Staat und seine Bürger', in *Staat und Staatlichkeit in der frühen römischen Republik*, ed. W. Eder. Stuttgart: 12–32.

1991. 'Who Rules? Power and Participation in Athens and Rome', in *City States in Classical Antiquity and Medieval Italy*, ed. A. Molho, K. Raaflaub, and J. Emlen. Ann Arbor – Stuttgart: 169–96.

1996. 'Republicans and sinners: the decline of the Roman Republic and the end of a provisional arrangement', in *Transitions to Empire. Essays in Graeco-Roman History 360–146 B.C. in Honor of E. Badian*, ed. R. W. Wallace and E. M. Harris. Oklahoma: 439–61.

ed. 1990b. *Staat und Staatlichkeit in der frühen römischen Republik.* Stuttgart.

Eilers, C. 1996. 'Silanus <and> Murena (*I.Priene* 121)', *CQ* 46: 175–82.

Evans R. J. 2007. 'The Sulpician law on debt: implications for the political elite and broader ramifications', *AClass* 50: 81–94.

Fantham, E. 1973. 'Aequabilitas in Cicero's political theory, and the Greek tradition of proportional justice', *CQ* 23: 285–90.

Ferrary, J.-L. 1984a. 'L'archéologie du 'De re publica' (2.2.4–37,63): Cicéron entre Polybe et Platon', *JRS* 74: 87–98.

1997. '*Optimates* et *populares*: le problème du role de l'idéologie dans la politique', in *Die späte römische Republik. La Fin de la République romaine. un débat franco-allemand d'histoire et d'historiographie*, ed. H. Bruhns, J.-M. David, W. Nippel. *Collection de l'École française de Rome* 235. Rome: 221–31.

2012. 'L'iter legis, de la rédaction de la rogatio à la publication de la lex rogata', in *Leges publicae. La legge nell'esperienza giuridica romana*, ed. J.-L. Ferrary. Pavia: 3–37.

ed. 1984b. *Leges publicae. La legge nell'esperienza giuridica romana*. Pavia.

Fezzi, L. 1999. 'La legislazione tribunicia di Publio Clodio Pulchro (58 a.C.) e la ricerca del consenso a Roma', *SCO* 47: 245–341.

2008. *Il tribuno Clodio*. Rome.

Finer, S. E. 1997. *The History of Government from the Earliest Times*. Volume II: *The Intermediate Ages*. Oxford.

Finley, M. I. 1983. *Politics in the Ancient World*. Cambridge.

Fiori, R. 2014. 'La convocazione dei comizi centuriati', *ZRG* 131: 60–176.

Flaig, E. 1995a. 'Entscheidung und Konsens. Zu den Feldern der politischen Kommunikation zwischen Aristokratie und Plebs', in *Demokratie in Rom? Die Rolle des Volkes in der Politik der römischen Republik*, ed. M. Jehne. *Historia* Einzelschriften 96. Stuttgart: 77–127.

1995b. 'Die *Pompa Funebris*. Adlige Konkurrenz und annalistische Erinnerung in der römische Republik', in *Memoria als Kultur*, ed. O. G. Oexle. Göttingen: 115–48.

2003. *Ritualisierte Politik: Zeichen, Gesten und Herrschaft in alten Rom*. Göttingen.

2004. 'Review of F. X. Ryan, *Rank and Participation in the Republican Senate*', *Gnomon* 76: 331–41.

Flower, H. I. 1996. *Ancestor Masks and Aristocratic Power in Roman Culture*. Oxford.

2010. *Roman Republics*. Princeton.

ed. 2014. *The Cambridge Companion to the Roman Republic*. 2nd edn. Cambridge. 1st edn. 2004.

Forsythe, G. 1988. 'The political background of the *Lex Calpurnia* of 149 B.C.', *AncW* 17: 109–19.

2005. *A Critical History of Early Rome. From Prehistory to the First Punic War*. Berkeley.

Fraccaro, P. 1957. 'La procedura del voto nei comizi tribute romani', in *Opuscula II. Studi sull'età della rivoluzione romana. Scritti di diritto public. Militaria*. Pavia: 235–54.

Frederiksen, M. W. 1966. 'Caesar, Cicero and the problem of debt', *JRS* 56: 128–41.

Frier, B. W. 1971. 'Sulla's propaganda and the collapse of the Cinnan Republic', *AJPh* 92: 585–604.

Fritz, K. von. 1954. *The Theory of the Mixed Constitution in Antiquity*. New York.

Gabba, E. 1976. *Republican Rome, the Army and the Allies*. Transl. P. J. Cuff. Oxford.

1984. 'Il consenso popolare alla politica espansionistica romana fra III et II sec. a.C.' in *The Imperialism of Mid-Republican Rome*, ed. W. V. Harris. *PMAAR* 29: Rome: 115–29.

1987. 'Maximus Comitiatus', *Athenaeum* 75: 203–5.

1988. 'Assemblee ed esercito a Rome fra IV e III sec.a.C.', in *Roma tra oligarchia e democrazia. Classi sociali e formazione del diritto in epoca medio-repubblicana.* Napoli: 41–54.

1990. 'Democrazia a Roma', *Athenaeum* 85: 266–71.

Garnsey, P. D. A. 1988. *Famine and Food Supply in the Graeco-Roman World.* Cambridge.

2010. 'Roman patronage', in *From the Tetrarchs to the Theodosians. Later Roman History and Culture, 284–450 CE*, ed. S. McGill. Cambridge: 33–54.

Gauthier, P. 1974. '"Générosité" romaine et "avarice" greque. Sur l'octroi du droit de cité', in *Mélanges d'histoire ancienne offerts a William Seston.* Paris: 207–15.

1981. 'La citoyenneté en Grèce et à Rome; participation et intégration', *Ktema* 6: 167–79.

1990. 'Quorum et participation civique dans les démocraties grecques', *CCG* 1: 73–99.

Gelzer, M. 1912. *Die Nobilität der römischen Republik.* Leipzig – Berlin. Rev. English edn. 1969. *The Roman Nobility.* Transl. R. Seager. Oxford: 1–140.

Giovannini, A. 1985. '*Auctoritas patrum*', *MH* 42: 28–36.

1990. 'Magistratur und Volk. Ein Beitrag zur Entstehungsgeschichte des Staatsrechts', in *Staat und Staatlichkeit in der frühen römischen Republik*, ed. W. Eder. Stuttgart: 606–36.

1995. 'Catilina et le problème des dettes', in *Leaders and Masses in the Roman World. Studies in Honor of Zvi Yavetz*, ed. I. Malkin and Z. W. Rubinsohn. Leiden – New York – Köln: 15–32.

2012. 'Le *senatus consultum ultimum*. Les mensonges de Cicéron', *Athenaeum* 100: 181–96.

Girardet, K. M. 1983. *Die Ordnung der Welt. Ein Beitrag zur philosophischen und politischen Interpretation von Ciceros Schrift De Legibus.* Historia Einzelschriften 42. Stuttgart.

Goldbeck, F. 2010. Salutationes. *Die Morgenbegrüssungen in Rom in der Republik und der frühen Kaiserzeit. Klio* Beifhefte 16. Berlin.

Golden, G. K. 2013. *Crisis Management during the Roman Republic. The Role of Political Institutions in Emergencies.* Cambridge.

Goldmann, F. 2002. '*Nobilitas* als Status und Gruppe. Überlegungen zum Nobilitätsbegriff der römischen Republik', in *Res publica reperta. Zur Verfassung und Gesellschaft der römischen Republik und des frühen Prinzipats. Festschrift für Jochen Bleicken zum 75. Geburtstag*, ed. J. Spielvogel. Stuttgart: 53–66.

Graeber, A. 2001. *Auctoritas Patrum. Formen und Wege der Senatsherrschaft zwischen Politik und Tradition.* Berlin.

Grieve, L. 1985. 'The reform of the *comitia centuriata*', *Historia* 34: 278–309.

1987. 'Proci patricii: a question of voting order in the centuriate assembly', *Historia* 36: 302–17.

Griffin, M. 1973. 'The tribune C. Cornelius', *JRS* 63: 196–213.

2009. ed. *A Companion to Julius Caesar*. Oxford.

Grimm, D. 2009. *Souveränität. Herkunft und Zukunft eines Schlüsselbegriffs*. Berlin.

Gruen, E. S. 1968. *Roman Politics and the Criminal Courts, 149–78 B.C.* Cambridge, MA.

1974. *The Last Generation of the Roman Republic*. Berkeley.

1990. 'Review of L. A. Burckhardt, *Politische Strategien der Optimaten in der späten römischen Republik*', *Gnomon* 62: 179–81.

1991. 'The Exercise of Power in the Roman Republic', in *City States in Classical Antiquity and Medieval Italy*, ed. A. Molho, K. Raaflaub, and J. Emlen. Ann Arbor – Stuttgart: 252–67.

1996. 'The Roman oligarchy: image and perception', in *Imperium Sine Fine. T. Robert S. Broughton and the Roman Republic*, ed. J. Linderski. *Historia* Einzelschriften 105. Stuttgart: 215–43.

2009. 'Caesar as politician', in *A Companion to Julius Caesar*, ed. M. Griffin. Oxford: 23–36.

Hackl, U. 1972. 'Das Ende der römischen Tribusgründungen 241 v. chr', *Chiron* 2: 135–70.

Hahm, D. E. 1995. 'Polybius' applied political theory', in *Justice and Generosity. Studies in Hellenistic Social and Political Philosophy*, ed. A. Laks and M. Schofield. Cambridge: 7–47.

Hall, U. 1964. 'Voting Procedure in Roman Assemblies', *Historia* 13: 267–306.

Hantos, Th. 1988. *Res publica constituta. Die Verfassung des Dictators Sulla*. *Hermes* Einzelschriften 50. Stuttgart.

Harris, W. V. 1985. *War and Imperialism in Republican Rome, 327–70 B.C.* Rev. ed. Oxford. 1st ed. 1979.

1989. *Ancient Literacy*. Cambridge, MA.

1990. 'On defining the political culture of the Roman Republic: some comments on Rosenstein, Williamson, and North', *CPh* 85: 288–94.

Heikkilä, K. 1993. 'Lex non iure rogata: Senate and Annulment of Laws in the Late Republic', in *Senatus Populusque Romanus. Studies in Roman Republican Legislation*, ed. J. Vaahtera. *Acta Instituti Romani Finlandiae* 13. Rome: 117–42.

Hellegouarc'h, J. 1972. *Le vocabulaire latin des relations et des partis politique sous la république*. 2nd edn. Paris. 1st edn. 1963.

Hermon, E. 1982. 'La place de la loi curiate dans l'histoire constitutionelle de la fin de la République romaine', *Ktema* 7: 297–307.

Hiebel, D. 2009. *Rôles institutionnel et politique de la contio sous la république romaine (287 – 49 av. J.-C.)*. Paris.

Hinard, F. 1985. *Les proscriptions de la Rome républicaine*. Paris – Rome.

Hölkeskamp, K.-J. 1990. 'Senat und Volkstribunat im frühen 3. Jh. v. Chr.', in *Staat und Staatlichkeit in der frühen römischen Republik*, ed. W. Eder. Stuttgart: 437–57. Repr. 2004. *Senatus populusque Romanus. Die politische Kultur der Republik – Dimensionen und Deutungen*. Stuttgart: 85–103.

1993. 'Conquest, competition and consensus: Roman expansion in Italy and the rise of the nobilitas', *Historia* 42: 12–39.

1994. Review of N. S. Rosenstein, *Imperatores Victi. Military Defeat and Aristocratic Competition in the Middle and Late Republic, Gnomon* 66: 332–41.

1995. 'Oratoris maxima scaena: Reden vor dem Volk in der politischen Kultur der Republik', in *Demokratie in Rom? Die Rolle des Volkes in der Politik der römischen Republik*, ed. M. Jehne. *Historia* Einzelschriften 96. Stuttgart: 11–49. Repr. 2004. *Senatus populusque Romanus. Die politische Kultur der Republik – Dimensionen und Deutungen.* Stuttgart: 219–56.

1996. '*Exempla* und *mos maiorum*: Überlegungen zum kollektiven Gedächnis der Nobilität', in *Vergangenheit und Lebenswelt. Soziale Kommunikation, Traditionsbildung und Historisches Bewusstsein*, ed. H.-J. Gehrke and A. Möller. Tübingen: 301–38. Repr. 2004. *Senatus populusque Romanus. Die politische Kultur der Republik – Dimensionen und Deutungen.* Stuttgart: 169–98.

2000. 'The Roman Republic: government of the people, by the people, for the people?', *SCI* 19: 203–23.

2004. *Senatus populusque Romanus. Die politische Kultur der Republik – Dimensionen und Deutungen.* Stuttgart.

2006. 'Konsens und Konkurrenz. Die politische Kultur der römischen Republik in neuer Sicht', *Klio* 88: 360–96.

2008. 'Hierarchie und Konsens. *Pompae* in der politischen Kultur der römischen Republik', in *Machtfragen. Zur kulturellen Repräsentation und Konstruktion von Macht in Antike, Mittelalter und Neuzeit*, ed. A. H. Arweiler and B. M. Gauly. Stuttgart: 79–126.

2009. 'Eine politische Kultur (in) der Krise? Gemässigt radikale Vorbemerkungen zum kategorischen Imperativ der Konzepte', in *Eine politische Kultur (in) der Krise? Die "letzte Generation" der römischen Republik*, ed. K.-J. Hölkeskamp and E. Müller-Luckner. Munich: 1–25.

2010. *Reconstructing the Roman Republic. An Ancient Political Culture and Modern Research.* Rev. edn., transl. H. Heitmann-Gordon. Princeton. 1st edn. 2004.

2011. *Die Entstehung der Nobilität.* 2nd edn. Stuttgart. 1st edn. 1987.

Hölkeskamp, K.-J. and E. Müller-Luckner eds. 2009. *Eine politische Kultur (in) der Krise? Die "letzte Generation" der römischen Republik.* Munich.

Hölkeskamp, K.-J. and E. Stein-Hölkeskamp eds. 2000. *Von Romulus zu Augustus. Grosse Gestalten der römischen Republik.* Munich.

Holleran, C. 2011. 'Migration and the urban economy of Rome', in *Demography and the Graeco-Roman World*, ed. C. Holleran and A. Pudsey. Cambridge: 155–80.

2012. *Shopping in Ancient Rome.* Oxford.

Hölscher, T. 1978. 'Die Anfänge der römischen Repräsentationskunst', *MDAI(R)* 85: 315–57.

2001. 'Die Alten vor Augen. Politische Denkmäler und öffentliches Gedächnis im republikanischen Rom', in *Institutionalität und Symbolisierung. Verstetigungen kultureller Ordnungsmuster in Vergangenheit und Gegenwart*, ed. G. Melville. Cologne: 183–211.

Hopkins, K. 1978. *Conquerors and Slaves*. Cambridge.
  1983. *Death and Renewal*. Cambridge.
  1991. 'From violence to blessing: symbols and rituals in ancient Rome', in *City States in Classical Antiquity and Medieval Italy*, ed. A. Molho, K. Raaflaub and J. Emlen. Ann Arbor – Stuttgart: 479–98.
Hopkins, K. and G. Burton 1983. 'Political succession in the late Republic (249–50 BC)', in *Death and Renewal*. Cambridge: 31–119.
Humm, M. 2000. 'Spazio e tempo civici: riforma delle tribù e riforma del calendario alla fine del quarto secolo a.C.', in *The Roman Middle Republic. Religion, Politics, and Historiography c. 400 – 133 B.C.*, ed. C. Bruun. *Acta Instituti Romani Finlandiae* 23. Rome: 91–119.
  2005. *Appius Claudius Caecus. La république accomplie*. Rome.
  2012. 'The curiate law and the religious nature of the power of Roman magistrates', in *Law and Religion in the Roman Republic*, ed. O. Tellegen-Couperus. Leiden: 57–84.
Hurlet, F. 2012. 'Démocratie à Rome? Quelle démocratie? En relisant Millar (et Hölkeskamp)', in *Rome, a City and Its Empire in Perspective. The Impact of the Roman World through Fergus Millar's Research*, ed. S. Benoist. Leiden: 19–43.
Jehne, M. 1993. 'Geheime Abstimmung und Bindungswesen in der römischen Republik', *HZ* 257: 593–613.
  1995a. 'Einführung: Zur Debatte um die Rolle des Volkes in der römischen Republik', in *Demokratie in Rom? Die Rolle des Volkes in der Politik der römischen Republik*, ed. M. Jehne. *Historia* Einzelschriften 96. Stuttgart: 1–9.
  1995b. 'Die Beeinflussung von Entscheidungen durch "Bestechung": zur Funktion des ambitus in der römischen Republik', in *Demokratie in Rom? Die Rolle des Volkes in der Politik der römischen Republik*, ed. M. Jehne. *Historia* Einzelschriften 96. Stuttgart: 51–76.
  2000a. 'Wirkungsweise und Bedeutung der centuria praerogativa', *Chiron* 30: 661–78.
  2000b. 'Jovialität und Freiheit. Zur Institutionalität der Beziehungen zwischen Ober- und Unterschichten in der römischen Republik', in *Mos Maiorum. Untersuchungen zu den Formen der Identitätsstiftung und Stabilisierung in der römischen Republik*, ed. B. Linke and M. Stemmler. *Historia* Einzelschriften 141. Stuttgart: 207–35.
  2000c. 'Rednertätigkeit und Statusdissonanzen in der späten römischen Republik', in *Rede und Redner. Bewertung und Darstellung in den antiken Kulturen*, ed. C. Neumeister and W. Raeck. Möhnesee: 167–89.
  2001. 'Integrationsrituale in der römischen Republik. Zur einbindenden Wirkung der Volksversammlungen', in *Integrazione Mescolanza Rifiuto. Incontri di popoli, lingue e culture in Europa dall'Antichità all'Umanesimo*, ed. G. Urso. Rome: 89–113. Repr. 2003. *Sinn (in) der Antike. Orientierungssysteme, Leitbilder und Wertkonzepte im Altertum*, ed. K.-J. Hölkeskamp, J. Rüsen, and E. Stein-Hölkeskamp. Mainz: 279–97.
  2005. 'Die Volksversammlungen in Mommsens Staatsrecht, oder: Mommsen als Gesetzgeber', in *Theodor Mommsens langer Schatten. Das römische*

Staatsrecht *als bleibende Herausforderung für die Forschung*, ed. W. Nippel and B. Seidensticker. Hildesheim: 131–60.

2006a. 'Who attended Roman assemblies? Some remarks on political participation in the Roman Republic', in *Repúblicas y ciudadanos. Modelos de participación cívica en el mundo antiguo*, ed. F. Marco Simón, F. Pina Polo, and J. Remesal Rodriguez. Barcelona: 221–234.

2006b. 'Römer, Latiner und Bundesgenossen im Krieg. Zu Formen und Ausmass der Integration in der republikanischen Armee', in *Herrschaft ohne Integration?* ed. M. Jehne and R. Pfeilschifter. Frankfurt a. M.: 243–67.

2006c. 'Methods, models and historiography', in *A Companion to the Roman Republic*, ed. N. Rosenstein and R. Morstein-Marx. Oxford: 3–28.

2009a. 'Caesar's Alternative(n). Das Ende der römischen Republik zwischen autonomen Prozess und Betriebsunfall', in *Eine politische Kultur (in) der Krise? Die "letzte Generation" der römischen Republik*, ed. K.-J. Hölkeskamp and E. Müller-Luckner. Munich: 141–60.

2009b. *Der Grosse Trend, der kleine Sachzwang und das handelde Individuum. Caesars Entscheidungen*. Munich.

2010. 'Die Dominanz des Vorgangs über den Ausgang. Struktur und Verlauf der Wahlen in der römischen Republik', in *Technik und Symbolik vormoderner Wahlverfahren*, ed. C. Dartmann, G. Wassilowsky, and T. Weller. *HZ* Beiheft 52. Munich: 17–34.

2011. 'Blaming the people in front of the people. Restraint and outbursts of orators in Roman *contiones*', in *Praise and Blame in Roman Republican Rhetoric*, ed. C. Smith and R. Corvino. Swansea: 111–25.

2013a. 'Politische Partizipation in der römischen Republik', in *Politische Partizipation. Idee und Wirklichkeit von der Antike bis in die Gegenwart*, ed. H. Reinau and J. von Ungern-Sternberg. Berlin: 103–44.

2013b. 'Konsensfiktionen in römischen Volksversammlungen', in *Genesis und Dynamiken der Mehrheitsentscheidung*, ed. E. Flaig and E. Müller-Luckner. Munich: 129–52.

2013c. 'Der römische Senat als Hüter des Gemeinsinns', in *Gemeinsinn und Gemeinwohl in der römischen Antike*, ed. M. Jehne and C. Lundgreen. Stuttgart: 23–50.

2013d. 'Feeding the *plebs* with words: the significance of senatorial public oratory in the small world of Roman politics', in *Community and Communication. Oratory and Politics in Republican Rome*, ed. C. Steel and H. Van der Blom. Oxford: 49–62.

2014a. 'Gerechtigkeitskonkurrenzen in der politischen Praxis der römischen Republik', in *Gerechtigkeit*, ed. G. Melville, G. Vogt-Spira, M. Breitenstein. Cologne – Weimar – Vienna: 58–73.

2014b. 'Das Volk als Institution und als diskursive Bezugsgrösse in der römischen Republik', in *Staatlichkeit in Rom? Diskurse und Praxis (in) der römischen Republik*, ed. C. Lundgreen. Stuttgart: 117–37.

ed. 1995c. *Demokratie in Rom? Die Rolle des Volkes in der Politik der römischen Republik*. *Historia* Einzelschriften 96. Stuttgart.

Johnson, T. and C. Dandeker 1989. 'Patronage: relation and system', in *Patronage in Ancient Society*, ed. A. Wallace-Hadrill. London – New York: 219–42.

Kaster, R. A. 2006. *Marcus Tullius Cicero. Speech on Behalf of Publius Sestius*. Oxford.

Keaveney, A. 2005. *Sulla. The Last Republican*. 2nd edn. London – New York. 1st edn. 1982.

Kloft, H. 1977. *Prorogation und ausserordentliche Imperien 326–81 v. Chr. Untersuchungen zur Verfassung der römischen Republik*. Meisenheim am Glan.

Kneissl, P. and V. Losemann eds. 1998. *Imperium Romanum. Studien zu Geschichte und Rezeption. Festschrift für Karl Christ zum 75. Geburtstag*. Stuttgart.

Kruschwitz, P. 2002. *Carmina Saturnia Epigraphica. Einleitung, Text und Kommentar zu den saturnischen Versinschriften. Hermes* Einzelschriften 84. Stuttgart.

Kunkel, W. 1973. *An Introduction to Roman Legan and Constitutional History*. 2nd edn., transl. J. M. Kelly. Oxford. 1st English edn. 1966; 6th German edn. 1972.

Laurence, R. 1994. 'Rumour and communication in Roman politics', *G&R* 41: 62–74.

Levick, B. 1981. 'Professio', *Athenaeum* 59: 378–88.

   1982. 'Morals, politics and the fall of the Roman Republic', *G&R* 29: 53–62.

Ligt, L. de 2012. *Peasants, Citizens and Soldiers. Studies in the Demographic History of Roman Italy 225 BC – AD 100*. Cambridge.

Linderski, J. 1990. 'The auspices and the Struggle of the Orders', in *Staat und Staatlichkeit in der frühen römischen Republik*, ed. W. Eder. Stuttgart: 34–48.

   ed. 1996. *Imperium sine fine. T. Robert S. Broughton and the Roman Republic. Historia* Einzelschriften 105. Stuttgart.

Linderski, J. and A. Kaminska-Linderski 1973. 'A. Gabinius A.f. Capito and the first voter in the legislative *comitia tribute*', *ZPE* 12: 247–52.

Linke, B. 1995. *Von der Verwandtschaft zum Staat. Die Entstehung politischer Organisationsformen in der frührömischen Geschichte*. Stuttgart.

   2005. *Die römische Republik von den Gracchus bis Sulla*. Darmstadt.

   2010. Review of M. Rieger, *Tribus und Stadt. Die Entstehung der römischen Walhbezirke im urbanen und mediterranen Kontext (ca. 750–450 v. Chr.)*, *Gnomon* 82: 177–9.

Linke, B. and M. Stemmler eds. 2000. *Mos Maiorum. Untersuchungen zu den Formen der Identitätsstiftung und Stabilisierung in der römischen Republik. Historia* Einzelschriften 141. Stuttgart.

Lintott, A. W. 1987. 'Democracy in the Middle Republic', *ZRG* 104: 34–52.

   1990. 'Electoral bribery in the Roman Republic', *JRS* 80: 1–16.

   1994. 'The crisis of the Republic: sources and source-problems', *CAH* IX. Cambridge: 1–15.

   1997. 'The theory of the mixed constitution at Rome', in *Philosophia Togata II: Plato and Aristotle at Rome*, ed. J. Barnes and M. Griffin. Oxford: 70–85.

   1999. *The Constitution of the Roman Republic*. Oxford.

Lo Cascio, E. 1997. 'Le procedure di *recensus* dalla tarda repubblica al tardo antico e il calcolo della popolazione di Roma', in *La Rome impériale. Démographie et logistique. Collection de l'École française de Rome* 230. Rome: 1–76.

Lovano, M. 2002. *The Age of Cinna. Crucible of Late Republican Rome. Historia* Einzelschriften 158. Stuttgart.

Luisi, N. D. 1995. 'Sul problema delle tabelle di voto nelle votazioni legislative: contributo all'interpretazione di Cic. "ad Att." 1,14,5', *Index* 23: 419–51.

Lundgreen, C. 2009a. 'Geheim(nisvoll)e Abstimmung in Rom', *Historia* 58: 36–70.

2009b. *Regelkonflikte in der römischen Republik. Geltung und Gewichtung von Normen in politischen Entscheidungsprozessen. Historia* Einzelschriften 221. Stuttgart.

2014a. 'Gesetze und die Grenzen ihrer Geltung: *leges* und konkurrierende Normen in der römischen Republik', in *Gesetzgebung und politische Kultur in der römischen Republik*, ed. U. Walter. Heidelberg: 108–67.

2014b. 'Staatsdiskurse in Rom? Staatlichkeit als analytische Kategorie für die römische Republik', in *Staatlichkeit in Rom? Diskurse und Praxis (in) der römischen Republik*, ed. C. Lundgreen. Stuttgart: 15–61.

ed. 2014c. *Staatlichkeit in Rom? Diskurse und Praxis (in) der römischen Republik*. Stuttgart.

Mackie, N. 1992. '*Popularis* ideology and popular politics at Rome in the first centuries B.C.', *RhM* 135: 49–73.

MacMullen, R. 1980. 'How many Romans voted?' *Athenaeum* 58: 454–7.

Malkin, I. and Z. W. Rubinsohn eds. 1995. *Leaders and Masses in the Roman World. Studies in Honor of Zvi Yavetz.* Leiden – New York – Köln.

Marco Simón, F., F. Pina Polo, and J. Remesal Rodríguez eds. 2012. *Vae victis! Perdedores en el mundo antiguo.* Barcelona.

Marcone, A. 2005. 'Tra antico e moderno. Democrazia e democrazie', in *Storia romana e storia moderna. Fasi in prospettiva*, ed. M. Pani. Bari: 85–100.

Marshall, A. J. 1984. 'Symbols and showmanship in Roman public life: the fasces', *Phoenix* 38: 120–41.

Marshall, B. A. 1984. 'Faustus Sulla and political labels in the 60's and 50's B. C.', *Historia* 33: 199–219.

1997. 'Libertas populi: the introduction of secret ballot in Rome and its depiction on coinage', *Antichthon* 31: 54–73.

Mayer, E. 2012. *The Ancient Middle Classes.* Cambridge, MA.

McCall, J. B. 2002. *The Cavalry of the Roman Republic.* London – New York.

Meier, C. 1956. 'Praerogativa centuria', *RE* suppl. 8: 567–98.

1965. 'Populares', *RE* suppl. 10: 549–615.

1968. 'Die loca intercessionis bei Rogationen', *MH* 25: 88–100.

1980. *Res publica amissa.* 2nd edn. Frankfurt. 1st edn. 1966.

1990. 'C. Caesar Divi filius and the formation of the alternative in Rome', in *Between Republic and Empire. Interpretations of Augustus and His Principate*, ed. K. A. Raaflaub and M. Toher. Berkeley: 54–70.

1997. 'Der griechische und der römische Bürger. Gemeinsamkeiten und Unterschiede im Ensemble gesellschaftlicher Bedingungen', in *Griechenland und Rom. Vergleichende Untersuchungen zu Entwicklungstendenzen und – höhepunkten der antiken Geschichte, Kunst und Literatur*, ed. E. G. Schmidt. Tbilisi – Erlangen – Jena: 41–66.

Meissner, B. 2000. 'Gaius Flaminius – oder: wie ein Aussenseiter zum Sündenbock wurde', in *Von Romulus zu Augustus. Grosse Gestalten der römischen Republik*, ed. K.-J. Hölkeskamp and E. Stein-Hölkeskamp. Munich: 92–105.

Melville, G. ed. 2009. *Institutionalität und Symbolisierung. Verstetigungen kulturel-ler Ordnungsmuster in Vergangenheit und Gegenwart*. Cologne.

Meyer, E. 1961. *Römischer Staat und Staatsgedanke*. 2nd edn. Zürich – Stuttgart. 1st edn. 1948.

Millar, F. 1984. 'The political character of the classical Roman Republic, 200–151 B.C.', *JRS* 74: 1–19.

1986. 'Politics, persuasion and the people before the Social War (150–90 B.C.)' *JRS* 76: 1–11.

1989. 'Political power in mid-Republican Rome: Curia or Comitium?' *JRS* 79: 138–50.

1995. 'Popular politics at Rome in the late Republic', in *Leaders and Masses in the Roman World. Studies in Honor of Zvi Yavetz*, ed. I. Malkin and Z. W. Rubinsohn. Leiden – New York – Köln: 91–113.

1998. *The Crowd in Rome in the Late Republic*. Michigan.

Mitchell, R. E. 1990. *Patricians and Plebeians. The Origins of the Roman State*. Ithaca, NY – London.

Molho, A., K. Raaflaub, and J. Emlen. eds. 1991. *City States in Classical Antiquity and Medieval Italy*. Ann Arbor – Stuttgart.

Mommsen, Th. 1854–5. *Römische Geschichte*. Leipzig.

1887. *Römisches Staatsrecht*. Leipzig.

Moreau, P. 2003. 'Donner la parole au peuple? Rhétorique et manipulation des *contiones* à la fin de la République romaine', in *Argumentation et discours politique. Antiquité grecque et latine, Révolution française, Monde contempor-ain*, ed. S. Bonnafous, P. Chiron, D. Ducard, and C. Levy. Rennes: 175–89.

Morel, J.-P. 1987. 'La topographie de l'artisanat et du commerce dans la Rome antique', in *L'urbs. Espace urbain et histoire Ier avant J.-C. – IIIe siècle après J.-C. Collection de l'École française de Rome* 98. Rome: 127–55.

Morley, N. 2009. 'The poor in the city of Rome', in *Poverty in the Roman World*, ed. M. Atkins and R. Osborne. Cambridge: 21–39.

Morstein-Marx, R. 1998. 'Publicity, popularity and patronage in the *commentar-iolum petitionis*', *ClAnt* 17: 259–88.

2004. *Mass Oratory and Political Power in the Late Roman Republic*. Cambridge.

2013. '"Cultural hegemony" and the communicative power of the Roman elite', in *Community and Communication. Oratory and Politics in Republican Rome*, ed. C. Steel and H. Van der Blom. Oxford: 29–47.

Morstein-Marx, R. and N. Rosenstein 2010. 'The transformation of the Republic', in *A Companion to the Roman Republic*, ed. N. Rosenstein and R. Morstein-Marx. Oxford: 625–37.

Mouritsen, H. 1998. *Italian Unification. A Study in Ancient and Modern Historiography, BICS* Suppl. 70. London.

2001. *Plebs and Politics in the Late Roman Republic.* Cambridge.

2004. 'Pits and politics: interpreting colonial fora in republican Italy', *PBSR* 72: 37–67.

2005. 'Review of R. Morstein-Marx, *Mass Oratory and Political Power in the Late Roman Republic*', *JRS* 95: 251–2.

2011a. 'Lottery and elections: containing elite competition in Venice and Rome', in *Competition in the Ancient World*, ed. N. Fisher and H. van Wees. Swansea: 221–38.

2011b. *The Freedman in the Roman World.* Cambridge.

2012. 'Review of E. Mayer, *The Ancient Middle Classes: Urban Life and Aesthetics in the Roman Empire, 100 BCE-250 CE*', *BMCR* 9: 40.

2013. 'From meeting to text: the *contio* in the late Republic', in *Community and Communication. Oratory and Politics in Republican Rome*, ed. C. Steel and H. Van der Blom. Oxford: 63–82.

2014. 'Pagane Lebensmodelle? Gods, *pietas*, and the Roman *maiores*', in *Der Mensch zwischen Weltflucht und Verantwortung. Lebensmodelle der paganen und der jüdisch-christlichen Antike*, ed. H.-G. Nesselrath and M. Rühl. Tübingen: 47–62.

2015a. 'The incongruence of power: the Roman constitution in theory and practice', in *A Companion to Greek Democracy and the Roman Republic*, ed. D. Hammer. Oxford: 146–63.

2015b. 'Status and social hierarchies: the case of Pompeii', in *Social Status and Prestige in the Roman World*, ed. A. Kuhn. Stuttgart: 87–114.

2015c. 'New Pompeian graffiti and the limits of Roman literacy', in *Antike. Kultur. Geschichte. Festschrift für Inge Nielsen zum 65. Geburtstag*, ed. S. Faust, M. Seifert, and L. Ziemer. Aachen: 201–14.

2017. 'Cicero's *familia urbana* and the social structure of late Republican Rome', in *Politische Kultur und soziale Struktur der römischen Republik*, ed. A.-C. Harders and M. Haake. Stuttgart: 215–30.

Nicholls, J. J. 1956. 'The reform of the comitia centuriata', *AJPh* 77: 225–54.

1967. 'The content of the lex curiata', *AJPh* 88: 257–78.

Nicolet, C. 1959. '"Confusio suffragiorum". A propos d'une réforme électorale de Caius Gracchus', *MEFRA* 71: 145–210.

1970. 'Le livre III des Res Rusticae de Varron et les allusions au déroulement des comices tributes', *REA* 72: 113–37.

1973. 'Polybe et les institutions romaines', in *Polybe*, ed. E. Gabba. *Fondation Hardt, Entretiens sur l'antiquité classique* 20. Vandoeuvres – Genève: 209–58.

1980. *The World of the Citizen in Republican Rome.* Transl. P. S. Falla. London. 1st edn. 1976.

1983. 'Polybe et la "constitution" de Rome: aristocratie et démocratie', in *Demokratia et aristokratia. À propos de Caius Graccuhs: mots grecs et réalités romaines*, ed. C. Nicolet. Paris: 15–35.

Nielsen, I. and B. Poulsen 1992. *The Temple of Castor and Pollux* I. Rome.

Bibliography

Nippel, W. 1980. *Mischverfassungstheorie und Verfassungsrealität in antike und früher Neuzeit.* Stuttgart.

1981. 'Die Plebs urbana und die Rolle der Gewalt in der späten römischen Republik', in *Von Elend der Handarbeit*, ed. H. Mommsen and W. Schulze. Stuttgart: 70–92.

1988. *Aufruhr und 'Polizei' in der römischen Republik.* Stuttgart.

1995. *Public Order in Ancient Rome.* Cambridge.

Nippel, W. and B. Seidensticker eds. 2005. *Theodor Mommsens langer Schatten. Das römische Staatsrecht als bleibende Herausforderung für die Forschung.* Hildesheim.

North, J. A. 1981. 'The development of Roman imperialism', *JRS* 71: 1–9.

1990. 'Politics and Aristocracy in the Roman Republic', *P&P* 126: 3–21.

2002. 'Introduction: Pursuing Democracy', in *Representations of Empire. Rome and the Mediterranean World*, ed. A. K. Bowman et al. Oxford: 1–12.

2007. 'The constitution of the Roman Republic', in *A Companion to the Roman Republic*, ed. N. Rosenstein and R. Morstein-Marx. Oxford: 256–77.

Oakley, S. 1993. 'The Roman conquest of Italy', in *War and Society in the Roman World*, ed. J. Rich and G. Shipley. London: 9–37.

Ostwald, M. 2000. *Oligarchia. The Development of a Constitutional Form in Ancient Greece. Historia* Einzelschriften 144. Stuttgart.

Paananen, U. 1972. *Sallust's Politico-Social Terminology.* Helsinki.

1993. 'Legislation in the *comitia centuriata*', in *Senatus Populusque Romanus. Studies in Roman Republican Legislation*, ed. J. Vaahtera. *Acta Instituti Romani Finlandiae* 13. Rome: 9–73.

Palmer, R. E. A. 1970. *The Archaic Community of the Romans.* Cambridge.

Pani, M. 1997. *La politica in Roma antica: cultura e prassi.* Rome.

Papi, E. 2002. 'La turba inpia: artigiani e commercianti del Foro Romano e dintorni (I sec. a.C. – 64 d.C.)', *JRA* 15: 45–62.

Patterson, J. R. 1999. *Political Life in the City of Rome.* London.

Perelli, L. 1982. *Il movimento popolare nell'ultimo secolo della repubblica.* Torino.

Perl, G. and I. El-Qalqili 2002. 'Zur Problematik der *lex Oppia* (215/195 v. Chr.)', *Klio* 84: 414–39.

Pfeilschifter, R. 2005. *Titus Quinctius Flamininus. Untersuchungen zur römischen Griechenlandpolitik. Hypomnemata* 162. Göttingen.

Phillips, D. A. 2004. 'Voter turnout in consular elections', *AHB* 18: 48–60.

Pina Polo, F. 1995. 'Procedures and Functions of Civil and Military Contiones in Rome', *Klio* 77: 203–16.

1996. *Contra arma verbis. Der Redner vor dem Volk in der späten römischen Republik.* HABES 22. Heidelberg.

2011. *The Consuls at Rome. The Civil Functions of the Consuls in the Roman Republic.* Cambridge.

2012. 'Veteres candidate: losers in the elections in Republican Rome', in *Vae victis! Perdedores en el mundo antiguo*, ed. F. Marco Simón, F. Pina Polo, and J. Remesal Rodríguez. Barcelona: 63–82.

Pittinger, M. R. P. 2008. *Contested Triumphs: Politics, Pageantry, and Performance in Livy's Republican Rome*. Berkeley.

Polverini, L. 2005. 'Democrazia a Roma? La costituzione repubblicana secondo Polibio', in *Popolo e potere nel mondo antico*, ed. G. Urso. Pisa: 85–96.

Powell, J. G. F. 1990. 'The tribune Sulpicius', *Historia* 39: 446–60.

Prugni, G. 1987. 'Quirites', *Athenaeum* 65: 127–61.

Raaflaub, K. A. 1991. 'City-state, territory and empire in classical antiquity', in *City States in Classical Antiquity and Medieval Italy*, ed. A. Molho, K. Raaflaub, and J. Emlen. Ann Arbor – Stuttgart: 565–88.

   1993. 'Politics and society in fifth-century Rome', in *Bilancio critico su Roma arcaica fra monarchia e repubblica. In memoria di Ferdinando Castagnoli. Atti dei convegni Lincei* 100. Rome: 129–57.

   2005. 'The conflict of the orders in archaic Rome: a comprehensive and comparative approach', in *Social Struggles in Archaic Rome. New Perspectives on the Conflict of the Orders*, ed. K. A. Raaflaub. 2nd edn. Berkeley: 1–46. 1st edn. 1986.

Rathbone, D. W. 1993. 'The *census* qualifications of the *assidui* and the *prima classis*', in *De Agricultura: In Memoriam Pieter Willem de Neeve*, ed. H. Sancisi-Weerdenburg et al. Amsterdam: 121–52.

Rich, J. W. 1976. *Declaring War in the Roman Republic in the Period of Transmarine Expansion*. Brussels.

   2012. 'Roman attitudes to defeat in battle under the Republic', in *Vae victis! Perdedores en el mundo antiguo*, ed. F. Marco Simón, F. Pina Polo, and J. Remesal Rodríguez. Barcelona: 83–111.

Richardson, J. H. 2008. 'Ancient historical thought and the development of the consulship (1)', *Latomus* 67: 328–41, 627–33.

Rieger, M. 2007. *Tribus und Stadt. Die Entstehung der römischen Wahlbezirke im urbane und mediterranen Kontext (ca. 750–450 v. Chr.)*. Göttingen.

Rilinger, R. 1976. *Der Einfluss des Wahlleiters bei den römischen Konsulwahlen von 366 bis 50 v. Chr. Vestigia* 24. Munich.

   1982. 'Die Interpretation des Niedergangs der römischen Republik durch "Revolution" und "Krise ohne Alternative"', *AKG* 64: 279–306.

   1989. '"Loca intercessionis" und legalismus in der späten Republik', *Chiron* 19: 481–98.

Ritter, H.-W. 1998. 'Zu Libertas und den Tabellargesetzen in der republikanischen Münzprägung', in *Imperium Romanum. Studien zu Geschichte und Rezeption. Festschrift für Karl Christ zum 75. Geburtstag*, ed. P. Kneissl and V. Losemann. Stuttgart: 608–14.

Robb, M. A. 2010. *Beyond* Populares *and* Optimates. *Political Language in the Late Republic. Historia* Einzelschriften 213. Stuttgart.

Robinson, A. 1994. 'Cicero's use of the Gracchi in two speeches before the people', *A&R* 39: 71–6.

Roddaz, J.-M. 2005. 'Popularis, populisme, popularité', in *Popolo e potere nel mondo antico*, ed. G. Urso. Pisa: 97–122.

Rogers, G. M. 2002. 'Polybius was right', in F. Millar, *Rome, the Greek World, and the East I. The Roman Republic and the Augustan Revolution*, ed. G. M. Rogers and H. M. Cotton. Chapel Hill – London: IX–XVI.

Rosenstein, N. 1990a. *Imperatores Victi. Military Defeat and Aristocratic Competition in the Middle and Late Republic.* Berkeley – Los Angeles – Oxford.

1990b. 'War, failure, and aristocratic competition', *CPh* 85: 255–65.

1995. 'Sorting out the lot in Republican Rome', *AJP* 116: 43–75.

Rosenstein, N. and R. Morstein-Marx eds. 2006. *A Companion to the Roman Republic.* Oxford.

Rosillo-López, C. 2010. *La corruption à la fin de la République romaine (IIe – Ier s. av. J.-C.). Aspects politiques et financiers. Historia* Einzelschriften 200. Stuttgart.

Rüpke, J. 1990. *Domi Militiae: die religiöse Konstruktion des Krieges in Rome.* Stuttgart.

Russell, A. 2013. 'Speech, competition, and collaboration: tribunician politics and the development of popular ideology', in *Community and Communication. Oratory and Politics in Republican Rome*, ed. C. Steel and H. Van der Blom. Oxford: 101–15.

Ryan, F. X. 1994. 'The praetorship of Favonius', *AJP* 115: 587–601.

1995. 'Sexagenarians, the bridge and the *centuria praerogativa*', *RhM* 138: 188–90.

1998. *Rank and Participation in the Republican Senate.* Stuttgart.

2001. 'Knappe Mehrheiten bei der Wahl zum Konsul', *Klio* 83: 402–24.

Sandberg, K. 1993. 'The *concilium plebis* as a legislative body during the Republic', in *Senatus Populusque Romanus. Studies in Roman Republican Legislation*, ed. J. Vaahtera. *Acta Instituti Romani Finlandiae* 13. Rome: 74–96.

2000. 'Tribunician and non-tribunician legislation in mid-Republican Rome', in *The Roman Middle Republic. Religion, Politics, and Historiography c. 400 – 133 B.C.*, ed. C. Bruun. *Acta Instituti Romani Finlandiae* 23. Rome: 121–40.

2001. *Magistrates and Assemblies. A Study of Legislative Practice in Republican Rome. Acta Instituti Romani Finlandiae* 24. Rome.

2004. 'Consular legislation in pre-Sullan Rome', *Arctos* 38: 133–62.

Santalucia, B. 2012. 'Le clausole autoprotettive delle leges', in *Leges publicae. La legge nell'esperienza giuridica romana*, ed. J.-L. Ferrary. Pavia: 116–37.

Santangelo, F. 2006. 'Sulla and the Senate: a reconsideration', *CCG* 17: 7–22

2008. 'Cicero and Marius', *Athenaeum* 96: 597–607.

2014. 'Roman politics in the 70s B.C.: a story of realignments?' *JRS* 1–27.

Scheid, J. 2003. *An Introduction to Roman Religion.* 2nd edn. Edinburgh. 1st edn. 1998.

Scheidel, W. 2004. 'Human mobility in Roman Italy, 1: the free population', *JRS* 94: 1–26.

Scheidel, W. and S. J. Friesen 2009. 'The size of the economy and the distribution of income in the Roman Empire', *JRS* 99: 61–91.

Schmidt, E. G. ed. 1997. *Griechenland und Rom. Vergleichende Untersuchungen zu Entwicklungstendenzen und –höhepunkten der antiken Geschichte, Kunst und Literatur.* Tbilisi – Erlangen – Jena.

Schofield, M. 1995. 'Cicero's definition of *Res Publica*', in *Cicero the Philosopher*, ed. J. G. F. Powell. Oxford: 63–83.

Scholz, P. 2011. *Den Vätern folgen. Sozialisiation und Erziehung der republikanischen Senatsaristokratie.* Berlin.

Schovánek, J. G. 1972. 'The date of M. Octavius and his *lex frumentaria*', *Historia* 21: 235–43.

Scobie, A. 1986. 'Slum, Sanitation, and Mortality in the Roman World', *Klio* 68: 309–433.

Seager, R. 2013. 'Polybius' distortions of the Roman constitution: a simpl(istic) explanation', in *Polybius and His World. Essays in Memory of F. W. Walbank*, ed. B. Gibson and T. Harrison. Oxford: 247–54.

Shackleton Bailey, D. R. 1965–70. *Letters to Atticus.* Cambridge.

1981. *Cicero. Epistulae ad Quintum Fratrem et M. Brutum.* Cambridge.

1986. '*Nobiles* and *novi* reconsidered', *AJPh* 107: 255–60.

Shatzman, I. 1975. *Senatorial Wealth and Roman Politics.* Brussels.

Sion-Jenkis, K. 2000. *Von der Republik zum Prinzipat. Ursachen für den Vervassungsvechsel in Rom im historischen Denken der Antike.* Palingenesia 69. Stuttgart.

Smith, R. E. 1957. 'The lex Plotia agraria and Pompey's Spanish veterans', *CQ* 7: 82–5.

Spielvogel, J. 1993. *Amicitia und res publica. Ciceros Maxime während der innenpolitischen Auseinandersetzungen der Jahre 59–50 v. Chr.* Stuttgart.

ed. 2002. *Res publica reperta. Zur Verfassung und Gesellschaft der römischen Republik und des frühen Prinzipats. Festschrift für Jochen Bleicken zum 75. Geburtstag.* Stuttgart.

Stanton, G. R. and P. J. Bicknell 1987. 'Voting in tribal groups in the Athenian Assembly', *GRBS* 28: 51–92.

Stasse, B. 2005. 'La loi curiate des magistrats', *RIDA* 52: 375–400.

Staveley, E. S. 1953. 'The reform of the comitia centuriata', *AJPh* 74: 1–33.

1969. 'The role of the first voter in the Roman legislative assemblies', *Historia* 18: 513–20.

1972. *Greek and Roman Voting and Elections.* London.

Steel, C. 2013. *The End of the Roman Republic, 146–44 BC. Conquest and Crisis.* Edinburgh.

2014. 'Rethinking Sulla: the case of the Roman senate', *CQ* 64: 657–68.

Steel, C. and H. Van der Blom eds. 2013. *Community and Communication. Oratory and Politics in Republican Rome.* Oxford.

Stein-Hölkeskamp, E. 2013. 'Macht, Memoria und Monumente: Marius, Sulla und der Kampf um den öffentlichen Raum', *Klio* 95: 429–46.

Stemmler, M. 1997. *Eques Romanus – Reiter und Ritter. Begriffsgeschichtliche Untersuchungen zu den Entstehungsbedingungen einer römischen Adelskategorie im Heer und in den comitia centuriata.* Prismata 8. Frankfurt a. M.

2000. 'Die römische Manipularordnung und der Funktionswandel der Centurien', *Klio* 82: 107–28.

2001. 'Institutionalisierte Geschichte. Zur Stabilisierungsleistung und Symbolizität historischer Beispiele in der Redekunst der römischen Republik', in *Institutionalität und Symbolisierung. Verstetigungen kultureller Ordnungsmuster in Vergangenheit und Gegenwart*, ed. G. Melville. Cologne: 219–40.

Stewart, R. 1998. *Public Office in Early Rome. Ritual Procedure and Political Practice*. Ann Arbor.

Strasburger, H. 1939. 'Optimates', *RE* 18.1: 773–98.

Straumann, B. 2011. 'Constitutional thought in the late Roman republic', *HPTh* 32: 280–92.

Stumpf, G. R. 1985. 'C. Atinius C.f. Praetor in Asia 122–121 v. Chr., auf einem Kistophor', *ZPE* 61: 186–90.

Syme, R. 1939. *The Roman Revolution*. Oxford.

1964. *Sallust*. Berkeley.

Tan, J. 2008. '*Contiones* in the age of Cicero', *ClAnt* 27: 163–201.

Tatum, W. J. 1999. *The Patrician Tribune Publius Clodius Pulcher*. Chapel Hill, NC – London.

2010. 'The *Plebiscitum Atinium* once more', in *Res Historica. Terra, Mare et Homines II. Studies in Memory of Professor Tadeusz Loposzko*, ed. H. Kowalski and P. Madejski. Lublin: 198–208.

2013. 'Campaign rhetoric', in *Community and Communication. Oratory and Politics in Republican Rome*, ed. C. Steel and H. Van der Blom. Oxford: 133–50.

Taylor, L. R. 1949. *Party Politics in the Age of Caesar*. Berkeley.

1957. 'The centuriate assembly before and after the reform', *AJPh* 78: 337–54.

1960. *The Voting Districts of the Roman Republic*. Rome.

1962. 'Forerunners of the Gracchi', *JRS* 52: 19–27.

1966. *Roman Voting Assemblies*. Ann Arbor.

Thommen, L. 1989. *Das Volkstribunat der späten römischen Republik. Historia Einzelschriften* 59. Stuttgart.

1995. 'Les lieux de la plèbe et de ses tribuns dans la Rome républicaine', *Klio* 77: 358–70.

Tiersch, C. 2009. 'Politische Öffentlichkeit statt Mittbestimmung? Zur bedeutung der *contiones* in der mittleren und späten römischen Republik', *Klio* 91: 40–68.

Timmer, J. 2008. *Altersgrenzen politischer Partizipation in antiken Gesellschaften*. Berlin.

2009. 'Auseinandertreten, wenn alle einer Meinung sind – Überlegungen zur discessio', *Klio* 91: 384–405.

Ungern-Sternberg, J. von 1970. *Untersuchungen zum spätrepublikanischen Notstandsrecht. Senatus consultum ultimum und hostis-Erklärung. Vestigia* 11. Munich.

1990. 'Die Wahrnehmung des "Ständeskampfes" in der römischen Geschichtsschreibung', in *Staat und Staatlichkeit in der frühen römischen Republik*, ed. W. Eder. Stuttgart: 92–102.

1991. 'Die politische und soziale Bedeutung der spätrepublikanischen *leges frumentariae*', in *Nourrir la plebe*, ed. A. Giovannini. Basel: 19–41.

1998. 'Die Legitimitätskrise der römischen Republik', *HZ* 266: 607–24.

2014. 'The crisis of the Republic', in *The Cambridge Companion to the Roman Republic*, ed. H. I. Flower 2nd edn. Cambridge: 78–98. 1st edn. 2004.

Urso, G. ed. 2005. *Popolo e potere nel mondo antico*. Pisa.

Vaahtera, J. 1990. 'Pebbles, points, or ballots: the emergence of the individual vote in Rome', *Arctos* 24: 161–77.

1993a. 'On the religious nature of the place of assembly', in *Senatus Populusque Romanus. Studies in Roman Republican Legislation*, ed. J. Vaahtera. *Acta Instituti Romani Finlandiae* 13. Rome: 97–116.

1993b. 'The origin of Latin *suffragium*', *Glotta* 71: 6–80.

ed. 1993c *Senatus Populusque Romanus. Studies in Roman Republican Legislation. Acta Instituti Romani Finlandiae* 13. Rome.

Vervaet, F. J. 2004. 'The *lex Valeria* and Sulla's empowerment as dictator (82–79 BCE), *CCG* 15: 37–84.

2009. 'Pompeius' career from 79 to 70 BCE: constitutional, political and historical considerations', *Klio* 91: 406–34.

Veyne, P. 1990. *Bread and Circuses*. Transl. E. Pearce. London.

Vervaet, F. J. 2000. 'La "plèbe moyenne" sous le Haut-Empire', *Annales (HSS)* 55: 1169–99.

Vishnia, R. F. 1989. 'Lex Atinia de tribunis plebis in senatum legendis', *MH* 46: 163–76.

1996. *State, Society, and Popular Leaders in Mid-Republican Rome*. London.

1998. 'The refusal of the centuriate assembly to declare war on Macedon (200 BC) – a reappraisal', *SCI* 17: 34–44.

2008. 'Written ballot, secret ballot and the *iudicia populi*. A note on the *leges tabellariae* (Cicero, *De legibus* 3.33–39)', *Klio* 90: 334–46.

Vlassopoulos, K. 2010. *Politics: Antiquity and Its Legacy*. London – New York.

Walbank, F. W. 1972. *Polybius*. Berkeley.

Wallace-Hadrill, A. 1989. 'Patronage in Roman Society: from Republic to Empire', in *Patronage in Ancient Society*, ed. A. Wallace-Hadrill. London – New York: 63–87.

2013. 'Trying to define and identify the Roman "middle classes"', *JRA* 26: 605–9.

ed. 1989. *Patronage in Ancient Society*. London – New York.

Waller, M. 2011. 'Victory, defeat and electoral success at Rome, 343–91 B.C.', *Latomus* 70: 18–38.

Wallinga, T. 1994. 'Ambitus in the Roman Republic', *RIDA* 41: 411–42.

Walter, U. 1998. 'Der Begriff des Staates in der griechischen und römischen Geschichte', in *Althistorisches Kolloquium aus Anlass des 70. Geburtstag von Jochen Bleicken*, ed. Th. Hantos and G. A. Lehmann. Stuttgart: 9–27.

2001. 'Die Botschaft des Mediums. Überlegungen zum Sinnpotential von Historiographie im Kontext der römischen Geschichtskultur zur Zeit der Republik', in *Institutionalität und Symbolisierung. Verstetigungen kultureller Ordnungsmuster in Vergangenheit und Gegenwart*, ed. G. Melville. Cologne: 241–79.

2004. Memoria *und* res publica. *Zur Geschichtskultur im republikanischen Rom.* Frankfurt a. M.

2009. 'Struktur, Zufall, Kontingenz? Überlegungen zum ende der römischen Republik', in *Eine politische Kultur (in) der Krise? Die "letzte Generation" der römischen Republik*, ed. K.-J. Hölkeskamp and E. Müller-Luckner. Munich: 27–51.

2014a. 'Ordnungszersetzung: der Fall der späten römsichen Republik', in *Aufruhr – Katastrophe – Konkurrenz – Zerfall. Bedrohte Ordnungen als Thema der Kulturwissenschaften*, ed. E. Frie and M. Meier. Tübingen: 83–115.

2014b. 'Meister der Macht ohne Formierung von Staatlichkeit: die römische Aristokratie', in *Staatlichkeit in Rom? Diskurse und Praxis (in) der römischen Republik*, ed. C. Lundgreen. Stuttgart: 91–116.

Ward, A. M. 1970. 'Politics in the trials of Manilius and Cornelius', *TAPhA* 101: 545–56.

2004. 'How democratic was the Roman Republic?' *NECJ* 31: 101–19.

Warrior, V. M. 1996. *The Initiation of the Second Macedonian War. An Explication of Livy Book 31. Historia* Einzeschriften 97. Stuttgart.

Welwei, K.-W. 1996. 'Caesars Diktatur, der Prinzipat des Augustus und die Fiktion der historischen Notwendigkeit', *Gymnasium* 103: 477–97.

2000. 'Lucius Iunius Brutus – ein fiktiver Revolutionsheld', in *Von Romulus zu Augustus. Grosse Gestalten der römischen Republik*, ed. K.-J. Hölkeskamp and E. Stein-Hölkeskamp. Munich: 48–57.

2002. 'Demokratische Verfassungselemente in Rom aus der Sicht des Polybios', in *Res publica reperta. Zur Verfassung und Gesellschaft der römischen Republik und des frühen Prinzipats. Festschrift für Jochen Bleicken zum 75. Geburtstag*, ed. J. Spielvogel. Stuttgart: 25–35.

Whitehead, D. 1991. 'Norms of citizenship in ancient Greece', in *City States in Classical Antiquity and Medieval Italy*, ed. A. Molho, K. Raaflaub, and J. Emlen. Ann Arbor – Stuttgart: 135–54.

Williamson, C. 1990. 'The Roman aristocracy and positive law', *CPh* 85: 266–76.

2005. *The Laws of the Roman People. Public Law in the Expansion and Decline of the Roman Republic.* Ann Arbor.

Winterling, A. 2008. '"Krise ohne Alternative" in alten Rom', in *Christian Meier zur Diskussion*, ed. M. Bernett, W. Nippel, and A. Winterling. Stuttgart: 219–39.

Wirszubski, C. 1950. *Libertas as a Political Idea at Rome during the Late Republic and Early Principate.* Cambridge.

Wiseman, T. P. 1971. *New Men in the Roman Senate 139 BC-AD 14.* Oxford.

1985a. *Catullus and His World.* Cambridge.

1994. 'The senate and the *populares*', *CAH* IX. Cambridge: 327–67.

1995. *Remus: A Roman Myth.* Cambridge.

1999. 'Democracy alla romana', *JRA* 12: 537–40.

2004. *The Myths of Rome.* Exeter.

2009. *Remembering the Roman People. Essays on Late-Republican Politics and Literature.* Oxford.

2010. 'The two-headed state: how Romans explained civil war', in *Citizens of Discord. Rome and Its Civil Wars*, ed. B. W. Breed, C. Damon, and A. Rossi. Oxford: 25–44.

ed. 1985b. *Roman Political Life 90 BC – AD 69*. Exeter.

Yakobson, A. 1992. '*Petitio* and *Largitio*: Popular Participation in the Centuriate Assembly of the Late Republic', *JRS* 82: 32–52.

1993. 'Dionysius of Halicarnassus on a democratic change in the centuriate assembly', *SCI* 12: 139–53.

1995. 'Secret ballot and its effect in the late Roman Republic', *Hermes* 123: 126–42.

1999. *Elections and Electioneering in Rome. Historia* Einzelschriften 128. Stuttgart.

2010. 'Traditional political culture and the people's role in the Roman Republic', *Historia* 59: 282–302.

Zecchini, G. 1997. *Il pensiero politico romano. Dall'età arcaica alla tarda antichità.* Rome.

2006. 'In margine a "Rekonstruktionen einer Republik" di K.-J. Hölkeskamp', *StudStor* 47: 395–404.

Ziolkowski, A. 1992. *The Temples of Mid-Republican Rome and Their Historical and Topographical Context.* Rome.

Index

Abbreviations

cos.	consul
cos. suff.	consul suffectus
pr.	praetor
aed. cur.	aedilis curulis
tr. pl.	tribunus plebis
q.	quaestor
flam. dial.	flamen Dialis